Environmental Groups
and Legal Expertise

Environmental Groups and Legal Expertise
Shaping the Brexit process

Carolyn Abbot and Maria Lee

First published in 2021 by
UCL Press
University College London
Gower Street
London WC1E 6BT

Available to download free: www.uclpress.co.uk

Text © Authors, 2021
Images © Authors, 2021

The authors have asserted their rights under the Copyright, Designs and Patents Act 1988 to be identified as the authors of this work.

A CIP catalogue record for this book is available from The British Library.

This book is published under a Creative Commons 4.0 International licence (CC BY 4.0). This licence allows you to share, copy, distribute and transmit the work; to adapt the work and to make commercial use of the work providing attribution is made to the authors (but not in any way that suggests that they endorse you or your use of the work). Attribution should include the following information:

Abbot, C., and Lee, M. 2021. *Environmental Groups and Legal Expertise: Shaping the Brexit process*. London: UCL Press. https://doi.org/10.14324/111.9781787358584

Further details about Creative Commons licences are available at http://creativecommons.org/licenses/

Any third-party material in this book is published under the book's Creative Commons licence unless indicated otherwise in the credit line to the material. If you would like to reuse any third-party material not covered by the book's Creative Commons licence, you will need to obtain permission directly from the copyright holder.

ISBN: 978-1-78735-860-7 (Hbk.)
ISBN: 978-1-78735-859-1 (Pbk.)
ISBN: 978-1-78735-858-4 (PDF)
ISBN: 978-1-78735-861-4 (epub)
ISBN: 978-1-78735-862-1 (mobi)
DOI: https://doi.org/10.14324/111.9781787358584

Contents

Table of legislation and draft legislation — xi
Table of cases — xv
List of abbreviations — xvii
Acknowledgements — xix
Executive summaries — xxi

1. Law and legal expertise for Brexit-environment: scope, meaning and method — 1
2. NGOs, lobbying and legal mobilisation — 27
3. Brexit and the journey to the Environment Act – interrupted — 49
4. Law and legal expertise — 79
5. Mobilising law in practice — 99
6. Lobbying in coalition — 125
7. Greener UK: influence and collaboration — 148
8. Conclusions — 174

Bibliography — 182
Index — 191

Detailed contents

1	**Law and legal expertise for Brexit-environment: scope, meaning and method**	**1**
	Introduction	1
	The UK environmental NGO community	3
	Brexit and the Environment Bill	5
	Some theoretical background	8
	NGO advocacy, influence and impact	10
	Method and methodology: the empirical material	14
	Participants in our research	15
	Other empirical work	18
	Outline of the book	19
2	**NGOs, lobbying and legal mobilisation**	**27**
	Introduction	27
	Insiders and outsiders: group status and group strategy	28
	Interest group status	31
	Insider group strategies: lobbying, advocacy and legal mobilisation	33
	Explaining and shaping NGO strategies	36
	Legal and political opportunities	37
	Resource-based theories	38
	Organisational culture and identity	43
	Conclusions	45
3	**Brexit and the journey to the Environment Act – interrupted**	**49**
	Introduction	49
	Environmental law: life before and after Brexit	51
	Enforcement and accountability	52
	Developing environmental law and standards	54
	Environmental principles	55

	The dynamics of political and legal opportunity: parliament and government 2016 to 2020	56
	June 2016 to June 2017: resistance to action on the environment	59
	June 2017 to January 2018: 'Green Brexit'	62
	January 2018 to late 2018: consultation and evolution	64
	Late 2018 to mid-2019: legislative drafts and political turmoil	68
	December 2019 to June 2020: getting Brexit done – interrupted	70
	Conclusions	74
4	**Law and legal expertise**	**79**
	Introduction	79
	The fragility of expertise	80
	Identifying expertise	85
	Knowledge, skills and experience	89
	Conclusions	95
5	**Mobilising law in practice**	**99**
	Introduction	99
	NGO lawyering	100
	Leadership and strategy	102
	Mobilising law in advocacy	106
	Law and communication	116
	The impact of legal expertise	118
	Conclusions	121
6	**Lobbying in coalition**	**125**
	Introduction	125
	Collaboration and environmental groups	127
	Collaboration as an opportunity: individual v collective resource	130
	Collaboration as a challenge	136
	Alignment of interests and compromise	137
	Profile, competition and identity	141
	Conclusions	145

7	**Greener UK: influence and collaboration**	**148**
	Introduction	148
	Influence and impact	149
	The Manifesto objectives	152
	Moving into detail	154
	Success, failure and influence	159
	The qualities of collaboration	161
	The nature of Brexit: salience for the sector	163
	People and trust	164
	Resources	166
	The future of collaboration and Greener UK	168
	Conclusions	170
8	**Conclusions**	**174**
	Introduction	174
	Political and legal opportunity	175
	Law and legal expertise in the environmental community	176
	Forming a successful collaboration	178
	Brexit is special, but lessons can be learned	179
	Conclusions: the future	181

Table of legislation and draft legislation

UK primary legislation

Agriculture Bill, 4, 7, 51

Climate Change Act 2008, 7, 11, 54, 103, 104, 114, 119

Draft Environment (Principles and Governance) Bill, 19, 66, 68, 69, 109, 110, 111, 119, 127, 151, 155, 156

Environment Bill, 2, 6–7, 9, 11, 12, 14, 15, 16, 18, 19, 22, 23, 24, 34, 38, 49, 63, 64, 65, 70, 71, 72, 73, 74, 103, 118, 127, 128, 130, 143, 149, 150, 151, 154, 159, 160, 161, 162, 163, 170, 174, 175, 176, 178, 179, 181

    Clauses 1–6, 73
    Clause 1, 76
    Clause 2, 76
    Clause 5, 76
    Clause 6, 76, 172
    Clause 7, 65
    Clause 8, 76
    Clause 9, 172
    Clause 13, 76
    Clause 16, 56
    Clause 18, 56
    Clause 19, 76
    Clause 25, 76
    Clause 26, 76
    Clause 130, 25
    Part 1, 6–7, 13, 51–6, 65, 179
    Substantive parts, 17, 51, 107, 126, 139–40, 146, 164,

Environment Act 1995, 7

EU Referendum Act 2015, 77

EU (Withdrawal) Act 2018, 6, 51, 61, 65, 66–8, 73, 75, 153, 172

> Sections 2–7, 24
> Section 6, 78
> Section 8, 77, 172
> Section 13, 67
> Section 16, 67–8, 78, 155, 172

EU (Withdrawal Agreement) Act 2020, 8, 24, 57, 67, 69, 72–3, 78, 154, 172

> Section 26, 73, 75

EU (Withdrawal Agreement) Bills, 67, 69, 70, 72

> Clause 31, 72

European Communities Act 1972, 6, 66

Fisheries Bill, 7, 51

Marine and Coastal Access Act 2009, 7, 108

Natural Environment and Rural Communities Act 2006, 7

Trade Bill, 4, 51

UK secondary legislation

The Climate Change Act 2008 (2050 Target Amendment Order 2019 No 1056), 78

EU legislation

Directive 92/43/EEC on the conservation of natural habitats and of wild fauna and flora [1992] OJ L 206/7 (Habitats Directive), 55, 60, 61, 111, 123

Directive 2000/60/EC establishing a framework for Community action in the field of water policy [2000] OJ L 327/1

> Article 15, 76

Directive 2009/147/EC on the conservation of wild birds [2009] OJ L 20/7 (Birds Directive), 60, 111, 123

Directive 2010/75/EU on industrial emissions (integrated pollution prevention and control) [2010] OJ L 334/17, 76

Directive 2011/92/EU on the assessment of the effects of certain public and private projects on the environment [2012] OJ L 26/1, 76

International

UNECE Aarhus Convention on Access to Information, Public Participation in Decision-Making and Access to Justice in Environmental Matters 1998, 76

UN Framework Convention on Climate Change, 12

Draft EU Withdrawal Agreement 2018, 68–9, 70, 112

Draft EU Withdrawal Agreement 2019, 70

Treaty on European Union

    Article 4, 75
    Article 19, 75

Treaty on the Functioning of the European Union, 55

    Article 11, 55
    Articles 258–60, 75

Table of cases

Domestic cases

R (on the application of ClientEarth) v Secretary of State for Environment, Food and Rural Affairs [2012] Env LR 18, 75

R (on the application of (1) ClientEarth (2) Marine Conservation Society) v Secretary of State for Environment, Food and Rural Affairs [2019] EWHC 2682 (Admin), 77

R (on the application of Miller) v Secretary of State for Exiting the EU [2017] UKSC 5; [2017] 2 WLR 583, 76, 97

R (on the application of Miller) v The Prime Minister [2019] UKSC 41; [2019] 3 WLR 589, 76, 97

European cases

Case 26/62 *Van Gend en Loos* [1963] ECR 1, 75

Case C-106/89 *Marleasing* [1990] ECR I-4135, 75

Case C-68/11 *Commission v Italy (air quality)* ECLI:EU:C:2012:815, 75

Case C-56/90 *Commission v UK (bathing waters)* [1993] ECR I-4109, 75

Case C-127/02 *Landelijke Vereniging tot Behoud van de Waddenzee v Staatssecretaris van Landbouw (Waddenzee)* [2004] ECR I-7405, 76

Case C-404/13 R (on the application of ClientEarth) v Secretary of State for the Environment, Food and Rural Affairs [2015] 1 CMLR 55, 75

List of abbreviations

CAP	Common Agricultural Policy
CJEU	Court of Justice of the European Union
DEFRA	Department for Environment, Food and Rural Affairs
EAC	Environmental Audit Committee
EFRA	Environment, Food and Rural Affairs
EIP	Environmental Improvement Plan
MP	Member of Parliament
NGO	Non-Governmental Organisation
OEP	Office for Environmental Protection
STS	Science and Technology Studies
TEU	Treaty on European Union
TFEU	Treaty on the Functioning of the European Union
UKELA	UK Environmental Law Association

Acknowledgements

Along with much of the rest of the human population at the time, we found ourselves in strange, and sometimes difficult, circumstances as we completed this book. And yet, it has been fun. We are grateful to all of the people who have helped. The participants in our project, those who allowed us to interview them and those who took part in our kick-off and closing events, have been extremely generous with their time and indeed expertise. We are grateful to them, for their help with this project and for their general good humour and kindness.

We have benefited enormously from very generous feedback on chapters from many people: Chiara Armeni, Charlie Burns, Ruth Chambers, David Baldock, Steve Fownes, Olivia Hamlyn, Chris Hilson, Jacqui Kinghan, Lucy Natarajan, Colin Reid, Elen Stokes, Lisa Vanhala and Steven Vaughan. This book is better than it would otherwise have been, thanks to their support. We are grateful to our students Bart Kruk and Molly Vann for their assistance.

We are grateful for a British Academy small grant to help with this project.

We are especially grateful to each other, to Steve and Louis, Thomas, Megan and Jake.

Carolyn Abbot and Maria Lee
Manchester and London
June 2020

Executive summaries

Chapter 1 Law and legal expertise for Brexit-environment: scope, meaning and method

Our purpose in this book is to explore the ways in which environmental NGOs use and understand law and legal expertise. We scrutinise the activity of environmental groups through a case study of Brexit's environmental implications, and the development of the UK Environment Bill, especially Part 1 of the Bill, entitled 'Environmental Governance'. Part 1 was developed expressly in response to the enormous impact of leaving the EU on UK environmental law. Although we conclude that Brexit created special opportunities and demands for legal expertise, our detailed analysis of this unusually law-heavy, and anomalously politically open, case study provides rich lessons on what NGOs 'do' with legal expertise, and why, and what legal expertise might do for them.

We set the scene for the rest of this book in chapter 1, outlining issues that underpin subsequent discussions, from the diversity of the environmental NGO sector in the UK, and the characteristics of key groups such as Greener UK, to the theoretical material developed in later chapters. Our work is based on literature review, the analysis of documents published by environmental NGOs, and semi-structured interviews with 17 individuals from different backgrounds who were engaged with the Brexit-environment debate.

Chapter 2 NGOs, lobbying and legal mobilisation

Lobbying and advocacy, terms which we use interchangeably to mean direct interactions with decision-makers, have been the main approach to the Brexit-environment debate by environmental NGOs. In this chapter, we provide insights into the complex and wide-ranging literature on NGOs, lobbying and their use of law ('legal mobilisation').

A number of important factors shape NGO activity. The literature on 'political opportunity' explores the multitude of factors external to an environmental group that influence its approach to social change. It focuses especially on those factors that determine the space for NGOs in decision-making fora, and the receptivity of decision-makers to NGO demands. The concept of 'legal opportunity' emerged from the political opportunity literature to embrace important features of the legal, political and social environment, which either limit or incentivise legal mobilisation. As we explore further in chapter 3, environmental NGOs have been operating in a complex and ever-changing web of political opportunities during our period of study.

Factors internal to the NGO movement are also crucial in shaping NGO activity and impact. Drawing on our interview data, we argue that legal expertise is thinly dispersed across the sector (with the obvious exception of ClientEarth), partly because of the financial cost of legal expertise. Organisational identity, ideas and values are also important to the availability and use of legal expertise in the environmental NGO community. An organisation's understanding of itself, and of law, is likely to be reflected in investment (or not) in law. In a self-perpetuating cycle, investment in legal resource determines the legal expertise in an organisation, which reverberates in the understanding of law, back to how much investment is thought necessary.

Chapter 3 Brexit and the journey to the Environment Act – interrupted

Groups seeking to influence post-Brexit environmental law and policy have faced an extraordinarily dramatic and dynamic political context. In this chapter, we recount the Brexit-environment saga from the referendum in June 2016 to a world responding to pandemic Covid-19 in June 2020. This period has seen three Prime Ministers, five Secretaries of State for the Environment and two General Elections. Government has veered from having no majority in parliament, to a working majority of 87 seats. Towards the end of our case study, Government and Parliament had to begin looking for new ways of working within and beyond Covid-19 'lockdown'.

We explore the political and legal opportunities available to environmental groups in this period, and identify hybrid political–legal opportunities, which are new to the literature. We highlight five elements of the Brexit process, overlapping and non-exhaustive, which have shaped the behaviour of environmental advocates: the relationship between parliament and executive, and the extraordinary shifts of power between them; the crucial legislation, and colossal amounts of government and parliamentary activity necessary to exit the EU; the increasing electoral significance of the environment for the governing Conservative Party; Secretary of State Michael Gove's adoption of a 'Green Brexit' rhetoric, underpinned by an 'equivalence' and 'governance gap' framing; the technically as well as politically demanding nature of Brexit.

The complex public drama of Brexit highlights the difficulties of generalising about NGO advocacy, but may also illuminate the use and appreciation of law and legal expertise more clearly than business as usual. Looking at our material through the lens of political, legal and hybrid opportunity confirms the emphasis of the literature on the partial shaping of NGO activities (in our case the use of law and legal expertise) by external factors. For much of the period of our case study, certainly between the two General Elections in 2017 and 2019, political opportunity opened doors for environmental groups, and a different set of opportunities would have led to different results, in terms of what NGOs did, what they achieved, and what we find in the rest of this book.

But political opportunity is complex. It shifts rapidly, and in different ways simultaneously hampers and enables environmental groups. Agility is crucial for environmental groups seeking to influence those with power.

Chapter 4 Law and legal expertise

In this chapter, we complicate our central organising concept of 'legal expertise'. There are many, diverse literatures on what 'expertise' is, its strengths and weaknesses, and what experts (expertise embodied) bring to the table. There is also a vast literature on the legal profession, what (expert) lawyers do and should do. We learn from these literatures that 'objectivity' is elusive, and idiosyncratic values and understandings of the world intrude into expert assessments. This undermines claims that experts are uniquely qualified to make decisions. Further, an over-emphasis of technical legal debate may have on occasion rendered crucial normative disagreement around Brexit-environment inaccessible.

We do not suggest that legal arguments are more important than arguments based on other forms of expertise, or on values. However, notwithstanding pockets of impressive legal expertise in the sector, our research suggests an undervaluing of legal expertise by environmental groups, and ambivalence towards legal specialisation. The diversity of the 'legal' in the Brexit-environment debate (from environmental law in all its diversity, to constitutional law, to trade law, etc.) has been extraordinary. Lawyers and non-lawyers alike may have underestimated just how difficult it is for 'generalists' to engage with this complexity and diversity.

The availability of (expert) resources and an organisation's understanding of expertise are mutually reinforcing: resources are not just a *practical* limit on what expertise is available, but spill into the very understanding of what *constitutes* expertise. The expertise available shapes not only what NGOs do, but also what they think they ought to do, and hence what (expert) resources they think they need. For as long as legal expertise is very thinly spread across the sector, it is hard to make the case that more is needed.

Chapter 5 Mobilising law in practice

We have been struck by the range of activities carried out by relatively few legal experts across even the largest organisations. Contributing to shaping advocacy is far from their priority, with case work and corporate work dominating, and litigation playing the starring role.

Legal expertise can make a number of contributions to advocacy. Understanding both the detailed implications of law, and the overarching frameworks and institutions that govern outcomes, can provide a different way of seeing the world, and a different way of changing the world. Law and legal experts play a significant role in shaping the rules of the social and economic game, in determining the way things get done. Many of our participants emphasised the authority and power of legal argument and saw legal expertise in environmental groups as an important equaliser. Law is one of the approaches available to convince influential audiences, and if government and other actors use legal expertise, environmental NGOs must too.

Legal expertise makes limited contributions to strategy and leadership within environmental NGOs, playing mainly a supportive role. Whilst we see indications of change, it is surprising and revealing that our participants did not see strategic leadership as a role for legal expertise: this is a sophisticated and well-resourced sector, dominated in practice by complex regulation, and our sample of interviewees is sensitive to law. The relative absence of legal expertise in leadership resonates again with the mutually reinforcing limitations on legal expertise in the community. Less legal expertise in the strategic brain of environmental groups both contributes to and reflects a relative absence of highly experienced legal experts in environmental groups; and overstretched legal capacity feeds out of and into a relatively weak engagement with the need for, and importantly the potential of, legal expertise.

Alongside a merely patchy interest in legal expertise, however, we have witnessed significant, skilful legal input into the public debate on Brexit-environment. We conclude from this that there is genuine, if under-developed, recognition of the importance of legal expertise, and that the sector impressively mustered its capacity in a crisis. Collaboration, discussed in the next two chapters, played a central role in that. We share the sense of our interviewees that legal expertise had considerable, if not uniquely significant, influence in the Brexit-environment debate. Combining this chapter's exploration of the heavy use of law with the sector's influence as a whole (chapter 7) reinforces this conclusion.

Chapter 6 Lobbying in coalition

Collaboration is an important part of our Brexit-environment story. We focus on Greener UK, a coalition established in 2016 with the sole purpose of working on the impact of Brexit on the environment. We think it is relatively uncontroversial to describe Greener UK as being at the centre of governance work on Brexit-environment. Working in coalition is, of course, not new to the sector. But our rich empirical data points to the fact that the sector's collaboration through Greener UK has been different, even special.

Working in coalition can have multiple advantages. We are especially interested in the way that drawing on collective resource has not only led to an efficient pooling of legal expertise, but has also deepened that expertise, creating more than the sum of its parts. But collaboration is challenging. Although collaboration creates efficiency in the pooling of resources, it has its own costs: the coalition itself needs to be resourced. The alignment of interests can be difficult, but if a coalition is to achieve its aims, it is vital that its member organisations reach consensus on goals and approaches. NGOs often compete (for recognition, funding, membership, etc.), so this is no easy task and can imply considerable profile sacrifice for individual organisations.

Chapter 7 Greener UK: influence and collaboration

Greener UK has been a crucially important actor in the environmental NGO sector's response to Brexit-environment. Our interviewees expressed almost unanimous, and in most cases unconditional, support for the work that Greener UK has done in shaping the post-Brexit environmental law landscape.

Identifying the 'success' of lobbying is extraordinarily challenging. Even what constitutes 'success' is likely to be contested. Establishing causation is extremely difficult, because of the significant external factors, explored in earlier chapters, at play in the Brexit process, and because of the many other actors who contributed to the debate alongside environmental NGOs. Having said that, we explore the influence of Greener UK on the Brexit-environment debate and the development of the Environment Bill, drawing on both our analysis of public documents produced by environmental NGOs, and the subjective perceptions of our interviewees. Although there have been tensions and unachieved objectives, and their approach might be contested, Greener UK has been broadly successful across two dimensions.

First, many elements of the Environment Bill (arguably even the existence of any Bill at all) can be traced to the work of Greener UK and its allies. And second, Greener UK has 'worked' as a collaboration: holding together over a long and difficult period, with constant activity as a coalition, and constant contributions from the member organisations. This was a strong and recurring theme from our interview data, and we identify three particular features of the Greener UK collaboration that have contributed to this dimension of success. First, consensus around the broad issues associated with Brexit, and the enormous salience of Brexit for the sector. Second, the careful attention to the working relationships and trust between the individuals involved. And third, the direct resourcing of Greener UK itself, making individuals responsible for ensuring that the collaboration worked.

There is a clear appetite for collaboration in the sector. Whatever happens next, the lessons of Greener UK should be learned and taken forward.

Chapter 8 Conclusions

The heterogeneity and complexity of the area we are examining (the nature of the sector, the nature of the problem), and the unique circumstances thrown up by Brexit, mean we must be cautious about drawing generalisations from our case study. But the learning from this project can, we believe, contribute to filling significant gaps in the scholarship and in practical knowledge in the sector.

Three tightly related themes have emerged most strongly from our work. First, the political and legal opportunities around Brexit have been fascinating, complex and unique. Our work confirms the emphasis in the literature on the influence of external political features on environmental groups' approaches to achieving their objectives. Second, we draw two ostensibly contradictory conclusions about the role of legal expertise in the community. We saw intense and sophisticated rallying of expertise around Brexit and the Environment Bill. And yet, we observed that legal expertise is thinly spread in environmental NGOs, and the understanding of the role and complexity of legal expertise is sometimes complacent. These limitations may be linked in a self-perpetuating cycle with the sector's internal context, especially cost and culture. Intervening to reduce the overstretching of legal capacity in the sector could have effects throughout these chains. The point would be not just to allow for more of the same, but to create space for more creative thinking about law and its contribution to the objectives of the environmental community. And third, a very powerful collaboration between environmental NGOs on Brexit has enjoyed a certain amount of success as discussed above. Greener UK has also had a strong impact on the use of law and legal expertise.

We write in strange and uncertain times. Careful and considered scrutiny of the Environment Bill as it continues its journey through Parliament is crucial, even if circumstances make that difficult. But a perfect Environment Act would not be the end of the story. The whole point of the 'governance gap' exercise was to provide a framework to assist civil society in holding the powerful to account. Using the Act will require yet more sustained, disciplined, careful, collaborative and at least partly legal work.

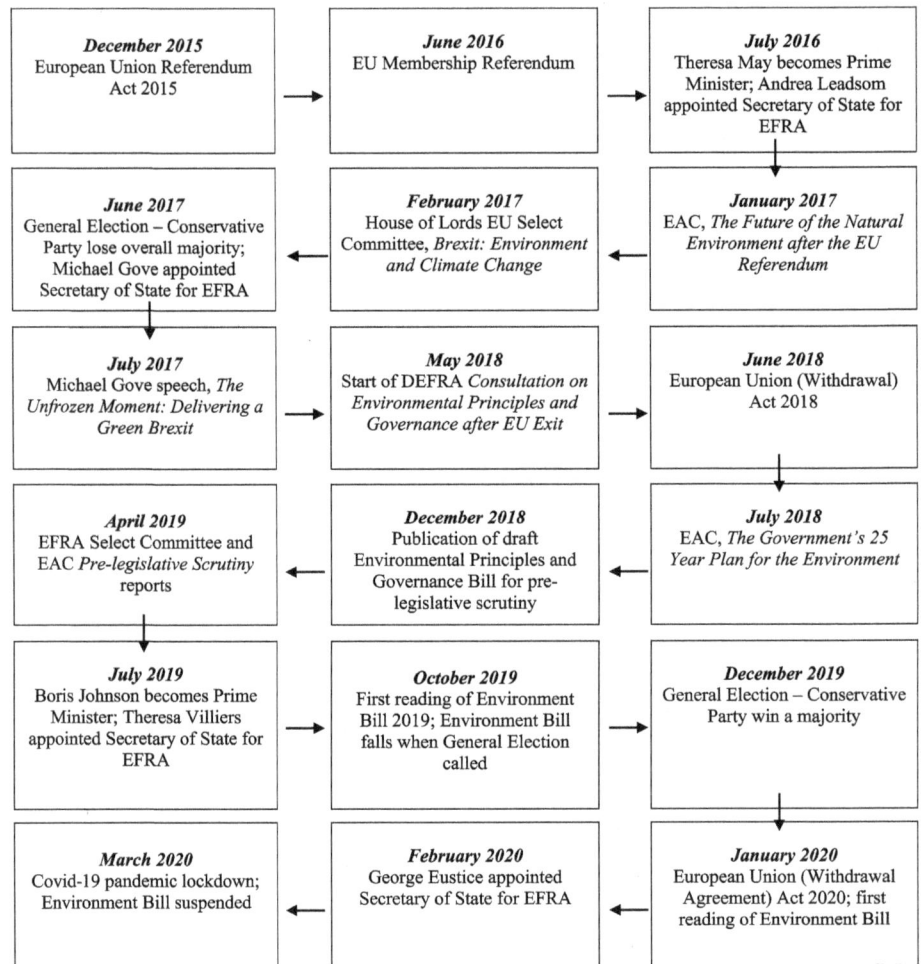

Figure 1 Brexit-environment timeline, December 2015 to June 2020 (source: authors).

1
Law and legal expertise for Brexit-environment: scope, meaning and method

Introduction

Environmental groups are a crucial part of environmental protection and improvement in the UK. They are diverse in size, sector, activity and funding; they take a range of approaches, from protests, demonstrations, petitions and campaigning to formal insider lobbying; they play different roles, including managing nature protection sites, carrying out scientific research, scrutinising public and private sector behaviour, as well as advocating for policy and legal change. Law and legal expertise are important tools in the persuasive armoury of environmental groups. Our main aim in this monograph is to enhance our understanding of the ways in which environmental groups use (or do not use) law and legal expertise in their public advocacy around environmental protection. Our interest in legal expertise and the role of law is broader than much of the social movement literature: we focus on legislation-making over case-making, and on the ways in which advocates of social and legal change use their knowledge of legal norms, rules and discourses to influence others. We explore this through the response of environmental groups to the UK's decision to leave the European Union (EU), or 'Brexit'.

We do not suggest in this book that legal expertise is always necessary in arguments for change, or more important than other sorts of expertise. But we do argue that legal expertise is one distinctive and important way of understanding and shaping the world. Our claims in this monograph turn around three tightly related themes. First, the political and legal opportunities around Brexit have been fascinating, complex and unique. We confirm the emphasis in the literature on the significance of external factors in shaping the activities of environmental groups: with a different set of political opportunities, we would be telling a very different story. Further, paying close attention to legal mobilisation *outside* judicial and quasi-judicial fora has allowed us to add to ideas of political and legal opportunity, identifying hybrid political–legal opportunities that create space for legal expertise in political fora. Second, we draw two ostensibly contradictory conclusions about the role of legal expertise in the environmental community. We argue that legal expertise may be under-utilised and under-appreciated in environmental groups, and that its role in advocacy is limited. And yet at the same time, we saw intense and sophisticated rallying of legal expertise around Brexit and the Environment Bill, and that seems to have had some impact. This suggests a genuine, if under-developed, valuing of legal expertise in the sector, and an impressive ability to muster resources in a crisis. This was in part enabled by what constitutes our third theme, namely the very powerful collaboration between environmental non-governmental organisations (NGOs) on Brexit, which has enjoyed (qualified) success in a number of different respects. Our work bears out the assumptions in much of the literature and practice that collaboration contributes positively to NGO work. We identify some of the key qualities of a successful collaboration.

Brexit has been and continues to be an enormous constitutional, political, economic and personal rupture. It also constitutes a massive change to the UK's laws and institutions of environmental protection, which had been shaped by EU membership since 1973. As such, it is a major challenge for the environmental NGO community. One of the many pieces of legislation that has been promised to ease the exit is the first wide-ranging UK environmental legislation for 25 years: the Environment Bill. The Bill is currently (June 2020) paused, due to the pandemic coronavirus Covid-19.

We do three things in this chapter to set the scene for the rest of the book. We begin with brief introductions to practical and theoretical contexts that feature throughout: the environmental NGO sector in the UK; Brexit and the Environment Bill; some of the theoretical context for our work (in particular legal mobilisation and political and legal opportunity theories); NGO advocacy, influence and impact. We touch on our methodology throughout this chapter and turn in detail to the two empirical elements of our work in the penultimate section. We end this chapter with an outline of the book.

The UK environmental NGO community

Environmental NGOs have developed in many ways since their emergence in the mid-nineteenth century.[1] Advances in our understanding of natural ecology have led to both an expansion in the range of issues considered, and a recognition that they extend beyond the local and national to the transnational and ultimately global. The number of NGOs, and public support for them, has increased dramatically in the UK and groups have become more institutionalised both internally (in terms of resources, staffing, etc.) and externally (in that they are recognised by governments[2] and other power-holders as authoritative voices that have access to important expertise on a range of issues).[3]

The diversity of environmental NGOs is astounding. There are large and small groups, groups that focus on broad or niche areas, groups that have national or international reach and groups founded by local communities to address particular local challenges. Some groups have a strong preference for certain tactics such as protest or litigation, whilst other groups would normally seek to initiate change through lobbying and media campaigns. Sources of funding also differ considerably. Some groups receive significant funding from public membership and sales to the public, others rely solely on individual donations, government grants and/or philanthropic funding.[4] The future of environmental NGO funding from all sources is of course a great unknown, given the economic and other impacts of the ongoing pandemic Covid-19 and the response to it.[5] It is difficult to predict how this crisis will affect the state of the sector.

The diversity of groups is reflected in the range of labels attached to NGOs: civil society organisations, community-based organisations, pressure groups, grassroots organisations, interest groups and environmental groups, to name but a few. Some of these labels may be associated with a particular type of group; for example, pressure groups as organisations that display a preference for more activist strategies, grassroots organisations as groups focused on local issues and/or action.

We know an NGO when we see one, but a commonly agreed definition is hard to find. Taken literally, 'NGO' is an umbrella term that could arguably cover any kind of organisation that is not a state. The literature, as we do, takes a narrower view. We use the term NGO to describe a not-for-profit public interest organisation that operates independently of government. Their purpose in our case is to address environmental issues and challenges. NGOs may pursue goals by seeking influence with public and private stakeholders using a range of direct strategies including lobbying, protest and litigation. Groups, including think tanks, may also look to influence change through the generation of knowledge to support environmental goals. Whilst we acknowledge the multiple labels attached to these organisations in this work, we simply use the terms 'environmental NGO' and 'environmental group' synonymously.

In the absence of specific numbers, one can only assume that there are thousands of environmental NGOs in the UK.[6] A 2013 Environmental Funders Network report concluded that one in ten adults was a member or supporter of a British environmental or conservation group.[7] A small number of groups have a relatively high income and staff numbers, and some of those also have a large membership base.[8] There is also a large number of much smaller organisations. Expertise is unevenly distributed across the sector. In light of this heterogeneity, the question of how and why certain groups pursue certain goals in certain ways is hugely complex and makes generalisations difficult if not impossible.

Two groups deserve particular mention in this introduction: ClientEarth and Greener UK. Launched in London in 2007, ClientEarth focuses on the use of law and legal expertise to achieve social change, and occupies an important place in the UK environmental NGO community. Made up of lawyers and environmental experts, it uses 'the power of the law to protect the planet and the people who live in it'.[9] Although perhaps best known for using litigation to achieve environmental change, ClientEarth works on all stages of the lifecycle of environmental law, from the science, to law and policy making, to implementation and enforcement.[10] ClientEarth regularly challenges the government and the private sector on their environmental ambitions.

Hosted by Green Alliance, an 'independent think tank focused on ambitious leadership for the environment',[11] Greener UK has been at the heart of the environmental sector's work on post-Brexit environmental law. It is a formal coalition of 13 major environmental groups with a combined membership of over eight million.[12] It was set up in 2016 with the aim of ensuring the maintenance and enhancement of environmental protections post-Brexit. As the Brexit-environment debate has become bigger and broader, the scope, remit and sheer size of Greener UK has expanded and evolved significantly. A lot of Greener UK's work on environmental principles and governance post-Brexit has been channelled through its Brexit Scenarios Group. Multiple pillars and task groups work on activities across a range of other areas, including teams working on the Environment, Agriculture and Trade Bills, and on EU negotiations. Its collaboration with other coalitions, including Wildlife and Countryside Link, adds a further layer of complexity to its organisational structure and governance. The Greener UK Board, chaired by the Executive Director of Green Alliance, oversees the work of the coalition and provides strategic direction. The Greener UK unit coordinates and drives forward the coalition's activities. The work of Greener UK features throughout this monograph, and we explore its work and its impact in detail in chapter 7.

Brexit and the Environment Bill

The UK joined the EU in January 1973. The EU membership referendum in June 2016 signalled the beginning of a tortuous process of leaving the EU, on 31 January 2020, with two general elections, two new prime ministers, and three postponements in between. An unprecedentedly dramatic parliamentary situation reflected the fact that for long periods, the hardest of no deal Brexits (leaving the EU without any arrangements in place to manage the exit or the future relationship), not leaving the EU at all, and a more managed exit (itself begging lots of questions), seemed more or less equally likely outcomes. Although the UK has now left the EU on the basis of agreement, the process of detachment is not over. The Withdrawal Agreement between the EU and the UK includes a transition or implementation period to the end of 2020,[13] during which the UK is fully bound by EU law, but plays no role in its institutions or decision-making processes. As we write (June 2020), the institutional arrangements for the relationship between the UK and the EU after the end of 2020 remain open.[14] The pandemic Covid-19 has interrupted and slowed down negotiations.

The EU has a large and distinctive body of law across the spectrum of substantive and procedural environmental matters. The EU's record on the environment is obviously imperfect, in ways too numerous to mention. The Common Agricultural Policy is widely criticised for allowing and even incentivising damaging agricultural practices. More generally, the EU has some obscure processes that take place, literally and metaphorically, at a distance from its citizens. It sometimes overly prioritises economic and trade interests over the environment. And good implementation has often been a weak spot. But the EU has powerful ways of making and sticking with environmental standards, and its size and strength have allowed it at times to pioneer and insist on ambitious objectives.

The EU has dominated the environmental arena in the UK. Although EU environmental law is not comprehensive, and can often be implemented by Member States in flexible ways, little is entirely untouched by EU law. EU Directives and Regulations have not been 'foreign' law; on the contrary, they create legally binding standards within the domestic legal system. The UK also participated in the EU's decision-making bodies, the main institutions of Commission, Council, Parliament, European Council and Court of Justice, as well as less high-profile bodies such as the European Environment Agency, and myriad technical and political committees and networks.[15]

Unpicking this relationship was always going to be a daunting challenge. The EU (Withdrawal) Act 2018 provided for the repeal of the European Communities Act 1972, the Act of Parliament that establishes the central place of EU law in the UK's domestic system, from the end of the transition period. But EU law is so deeply embedded in UK law that the loss of EU law overnight by repeal of the 1972 Act would leave a gaping hole. The 2018 Act creates a new category of 'retained law', which allows for the body of EU law to survive in UK law on exit day, for subsequent amendment or repeal if desired.[16]

Retained EU law includes 'EU-derived domestic legislation' and 'direct EU legislation'. The main type of EU-derived domestic legislation is secondary legislation that was passed under the European Communities Act 1972 (and so needs to be 'saved' on repeal of that Act), but the definition extends to statutory instruments passed under other legislation, and indeed to primary legislation. Direct EU legislation is legislation that has effect before exit day, without having been transposed into domestic law, most significantly the law contained in EU Regulations.

But some environmentally significant EU legal arrangements are not retained by the 2018 Act. In chapter 3 we discuss the EU measures that enhance the accountability of government for the implementation and enforcement of environmental law, EU approaches to developing new environmental standards and the environmental principles found in the EU treaties. Recognition that losing these features of EU law would leave what became known as a 'governance gap', provided the starting point for the Environment Bill. Part 1 of the Bill, entitled 'Environmental Governance', is the focus of this book. It contains a framework for setting legal targets on matters relating to the natural environment, and for creating, updating and monitoring environmental policy within a legislative framework. It contains provisions requiring a government policy statement on environmental principles. And chapter 2 of Part 1 of the Environment Bill provides for the creation of a new body called the Office for Environmental Protection (OEP), designed to monitor government and other public bodies for their compliance with environmental law: a body to regulate the regulators.

But this legislative moment has also been an opportunity for reshaping UK law in other areas. The Environment Bill is a wide-ranging and enormous (133 clauses, 19 schedules, over 240 pages) piece of framework legislation, granting powers and providing more or less substance on issues from plastic pollution to smoke control, to natural capital and nature recovery networks. It is the first proposed wide-ranging UK (or English)[17] environmental legislation since the Environment Act 1995. The intervening 25 years saw a number of important acts on single subjects and relatively narrow (but significant) institutional change (e.g. Natural Environment and Rural Communities Act 2006, Climate Change Act 2008, Marine and Coastal Access Act 2009, various planning acts). There was nothing of the scope and significance of the Bill.

The environmental NGO community, and others, worked extraordinarily hard advocating for the introduction of the Environment Bill, and then shaping its content. As we argue in chapter 7, they have enjoyed major, although not complete, success.

The environmental implications of Brexit, and its stimulation of the Environment Bill, provide an opportune case study for our work. Although the edges of the process are blurred, the more or less self-contained 'story' of the Bill within the period since the Brexit referendum,[18] and the relative stability of the main actors (especially Greener UK), provide a firm core for assessing arguments made by environmental groups. Moreover, this is a hugely significant moment: the Environment Bill will shape UK or English environmental law for a generation, and this book will not be the last word on its genesis.

Our focus on a single Part of a single Bill narrows down our case study of Brexit-environment. Principles and governance have been a constant and significant focus for NGO activity since the 2016 referendum and provide a useful lens through which to consider the role of law and legal expertise in NGO advocacy. We do not, however, intend to dismiss the involvement of the community in the broader environmental debate. In particular, environmental NGOs have engaged intensively around the development of three other environmentally significant 'Brexit bills': fisheries, agriculture and trade. Our view is that the benefits of a focused case study outweigh the limitations of scope. For similar reasons, we focus on the UK/English perspective, from Whitehall and Westminster. The UK's territorial constitution has been a sensitive part of the Brexit journey.[19] Both Northern Ireland and Scotland voted to remain in the EU in the 2016 referendum. The Welsh Assembly, the Northern Ireland Assembly[20] and the Scottish Parliament *all* withheld consent from the EU (Withdrawal Agreement) Act 2020,[21] which approved the Withdrawal Agreement between the UK and the EU, and the UK's exit from the EU.[22] Withholding consent has no legal impact, but highlights the spatial and constitutional aspect of passionate political divides over Brexit. Further, where particular environmental powers and responsibilities, previously held at EU level, sit after Brexit (with the UK government or the other governments or executives) is constitutionally sensitive. Common EU baselines, and common membership of the EU single market, have meant that environmental discordance between the UK's countries has been kept to a minimum.[23] Our self-limitation to English (mainly)/UK law and Whitehall/Westminster provides for a different, more focused, discussion than a comparative assessment of the four jurisdictions.

The case study methodology has well-rehearsed limitations and advantages, in particular around its positive potential for very fine-grained analysis of social life, versus the challenges of more general applicability. We cannot make simple claims for the generalisability of the conclusions in this book. Indeed, we conclude that Brexit provided special opportunities for, and made special demands on, law and legal expertise. We do, however, think that there are lessons to be learned from our case study, in part even *because* of the particular demands and opportunities presented by Brexit.[24] Our purpose is to explore and better understand the ways in which environmental NGOs use and understand law and legal expertise, and the political and legal contexts that incentivise or restrict the use of law and legal expertise. Our unusually law-heavy and anomalously politically open case study (see chapter 3) provides rich lessons on what NGOs do with law. The call on legal expertise was particularly intense in this case, but the challenges faced by the sector remained – challenges around resources and internal culture for example – as discussed further throughout this book. The nature of our case study means that when we identify challenges or limitations in the appreciation of legal expertise here, they are likely to be even more acute in other cases.

Some theoretical background

This book contributes to the literature on 'legal mobilisation' by (environmental) NGOs. As an umbrella term, legal mobilisation refers to the use of law in NGO efforts to shape social change.[25] Part of the purpose of developing a discourse around 'legal mobilisation' was precisely to broaden the preoccupations of the literature beyond courts and 'impact litigation'.[26] Nevertheless, the scholarship continues to be dominated by a consideration of legal rights claims through the courts, or other formal institutions.[27] Indeed, some argue that the phrase 'legal mobilisation' should properly be reserved for 'the use of law in an explicit, self-conscious way through the invocation of a formal, institutional mechanism', especially (although not only) a court.[28] Focusing on the response to Brexit, and the work on various iterations of the Environment Bill, takes us well beyond litigation, even broadly defined to include 'the presentation of claims to be decided by the courts (or court-like agencies) and the whole penumbra of threats, feints and so forth, surrounding such presentation'.[29]

We are seeking to assess the role of legal expertise, how law is mobilised, beyond litigation, beyond the court room or other quasi-judicial spaces. We recognise, however, that drawing lines between litigation and 'not' is neither straightforward nor necessarily helpful. Most cases started never reach the court room, and most disputes get nowhere near becoming cases. Further, when NGOs campaign or lobby around legal obligations, the threat of litigation may be implicit. And much careful legal work is often necessary to turn successful litigation into meaningful action.[30]

The emphasis on litigation in the legal mobilisation scholarship, and also practice, reflects a well-known academic preference for courts and cases as 'the star of the show',[31] over statutes and legislatures.[32] Cases are appealing, for their human and visceral quality in the retelling, for their apparently sudden eventfulness in campaigning, for their visibility and apparent speed.[33] Whilst there might be good practical campaigning reasons to prefer particular approaches, it is short-sighted to pass over the many ways in which legal expertise shapes the world outside rights claiming or litigation. A rehearsal of legislation's crucial part in the legal landscape is probably not necessary for the current audience: its role in adapting law to changing circumstances, negotiating a path through contentious, complex issues,[34] embracing and working through social disagreement,[35] solidifying and increasing the enforceability of the concessions.

A range of factors influence environmental groups' approach to change. Factors internal to the environmental group, including resources, identity, ideas and values, contribute to NGO strategy.[36] Political opportunity theories argue that the approaches taken, and their effectiveness, are shaped (not determined) by external factors:

'The basic premise is that exogenous factors enhance or inhibit prospects for mobilization, for particular sorts of claims to be advanced rather than others, for particular strategies of influence to be exercised, and for movements to affect mainstream institutional politics and policy.'[37] We conclude that both internal and external factors have shaped environmental groups' activities and their ability to achieve their objectives over the past four years.

The main interest of political opportunity theories was initially in the relationship between strategies of protest, outside of orthodox political spaces, and conventional political activity within institutions.[38] Legal opportunity theory was developed to add more thoughtful consideration of law to the lobbying/protest dyad, analysing what influences the choice of and success of legal mobilisation.[39] The legal opportunity literature focuses almost entirely on efforts to advance social change through litigation, exploring the issues that facilitate or inhibit legal action.[40] In seeking to understand legal mobilisation around Brexit, we expand the literature on lobbying by looking at the role of legal expertise in political advocacy, and the literature on legal mobilisation by looking at the role of law outside judicial and quasi-judicial fora. In addition to political or legal opportunities, we identify what we call hybrid political–legal opportunities, a space within which arguments based in law and legal expertise may be particularly politically powerful.

NGO advocacy, influence and impact

One of the many ways in which NGOs try to influence the state of the world is through what we term, interchangeably, 'advocacy' or 'lobbying'. Either advocacy or (less intuitively) lobbying[41] can involve campaigning activities to influence public opinion, as well as direct contact with policy elites. We are concerned with the latter: 'insider' advocacy or lobbying, an 'information-based interaction between groups and organizations and government'[42] with the aim of influencing policy formulation, law-making and decision-making. 'Lobbying' can sometimes imply illegitimate influence over political decision-making, but the scholarship generally implies no such negative intent, and nor do we. Moreover, we are not concerned with the activities of commercial or professional lobbyists who are paid by clients to leverage influence with power-holders (public and private) but instead, focus on lobbying by environmental groups.

We have some sympathy for the critique that the use of legal expertise may be inherently conservative and status quo preserving, that it might colonise more activist or inclusive approaches to change.[43] 'Outsider' groups[44] may provide a sense of the perceived limits of legal strategies: the language of Extinction Rebellion, for example, at least in spring/summer 2019, gives a sense that law and negotiation within established institutions have failed.[45] Lisa Vanhala describes (with caveats) Greenpeace (often seen as towards the outsider end of any spectrum) as having 'a skeptical orientation toward what can be achieved by relying on the legal framework alone'; environmental law is described by one of her participants as 'a fig leaf covering dirt'.[46] Although we think that there is such a thing as activist or radical law,[47] we accept that our decision to focus on law and formal engagement around Brexit may leave an important, more radical, part of the environmental movement (and Brexit) unexamined.

Environmental groups have to make important decisions when designing an approach to their objectives. Where choices are to be made, NGOs will ultimately choose those approaches that they believe are likely to be most effective in achieving their goals. There is a rich literature on measuring the impact or influence of NGO action. This includes significant debates on the impact of litigation, and its ability to contribute (both directly and indirectly) to social change.[48] And there is some consideration of the impact of lobbying (across different jurisdictions, different policy areas and different branches of government), although relatively little on the UK specifically, or on the impact of lobbying using arguments based on law or legal expertise.[49]

The methodological literature is clear: assessing impact is incredibly complex. Even taking the extreme case of Friends of the Earth's 'Big Ask' campaign for the Climate Change Act 2008, very widely accepted to be impactful,[50] there would be a lot to think about. Other factors intervene (much of our book revolves around the significance of 'other' factors in the evolution of the Environment Bill), and success is rarely complete (Friends of the Earth did not get everything they wanted). An additional complicating factor is that even if there is evidence of influence, the outcome may not necessarily be viewed as a success. For example, a very weak Climate Change Act would have demonstrated Friends of the Earth's influence, but not necessarily success. NGO objectives may not always be easily identifiable, for example in the difference between what NGOs publicly demand, and what they privately hope for. Nor is lobbying generally a zero-sum game, in which policy outcomes are measured on a 'winner-takes-all' basis. As noted by Christine Mahoney, 'if they get nothing but prevented something worse, have they succeeded? If they got some of what they wanted but not all, have they failed?'[51] Lobbying may make no difference to the specific outcome, but may influence the political assumptions of the future. Would this be a 'victory' for interest groups? And even if the outcome is perceived as a success, to what extent can that outcome be attributed to the lobbying activities of a particular group or groups, or indeed the use of particular arguments in advocacy (such as those based on law and legal expertise)? What is clear is that sometimes lobbying seems to work and sometimes it does not.[52]

In chapter 7, we adopt and adapt Michelle Betsill and Elisabeth Corell's powerful framework for measuring influence. They argue (in the context of international law and lobbying) that there are two dimensions to influence: '(1) the intentional transmission of information by NGOs and (2) alterations in behavior in response to that information.'[53] The first dimension in the framework can be evidenced by, for example, NGO activities, access to (in their case, international) negotiations, and resources, all of which provide an insight into how NGOs shared information and the types of information provided. Betsill and Corell are critical of an overemphasis in the literature of this side of the equation; it is of course possible that NGOs will be very active in negotiations without other actors altering their behaviour in response. The second dimension, which focuses on behavioural alteration, is perhaps most easily evidenced if the final text reflects NGO wording, although even that does not necessarily indicate causation. Betsill and Corell advocate the use of diverse methodologies to provide robust conclusions on influence, including process tracing, which involves the construction of a chain of evidence linking NGO sharing of information, actors use (or not) of that information and the effects (or not) of that information.[54]

Our work has not been designed to draw absolute conclusions on the impact of NGOs. As discussed in later chapters, the journey to what will (may) become the Environment Act was tortuous, and environmental NGOs interjected vigorously at numerous points with numerous other actors, using legal and other forms of expertise heavily in their arguments. As Matthew Paterson says of NGO activity during the UN Framework Convention on Climate Change, 'it is hard to conceive' that all of their activities 'were without effect'.[55] But environmental NGOs were far from the only influential feature of the landscape, which included for example the effects of young voters in the 2017 general election[56] and the school strike and Extinction Rebellion in 2019. And it is also of course early to be thinking about impact. The impact of all of this advocacy on the environment depends on continued activity over the coming years; and at the time of writing, the Environment Bill has been postponed due to the Covid-19 pandemic.

We do however draw some conclusions, in chapters 5 to 7, on the role of the sector around Brexit. We develop our methodology further in those chapters. We use our analysis of Select Committee submissions, plus a reading of some other public communications on Brexit-environment, to identify key NGO ideas and demands that were strongly made during the Brexit-environment debate. We do not aim to be comprehensive, but rather to identify some illustrative issues and areas. We explore specifically Greener UK's demands, for two main reasons. Most importantly, Greener UK represents a significant part of the community on the issues at the heart of our case study, and so provides a rough proxy for sectoral demands and success. More prosaically, ensuring a systematic analysis of an individual NGO's demands would be problematic as websites evolve and old material has been removed. However, we do not intend to suggest that Greener UK is responsible for all of the positive outcomes of the sector's work in this area. Most obviously, the active and energetic collaboration by a large number of NGOs is what made Greener UK what it is (as discussed in chapters 6 and 7). Equally importantly, the impact of work by those NGOs from within and outside the coalition, and other actors such as practitioners and academics, is impossible to separate from the impact of Greener UK.

Bearing in mind Betsill and Corell's cautions, we explore whether the demands of Greener UK shaped the content and depth of the public (especially parliamentary and government) discussion of Brexit-environment, and whether they found their way into parliamentary conclusions, government documents, and ultimately the Bill. Further, whilst our interviews did not set out to 'measure' impact, our interviewees shared some useful insights on the impact of environmental group lobbying around Brexit. We conclude that Greener UK had considerable success in shaping the Brexit-environment debate and the existence and content of Part 1 of the Environment Bill. It did not, of course, get everything it wanted and it will no doubt be subject to criticism over detailed decisions.

If it is difficult to measure a sector's overall influence on a debate, drawing confident conclusions on the role of particular arguments (those based on law and legal expertise) is almost impossible. The special circumstances of Brexit, discussed in chapter 3, have however enabled us to shine a brighter light than usual on law, and as discussed in chapter 5 (pages 118–20) we share the sense of many of our interviewees that legal expertise had *some* impact on the debate and the existence and content of the Bill. The strong place for legal expertise in this broadly successful advocacy campaign provides some additional indirect evidence for the impact of legal expertise.

Method and methodology: the empirical material

Turning to our empirical material, it is important before we go further to address the fact that one of us (Maria) has been working on the environmental implications of Brexit since well before the referendum,[57] in an academic as well as 'public service' context.[58] She has to some extent participated in, and contributed to shaping, the phenomena being investigated. Her (unpaid) membership of Greener UK's Brexit Scenarios Group since early 2017 has involved reasonably consistent attendance at monthly and then fortnightly two-hour meetings, and many email exchanges on specific issues. This involvement was particularly intense between mid-2017 and summer 2019. The relationship with Greener UK emerged organically and informally rather than from recruitment or appointment, and has been longer and deeper than probably anyone either intended or would have predicted. Occasionally, Maria's observations as something of an 'insider' will enrich our discussion. This is, however, far from an insider account. Maria's involvement came out of a desire to use her knowledge of EU environmental law to counter her dismay at Brexit, including its environmental impacts,[59] not to research her Greener UK colleagues. Her involvement is anyway peripheral to those working full time in environmental groups, or in environmental groups on Brexit specifically. This project is driven by both authors' longstanding interest in participation and expertise (and hence NGOs),[60] as well as curiosity about what we saw taking place in NGOs, set against the scholarly emphasis on litigation.

We should also say at this point that the restrictions imposed as a result of the pandemic coronavirus Covid-19 had some impact on our methodology. The two authors were unable to meet physically as planned and so completed the research and writing together online. A very small amount of material that we would otherwise have read has not been available. The follow-up interviews in March and April 2020 had always been planned remotely, primarily for the convenience of the interviewees. More generally, we had expected to know the fate of the Environment Bill by the time of completing this manuscript. The very severe impacts of Covid-19 and the associated restrictions on gatherings and movement have had a major impact on the progress of the Environment Bill. We return to this in chapter 3. Further, the profound implications of the virus, and the global response to it, will have unpredictable impacts on the issues we have been researching.

Participants in our research

We conducted semi-structured interviews with 17 people. We drew on personal knowledge of the field and personal contacts, plus their recommendations, to identify potential interviewees. We sought individuals with diverse professional backgrounds, as below. For richness of insight into our case study, we sought out interviewees with a common interest in Brexit-environment and/or the Environment Bill. Probably unsurprisingly, but with implications for our work, our NGO participants had all at some point worked with or for the Greener UK coalition. Our analysis for the same reason has tended towards the larger, more 'establishment' side of the NGO movement, and that is bound to be reflected in our conclusions.

We made initial contact by email, and most of those whom we approached agreed to be interviewed; in total five people either did not respond or were unwilling or unable to be interviewed. Ten of our participants were employed by environmental NGOs (including think tanks). Some of these NGOs are well established whilst others have been formed more recently, and we have included both membership and non-membership NGOs. They are all active nationally, and in some cases have an explicit European or international remit. Between them, they span a broad range of environmental interests, including species and landscape protection, pollution and climate change. Seven of our interviewees were not employed by environmental NGOs, but have worked with such groups, and in some cases have been employed by such groups in the past: two worked in large philanthropic re-granting organisations with a good overview of the NGO community; two worked in private practice; two were senior actors in government or non-departmental public bodies; and one was an academic with strong links to legal practice. These interviewees provided useful alternative and additional perspectives to the self-reported views of the other participants.

Most of our interviewees were deeply involved in the activity around Brexit, the rest were at least familiar with the debate. Ten of our interviewees have a legal background (i.e. have studied law at undergraduate or postgraduate level), although not all of those have professional legal qualifications. At the time of the interviews, they had between one and over forty years of experience working in or with environmental

NGOs. All worked primarily in England, although some have been and continue to be involved in Brussels, Wales and Scotland.

At the same time as Maria's closeness to the Brexit-environment community, discussed above, creates advantages of insight, understanding and access, it generates methodological challenges.[61] To the extent that Maria's vision of her own role in the world is law-heavy, any influence she may have had on people or outputs may resonate in a particular approach to law by certain interest groups, or more specifically by our participants. She has contributed her own legal expertise to the communal effort, and that may sometimes be reflected in NGO expertise. Further, because of the very significant role of Greener UK in NGO activity on Brexit/environment, most of our interviewees had met Maria since the referendum, if not before. All of our interviewees except for two knew Maria, in some cases through meeting on a couple of occasions, but in other cases through an ongoing friendly, professional relationship, over many months or years. We are very aware that the simple human desires to be nice and to be liked, which might turn into saying what the interviewee thinks the interviewer wants to hear, might be amplified in this case.

But researchers and researched are always in a relationship of some sort, and the values and perspectives of the researcher are always present. There is no direct relationship of power in our case, and our interviewees are elite actors in the sense of having skills and experience that set them apart.[62] But we are conscious that in some cases a large gap in experience between researchers and interviewees, together with pre-existing relationships, may have introduced a perceived hierarchy; although many of our interviewees far outstripped our experience and knowledge of the area. We have endeavoured to maintain our critical independence. Critical 'reflexivity' requires 'the researchers' self-understanding of the research process ... their ability to "question" the testimony of respondents (are they telling me what *I* want to hear?) and ... their awareness of the development of the emerging theory (am I seeing what *I* want to see?)'.[63] It has helped to have two equally experienced researchers jointly conducting interviews (with one exception) and jointly engaging in interpretation. Maria's pre-existing relationships with our interviewees is, to some extent, countered by Carolyn having met only two of the interviewees prior to commencement of this project.

The community involved in this work is small. To maintain anonymity, we are not identifying the characteristics of individual interviewees, or the organisations they represent. Other than in our discussion of the Greener UK coalition, we are not attempting to ascribe particular approaches to particular organisations, for example large or small, or types of individual, for example by qualification or experience. The occasional exception is where we draw distinctions, which are also drawn by many of our interviewees, between ClientEarth and other NGOs. Law is at the core of the culture of ClientEarth, and so we might expect them to have particular insight into the role of law and legal expertise.

We held a small 'kick-off' event in April 2019, before starting the interviews, with five NGO actors and one other academic, gathering useful insights on NGO perspectives, which helped us to shape our interview questions in more detail, and revealed additional lines of inquiry. Our first interview, which we used as a pilot to assess questions, timing and themes, as well as to gather data, was in May 2019. The next 14 interviews were carried out in two weeks in July 2019 and assessed on a preliminary basis over the summer. It was clear that we could enrich our data; we carried out two further interviews (16 and 17), in October 2019 and February 2020.

It was apparent from our first interview onwards that we would want to explore collaboration between NGOs. Our analysis of the interviews suggested, as discussed in chapters 6 and 7, that the sector's shared objectives on Brexit provided a particularly favourable context for collaboration. We (and some of our interviewees) suspected that collaboration might be more challenging around the provisions of the, at that point unarticulated, 'second part' of the Environment Bill, dealing with a whole range of substantive environmental matters.[64] As a result, we decided to carry out some shorter follow-up interviews by Zoom or Skype. We approached most of the initial interviewees who had been working in environmental groups both at the time of our original interviews and in February 2020.[65] Of nine requests, we had eight positive responses. We carried out these supplementary interviews in March and April 2020.

Both the first and follow-up interviews were semi-structured, around a common set of core questions, which were slightly different for those employed by NGOs and the others. All participants agreed to be recorded. Interviews were transcribed by a professional transcriber. One of us listened to each of the recordings, checking the transcript and our understanding. All responses were anonymised and anonymised identifiers are used in this monograph.[66] When the identity of the participant might be revealed, we do not attribute the quotation. We have very lightly edited the quotations for the benefit of readers.

With one exception, both researchers participated in all of the interviews. We each initially analysed the transcripts independently, making a list of themes according to which we highlighted the transcripts.[67] We met to discuss the themes, then exchanged and merged our themes and documents. We did the same thing with interviews 16 and 17, and with our follow-up interviews. We each re-read the whole set of transcripts at least twice, as well as referring back to them from time to time. Drawing conclusions from our interview data was an iterative and collaborative exercise.[68] We gave our participants the opportunity to check the interview quotations used in the book, and occasionally as a result removed the identifier to maintain anonymity.

We held a closing event in June 2020, where we tested some of our conclusions. This event was for NGOs and the funding community. With permission, we have included some quotations from the event in what follows.

Other empirical work

For external evidence of what environmental groups actually do with law, and to get some sense of a broader community's activity on Brexit, we also analysed public documents produced by environmental NGOs. Submissions to parliamentary Select Committee inquiries on Brexit and the environment[69] are an accessible and coherent body of material. Given the politics of Brexit, discussed in chapter 3, Select Committees absorbed a considerable amount of NGO activity on Brexit and what became the Environment Bill. Select Committees are a 'key site of influence for external pressure groups',[70] and they do seem to have nuanced as well as some direct impact on government and others.[71] We have not systematically analysed 'behind closed doors', face-to-face or written interactions with government and parliamentarians. We recognise that this is important, but the public-facing work is sufficient to place alongside what interviewees told us.

We read or re-read all Select Committee reports on Brexit and the environment. We identified six Select Committee reports (five inquiries), plus the work to date of the Environment Bill Committee, for closer analysis:

– Environmental Audit Committee, *The Future of the Natural Environment after the EU Referendum* 6th Report of Session 2016–17 HC 599 (report in January 2017);

- House of Lords European Union Select Committee, *Brexit: Environment and Climate Change*, 12th Report of Session 2016–17 HL Paper 109 (report in February 2017);
- Environmental Audit Committee, *The Government's 25 Year Plan for the Environment* 8th Report of 2017–19 HC 803 (report in July 2018);
- Joint call for evidence, Environment, Food and Rural Affairs Committee, *Pre-Legislative Scrutiny of the Draft Environment (Principles and Governance) Bill*, 14th Report of 2017–19 HC 1893;
- Environmental Audit Committee, *Scrutiny of the Draft Environment (Principles and Governance) Bill* 18th Report of 2017–19 HC 1951 (reports in April 2019);
- Written and oral evidence submitted to the House of Commons Public Bill Committee, *Environment Bill*.

These reports, from the first submission of evidence to the latest activity of the Public Bill Committee, takes us from the end of 2016 (shortly after the referendum), and involves four different Select Committees, plus one Public Bill Committee. The Select Committee inquiries all address the environmental impacts of Brexit, but across a range of areas. The context and detail of these inquiries are explored further in chapter 3, and our analysis of NGO inputs in chapters 5 and 7.

We analysed only written submissions, with two exceptions: the House of Lords inquiry, which did not make a call for written evidence, but invited oral evidence; and the Public Bill Committee, to get a broader sense of input at this crucial stage. We analysed over 130 written submissions, which amounted to several hundred pages of material, going beyond the organisations represented by our interviewees, and beyond England. The purpose of this analysis was to see how law is used in a particular type of advocacy, enriching and supplementing the interview data. One of us carried out an initial, detailed assessment, and the other reviewed a sample of submissions from all six reports. Our review of this material provides insights into the role of law in this particular public debate, and provides additional data to set alongside the interviews.

Outline of the book

In chapter 2 (NGOs, lobbying and legal mobilisation), we provide insights into the complex and wide-ranging literature on NGOs, lobbying and their use of law ('legal mobilisation'). This includes a discussion of political and legal opportunity introduced above, and of those factors that are internal to the NGO movement and are also crucial in shaping NGO activity and impact. Drawing on our interview data, we argue that legal expertise is thinly dispersed across the sector (with the obvious exception of ClientEarth), partly because of the financial cost of legal expertise. Organisational identity, ideas and values are also important to the availability and use of legal expertise in the environmental NGO community. An organisation's understanding of itself, and of law, is likely to be reflected in investment (or not) in law. In a self-perpetuating cycle, investment in legal resource determines the legal expertise in an organisation, which reverberates in the understanding of law, back to how much investment is thought necessary.

Groups seeking to influence post-Brexit environmental law and policy have faced an extraordinarily dramatic and dynamic political context. In chapter 3 (Brexit and the journey to the Environment Act – interrupted), we recount the Brexit-environment saga from the referendum in June 2016, to a world responding to pandemic Covid-19 in June 2020. We explore the political and legal opportunities available to environmental groups in this period, and identify hybrid political–legal opportunities, which are new to the literature. We highlight five elements of the Brexit process, overlapping and non-exhaustive, which have shaped the behaviour of environmental advocates: the relationship between parliament and executive, and the extraordinary shifts of power between them; the crucial legislation, and colossal amounts of government and parliamentary activity, necessary to exit the EU; the increasing electoral significance of the environment for the governing Conservative Party; Secretary of State Michael Gove's adoption of a 'Green Brexit' rhetoric, underpinned by an 'equivalence' and 'governance gap' framing (which we also examine in some detail here); the technically as well as politically demanding nature of Brexit.

The complex public drama of Brexit highlights the difficulties of generalising about NGO advocacy, but may also illuminate the use and appreciation of law and legal expertise more clearly than business as usual. Looking at our material through the lens of political, legal and hybrid opportunity confirms the emphasis of the literature on the partial shaping of NGO activities (in our case the use of law and legal expertise) by external factors. For much of the period of our case study, certainly between the 2017 and 2019 General Elections, political opportunity opened doors for environmental groups. A different set of opportunities would have led to different results, in terms of what NGOs did, what they achieved, and what we find in the rest of this book.

But political opportunity is complex. It shifts rapidly, and in different ways simultaneously hampers and enables environmental groups. Agility is crucial for environmental groups seeking to influence those with power.

In chapter 4 (Law and legal expertise), we complicate our central organising concept of 'legal expertise'. There are many, diverse literatures on what 'expertise' is, its strengths and weaknesses, and what experts (expertise embodied) bring to the table. There is also a vast literature on the legal profession, what (expert) lawyers do and should do. We learn from these literatures that 'objectivity' is elusive, and idiosyncratic values and understandings of the world intrude into expert assessments. This undermines claims that experts are uniquely qualified to make decisions. Further, an overemphasis of technical legal debate may have on occasion rendered crucial normative disagreement around Brexit-environment inaccessible.

We do not suggest that legal arguments are more important than arguments based on other forms of expertise, or on values. However, notwithstanding some impressive legal expertise in the sector, our research suggests an undervaluing of legal expertise by environmental groups, and ambivalence towards legal specialisation. The diversity of the 'legal' in the Brexit-environment debate (from environmental law in all its diversity, to constitutional law, to trade law) has been extraordinary. Lawyers and non-lawyers alike may have underestimated just how difficult it is for 'generalists' to engage with this complexity and diversity.

The availability of (expert) resources and an organisation's understanding of expertise are mutually reinforcing: resources are not just a *practical* limit on what expertise is available, but spill into the very understanding of what *constitutes* expertise. The expertise available shapes not only what NGOs do, but also what they think they ought to do, and hence what (expert) resources they think they need. For as long as legal expertise is very thinly spread across the sector, it is hard to make the case that more is needed.

We have been struck by the range of activities carried out by relatively few legal experts across even the largest organisations. Contributing to shaping advocacy is far from their priority, with case work and corporate work dominating, and litigation playing the starring role. Chapter 5 (Mobilising law in practice) explores the contribution of legal expertise to advocacy. Understanding both the detailed implications of law, and the overarching frameworks and institutions that govern outcomes, can provide a different way of seeing the world, and a different way of changing the world. Law and legal experts play a significant role in shaping the rules of the social and economic game. Many of our participants emphasised the authority and power of legal argument and saw legal expertise in environmental groups as an important equaliser. Law is one of the approaches available to convince influential audiences, and if government and other actors use legal expertise, environmental NGOs must.

Legal expertise makes limited contributions to strategy and leadership within environmental NGOs, playing mainly a supportive role. Whilst we see indications of change, it is surprising and revealing that our participants did not see strategic leadership as a role for legal experts: this is a sophisticated and well-resourced sector, dominated in practice by complex regulation, and our sample of interviewees is sensitive to law. The relative absence of legal expertise in leadership resonates again with the mutually reinforcing limitations on legal expertise in the community. Less legal expertise in the strategic brain of environmental groups both contributes to and reflects a relative absence of highly experienced legal experts in environmental groups; and over-stretched legal capacity feeds out of and into a relatively weak engagement with the need for, and importantly the potential of, legal expertise.

Alongside a merely patchy interest in legal expertise, however, we have witnessed significant, skilful legal input into the public debate on Brexit-environment. We conclude from this that there is genuine, if under-developed, recognition of the importance of legal expertise, and that the sector impressively mustered its capacity in a crisis. Collaboration, discussed in the next two chapters, played a central role in that. We share the sense of our interviewees that legal expertise had considerable, if not uniquely significant, influence in the Brexit-environment debate. Combining this chapter's exploration of the heavy use of law with the sector's influence as a whole (chapter 7) reinforces this conclusion.

In chapter 6 (Lobbying in coalition) we explore an important part of our Brexit-environment story: collaboration. We focus on Greener UK. We think it is relatively uncontroversial to describe Greener UK as being at the centre of governance work on Brexit-environment. Working in coalition is, of course, not new to the sector. But our rich empirical data points to the fact that the sector's collaboration through Greener UK is different, even special.

Working in coalition can have multiple advantages. We are especially interested in the way that drawing on collective resource has not only led to an efficient pooling of legal expertise, but has also deepened that expertise, creating more than the sum of its parts. Greener UK's collaboration with Wildlife and Countryside Link on the more expansive parts of the Environment Bill has enabled the sector to extend its reach further and utilise its expertise in a range of areas. But collaboration is challenging. Although collaboration creates efficiency in the pooling of resources, it has its own costs: the coalition itself needs to be resourced. The alignment of interests can be difficult, but if a coalition is to achieve its aims, it is vital that its member organisations reach consensus on goals and approaches. NGOs often compete (for recognition, funding, membership, etc.), so this is no easy task and can imply considerable profile sacrifice for individual organisations.

In chapter 7 (Greener UK: influence and collaboration), we explore the role of Greener UK, a crucially important actor in the environmental NGO sector's response to Brexit-environment. Our interviewees expressed almost unanimous, and in most cases unconditional, support for the work that Greener UK has done (and continues to do) in shaping the post-Brexit environmental law landscape.

As discussed above, identifying the 'success' of lobbying is extraordinarily challenging. Having said that, we explore the influence of Greener UK on the Brexit-environment debate and the development of the Environment Bill, drawing on both our analysis of public documents produced by environmental NGOs, and the subjective perceptions of our interviewees. We conclude that certain elements of the Environment Bill (arguably even the existence of any Bill at all) can be traced to the work of Greener UK and its allies.

Another way of understanding the 'success' of Greener UK is the way it has 'worked' as a collaboration: holding together over a long and difficult period, with constant activity as a coalition, and constant contributions from the member organisations. This was a strong and recurring theme from our interview data, and we identify three particular features of the Greener UK collaboration that have contributed to this aspect of success. First, consensus around the broad issues associated with Brexit, and the enormous salience of Brexit for the sector. Second, the careful attention to the working relationships and trust between the individuals involved. And third, the direct resourcing of Greener UK itself, making individuals responsible for ensuring that the collaboration worked.

There is a clear appetite for collaboration in the sector. Whatever happens next, the lessons of Greener UK should be learned and taken forward.

In chapter 8, we draw some conclusions. The heterogeneity and complexity of the area we are examining (the nature of the sector, the nature of the problem), and the unique circumstances thrown up by Brexit, mean we must be cautious about drawing generalisations from our case study. But the learning from this project can, we believe, contribute to filling significant gaps in the scholarship and in practical knowledge in the sector.

In this chapter, we return to the three themes identified in the introduction above: around political and legal opportunities, about the role of legal expertise in the environmental community and about collaboration around Brexit-environment. We write in strange and uncertain times. Careful and considered scrutiny of the Environment Bill as it continues its journey through Parliament is crucial, even if circumstances make that difficult. But a perfect Environment Act would not be the end of the story. The whole point of the 'governance gap' exercise was to provide a framework to assist civil society in holding the powerful to account. Using the Act will require yet more sustained, disciplined, careful, collaborative and at least partly legal work.

Notes

1. For a recent appraisal of the environmental movement see Berny and Rootes 2018.
2. We capitalise 'Government' and 'Parliament' when we refer to a particular Government or Parliament (e.g. the 2017 Theresa May Government), but not when we refer to government or parliament generally (e.g. throughout the period of our case study).
3. Van Der Heijden 1997 argues that the degree of institutionalisation varies from one country to another, and is determined primarily by the political opportunity structure of the country in question.
4. Miller, Cracknell and Williams 2017, 8–9.
5. Some emergency funds are open to environment-orientated organisations. See further Environmental Funders Network 2020.
6. Quantitative data on the environmental NGO community is patchy at best. For a discussion of why this is so, and a useful (but now rather dated) account of the sector see Clifford et al. 2013.
7. Cracknell, Miller and Williams 2013, 8. More recent sector-wide data are not available. However, we can see that membership numbers for individual environmental groups have grown since 2013 (e.g. National Trust membership has risen year on year, National Trust 2019).
8. Vanhala 2018a, 388.
9. https://www.clientearth.org/ accessed 1 July 2020. ClientEarth is not the only NGO to focus on law; we discuss the UK Environmental Law Association (UKELA) further in chapter 5.
10. Goodman and Thornton 2017, 57–58.
11. https://green-alliance.org.uk/ accessed 1 July 2020.
12. https://greeneruk.org/. The members of Greener UK are WWF, Friends of the Earth, Greenpeace, RSPB, ClientEarth, Marine Conservation Society, Green Alliance, National Trust, Wildlife Trusts, Woodland Trust, CPRE, E3G and Wildfowl and Wetlands Trust.
13. The Withdrawal Agreement (Agreement on the Withdrawal of the United Kingdom of Great Britain and Northern Ireland from the European Union and the European Atomic Energy Community 2019) refers to a 'transition' period, the EU (Withdrawal Agreement) Act 2020, an 'implementation' period.
14. Simply put, the closer the relationship between the EU and the UK at the end of 2020, the greater the EU role in UK environmental standards.
15. Lee 2014; Kingston, Heyvaert and Cavoski 2017.
16. Sections 2–7.

17 Most of the Bill applies to England only, although parts of the Bill apply more broadly. Part I applies to England only, with the exception of the possibility of extension of the OEP to Northern Ireland. See Clause 130 and Explanatory Notes.
18 Although it does build on earlier work done by the environment movement on environmental legislation.
19 E.g. Tierney 2019.
20 The Northern Ireland Assembly was suspended between January 2017 and January 2020.
21 Sargeant 2020.
22 The European Parliament approved the Withdrawal Agreement on 29 January 2020.
23 England took a different approach from the other countries when EU law was changed to allow objections to authorised GMOs; see Lee 2016.
24 See Flyvbjerg 2006 on the distinction between generalisability and general lessons, also on the value of atypical cases.
25 McCann 2004 describes legal mobilisation as a synthetic approach, attentive to the law and society and law and social movement literatures.
26 For a very useful discussion of the field, see Cummings 2018.
27 McCann 2008 and Cummings 2018. Boukalas 2013 explores non-court work, although he explicitly attributes an advocacy approach to the unavailability or failure of litigation and street protest, 413–14; Ghose 2005 offers a practical guide; Goodman and Thornton 2017 is an interesting history of ClientEarth. At a more detailed level, see e.g. Hilson 2009, 999 on 'citizens' weapons inspections'; Enright et al. 2021 on abortion rights in Ireland.
28 Lehoucq and Taylor 2020.
29 Galanter 1974, 165.
30 Kinghan and Vanhala 2019.
31 Duxbury 2012, 69, discussing Dworkin in particular, but making a more general point.
32 E.g. Duxbury 2012; Waldron 1999; Scotford 2021.
33 The conservatism and rejection of 'politics' that accompanies the more positive rejection of legislation in parts of academia (see Cane 2005) is probably reversed in the environmental movement. However, the two areas may share an implicit instrumental desire to side-step politics.
34 E.g. Scotford and Minas 2019.
35 Waldron 1999.
36 Kitschelt 1986; Hilson 2002.
37 Meyer and Minkoff 2004, 1457–8.
38 Meyer and Minkoff 2004; Kitschelt 1986.
39 Hilson 2002.
40 Scheingold 2004; Vanhala 2018a.
41 De Bruycker and Beyers 2019 refers to 'outsider lobbying', 57.
42 Jordan 2009, 371.
43 Cummings 2018 provides a good overview of the history. See also e.g. McCann 2008 and contributions to Philippopoulos-Mihalopoulos and Brooks 2017.
44 See the discussion of the classic divide in the social movement/NGO literature between 'insiders' and 'outsiders', discussed in chapter 2, and between radical action and incremental steps.
45 See e.g. Yamin 2019.
46 Vanhala 2018a, 400.
47 Consider e.g. Stone 1972, McAuslan 1980 or ecocide law put forward by Polly Higgins, https://ecocidelaw.com/ accessed 1 July 2020.
48 See for example Scheingold 2004; Epp 2008; Vanhala 2018b. For an excellent summary of the literature see Vanhala and Kinghan 2018.
49 E.g. Page 1999. In the EU environmental context, see Richards and Heard 2005 and at international level Betsill and Corell 2001; Paterson 1996.
50 Carter and Childs 2018 plus the academic, political and media sources cited therein.
51 Mahoney 2007, 37.
52 For detailed insight into the complexity of the empirical work on lobbying in a US context, see Baumgartner and Leech 1998.
53 Betsill and Corell 2001, 72. Also see Corell and Betsill 2008.
54 For an excellent survey of process tracing as a qualitative technique in the study of causal mechanisms see Vanhala 2017.

55 Paterson 1996.
56 Chapter 3 (page 62).
57 E.g. joint UK Environmental Law Association/Society of Legal Scholars conference, *The Environmental Impacts of Brexit* (Bristol), and oral evidence to Environmental Audit Committee 2016.
58 Lee 2018b.
59 Lee 2018b.
60 E.g. Lee and Abbot 2003; Abbot and Lee 2015.
61 Webley 2010.
62 This is 'elite-lite' interviewing, where we share some of the elite characteristics of the interviewees, Vaughan 2013.
63 Bailey, White and Pain 1999, 172, citation omitted.
64 Webley 2010, 932 on response to 'changing conditions, perceptions and findings' through 'fluid' research design.
65 Two interviewees had changed employers from or to an NGO between these dates.
66 In advance of each interview we provided interviewees with a Participant Information Sheet outlining, amongst other things, the provisions made for ensuring confidentiality and anonymity. We sought appropriate approval from our institutional Research Ethics Teams.
67 We worked by hand, rather than using coding software such as NVivo; we preferred to return to the materials multiple times, and consider the context of statements.
68 See e.g. Webley 2010 and Bailey, White and Pain 1999 on grounded theory.
69 The inquiry carried out before the referendum is also of interest, Environmental Audit Committee 2016.
70 Russell and Cowley 2016, 133.
71 Benton and Russell 2013.

2
NGOs, lobbying and legal mobilisation

Introduction

A diverse and voluminous literature is preoccupied with efforts to explain or assess the spectrum of activities and approaches adopted by NGOs. These activities and approaches range from efforts to mobilise public opinion (through protests, demonstrations, petitions, campaigning and the like), to direct appeals to political elites, and to the pursuit of policy goals through the courts. In this chapter, we draw selectively on some of the key themes of this literature, as well as our interview data, to begin our task of exploring the use of law and legal expertise by environmental NGOs.

As we explained in chapter 1, by contrast with much of the literature on social movement 'legal mobilisation', we are concerned with the role of legal expertise beyond litigation (even broadly defined), and beyond the use of law in quasi-judicial spaces.[1] This requires an expansive approach to legal mobilisation, embracing 'any process by which individuals or collective actors invoke legal norms, discourse or symbols to influence policy or behaviour'.[2] We are particularly concerned with legal mobilisation in NGO insider lobbying or advocacy around Brexit's environmental impact,[3] an 'information-based interaction between groups and organizations and government'[4] that aims to influence policy formulation and decision-making.

We begin this chapter with an overview of the literature on interest group 'insider' or 'outsider' status. The environmental groups most heavily involved in the Brexit-environment debate were consummate insiders, with considerable access to the powerful and limiting themselves almost entirely to insider activities. The insider/outsider divide is a useful first step in thinking about our research, and the ways in which NGOs seek to enhance their influence on power-holders. It is, however, far from complete as a framework for assessing interest group behaviour, and so we then turn to other factors identified in the literature as shaping interest group strategies and approaches. We start with external influences, discussing the literature on political and legal opportunity, which we explore through the rest of this monograph, especially in chapter 3. We then turn to the dynamics within the organisation that shape interest group activity. First, we look at resource-based theories, and conclude (with provisos) that the resource of legal expertise is spread very thinly through the environmental NGO community in England, in part because of the (perceived) financial cost of such expertise. We then turn to the effect of what might broadly be called organisational identity or cultural approaches ('identity, ideas and values'[5]) on the use of legal expertise by environmental groups. We argue that the way an organisation understands itself feeds into its capacity and willingness to use legal expertise. Importantly, no single theory can explain the choices that interest groups make in pursuance of their goals.

Insiders and outsiders: group status and group strategy

A vast political science literature seeks to understand the place of interest groups in the process of law- and policy-making. This literature has made a distinction between insider and outsider groups; groups with privileged access and status ('insiders') and those without ('outsiders'). As we discuss further below, this distinction is not without its critics. Amongst other things, the insider/outsider typology is not a binary variable, but sits on a sliding scale, with some groups having more access to power-holders than others at different times and in different contexts. However, insidership suggests a relationship in which groups are more likely to be invited to take part and listened to when they do, and the theory allows us to attribute 'influence to some groups and impotence to others'.[6] 'Consultation' is a term used a good deal in this literature, in that insider groups are more heavily consulted. Consultation can refer to formal public consultation opportunities, for example DEFRA's *Consultation on Environmental Principles and Governance after EU Exit* (the *EPG Consultation*),[7] or Select Committee calls for evidence. The identification of insiders and outsiders denotes, however, that not all are equal in these apparently open processes. Further, 'consultation' might include less public, informal events, for example, direct NGO communications such as briefings or letters, behind closed doors meetings with officials, or dealings with influential figures or organisations outside government or parliament.

Law and policy-makers 'are likely to be scanning the horizon for groups who may be able to aid them in policy formulation' and the 'policy-relevant group can simplify the policy making task'.[8] One of our interviewees recognised that there may be different reasons for seeking out a coalition of interest groups:

> ... the most cynical – it's ticking the box if somebody says, well you know, talk to civil society. Or it might be, 'Yeah, we really want to talk to civil society, want to know what they think.' And other times it feels more, 'Well you've got some competence, you know what's going on. You're sufficiently well informed about what civil servants are doing' (Interviewee 3).

Wyn Grant is commonly acknowledged as pioneering the early British literature on insider and outsider groups.[9] In one of his earliest contributions Grant stated that:

> The basic distinction in this paper between insider groups and outsider groups, is a distinction based on interest group strategies, by which is meant the combination of modes of action used by an interest group to attain its goals. It must be emphasised that the acquisition of insider or outsider status by a group involves both a decision by government and a decision by the group concerned. The basic aim of such insider groups is to establish a consultative relationship whereby their views on particular legislative proposals will be sought prior to the crystallisation of the Government's position.[10]

For Grant, insider groups display three key characteristics.[11] First, government and parliamentarians recognise these groups as legitimate spokespersons for particular issues or concerns. Second, once some legitimacy is secured, these groups are allowed to engage in dialogue with decision-makers. And third, they agree (albeit implicitly) to abide by the rules and put forward well-researched, accurate and truthful cases to support their claims. These insider groups would therefore be involved in regular, meaningful consultation with government (and other public officials), whereas outsider groups would not. In his view, most groups would adopt, wherever possible, insider strategies due to their greater likelihood of success.[12]

The labels 'insider' and 'outsider', as well as being applied to NGOs (as a question of status), may also be applied to the channels or strategies of interest group influence.[13] The 'insider' label (both in terms of strategy and status), we suggest, can be legitimately applied to many (not all) of the individual environmental NGOs participating in the Greener UK coalition, and most of their activities on Brexit understood as insider strategies. Green Alliance (the think tank that hosts Greener UK) has also adopted an insider approach when seeking influence. As noted by Rebecca Willis, founder of Green Alliance's Climate Leadership Programme:

> Green Alliance [...] were so proud of their close relationship with government and politicians that they named their magazine Inside Track. Everyone who has worked at Green Alliance could give you a few good stories about how a particular tax measure, environmental standard or policy proposal emerged from a carefully designed process of research and influencing.[14]

In this light, it is not surprising that the Greener UK coalition has carefully cultivated trusted insider status and used insider techniques. In discussing the potential role of other environmental group coalitions (notably Wildlife and Countryside Link) in the Brexit-environment process, one of our interviewees acknowledged the 'need for a coalition that could tap into the heart of Westminster at a more strategic level and would have the political access' (Interviewee 2).[15] Greener UK has indeed focused almost all of its energy on the lobbying of Westminster and Whitehall. The insider approach was described by one of our interviewees:

> At the end of the day, if you think about what parliamentarians are doing, they're like all of us, they're turning up to do their job because they want to do a good job, they believe in what they're doing and they have an opportunity to effect change for the better. Our job is to help them in that role and, you know, it's a privileged position to be in, I think, to be able to play that sort of advisory role. But if you don't do it in a kind of respectful and trust-based way, you're only gonna get so far (unattributed).

Whilst insiderness best describes Greener UK's approach to influence, it has mobilised broader publics in other ways, perhaps most notably through co-coordinating (with the Climate Coalition) *The Time is Now* mass lobby for climate, nature and people.[16] This 'was really the first time that they collectively have gone to their supporters, mobilised their supporters. Showed Parliament, "Look, our supporters are with us on this"' (Interviewee 11).

The predominance of insiderness was not without criticism: 'if I had a criticism of Greener UK, it's been such an inside-track organisation. Like its primary audience has been DEFRA. And its other primary audience has been parliament' (Interviewee 11). In discussing Greener UK's strategic approach to Brexit, another participant felt that there 'was a bit of a gap in that the coalition, you could see that, at times, campaigning would be helpful' (Interviewee 16). Further, changes in political and legal opportunities (see below and chapter 3) prompted one interviewee to query whether a shift in Greener UK's strategic approach may be needed:

> Greener UK has prioritised a sort of inside-track approach and kind of developing a close and friendly relationship with government, which I think made sense when we first set up. I think as that's progressed, it's become less effective as an approach overall, because of the changing nature of parliament, and then with the final, big landslide victory in December last year, saying, 'Well hang on, is this a government we can do business with?' (unattributed).

Grant's insider/outsider model, whilst widely applauded, has given 'rise to contradictions and confusions', and moreover, 'the terms have more to offer than a rudimentary dichotomy of the group world'.[17] The literature proceeds along two broad themes. First, it has been suggested that Grant's model presents an overly simplified model of interest group classifications, and we address some of the nuance below. Second, Grant's model arguably conflates two different, albeit closely related, phenomena in interest group influence, namely status and strategy. In recognition of this latter point, we look at status and strategy independently.

Interest group status

The insider or outsider status of interest groups speaks primarily to how these groups are perceived by those with power. Crucially, as discussed further below, group status 'is conditional upon government granted legitimacy: it is *ascribed* by policymakers to the group'.[18] Grant and others have developed the basic distinction between insider and outsider groups to acknowledge the complexity of group status.[19] William Maloney and colleagues, for example, distinguish between 'core' insider groups (those groups that regularly participate in a wide variety of issues over a broad policy area), 'specialist' insider groups (groups that participate in a particular area) and 'peripheral' insider groups (where participation has insider features but where influence is marginal at best).[20] In terms of outsider status, they distinguish between outsiders by ideology or goal, and outsiders by choice; neither group pursues insider-style strategies. A third category – thresholders – can be 'characterised by strategic ambiguity and oscillation between insider and outsider strategies'.[21] These groups are neither insiders nor outsiders but can be both.

Despite the more nuanced approach taken by many writers, the usefulness of the insider/outsider distinction remains controversial. Not only do groups display both insider and outsider characteristics, but insider status is very widely spread. Almost all (UK) interest groups seem to enjoy at least peripheral insider status. Edward Page's survey of 381 interest groups revealed (albeit cautiously) that 40 per cent of groups displayed all three of the insider characteristics that he used in his research (frequent contacts with at least one Ministry, consultation on almost all matters within their field and the ability to influence).[22] Fewer than 1 in 12 displayed no insider characteristics and were classed as pure outsiders. Page's research also suggests that the status and influence of groups varies from issue to issue, such that groups cannot easily be classified as *either* insiders *or* outsiders. Nevertheless, however complex and contested the ascription of 'a' status to groups, and however it is labelled, the idea that some groups are heard louder than others is important.

As suggested above, the status ascribed by those whom the NGO seeks to influence is crucial. Here, interest group resources (economic power, knowledge, expertise, etc.) are important in framing perceptions of legitimacy. David Truman recognised the significance of both technical and political knowledge – technical expertise and political sophistication strengthen a group's credibility with decision-making – as early as the 1950s.[23] Groups are provided with an opportunity to shape law and policy in return for the resources (often information and expertise) that are needed to ensure a reasonable, realistic and working policy.[24] Sheila Jasanoff calls the connection by NGOs of knowledge about the world (sometimes but not always scientific knowledge) with actions designed to advance particular goals the 'knowledge–action link'. She argues that the knowledge–action link is at the core of NGO activity in the law- and policy-making arena and is what 'gives NGOs their primary points of political intervention'.[25] As suggested above, 'Groups may be actively pursued because they are the possessors of "indispensable information" which decision-makers seek.'[26] That this speaks to legitimacy and credibility was acknowledged by one of our interviewees:

> You know, sometimes governments like NGOs like us, because we're very scientific, we're very evidence-based and they know they can rely on our credibility [...] So we actually have really good access sometimes to government, to be able to influence policy (unattributed).

The importance of interest group status and legitimacy applies equally to coalitions of NGOs, such as Greener UK. Here too, resources are important. One of our interviewees, in talking about the membership profile of Greener UK, commented that 'You do definitely get some legitimacy from representing a big organisation, especially if it's got a lot of members. But you also get legitimacy through sort of whether you're competent, whether you're plausible, whether you actually understand what's going on, why you're in the meeting' (Interviewee 3).[27]

These resource-based exchange theories are not the only factors that may be relevant in determining group status. Some question whether pursuing an insider strategy (such as making 'reasonable' demands, whilst engaging in formal consultation) may be a precondition to (or at least enhance the prospects of) insider status.[28] An insider strategy will not necessarily lead to insider status, however, as evidenced by, for example, David Marsh and colleagues' study of the Countryside Alliance's campaign on fox hunting.[29] Furthermore, it could be argued that the state seeks out those groups who are likely to be their allies, and so interest groups who are inclined to agree with a particular (government) position are more likely to be afforded insider status.[30] Again, this overlaps with some of the discussion below, and we return to this in chapter 3.

Insider group strategies: lobbying, advocacy and legal mobilisation

The literature considering the range of approaches that interest groups can take describes and labels those strategies in a variety of ways. As discussed above, Grant's insider/outsider typology is one approach to group strategy. Outsider strategies include the use of protests and campaigns to generate pressure on power-holders indirectly by appealing to the public at large. They can also include the use of litigation, which can place indirect pressure on power-holders, but also in some cases compel them to take action.[31] Such outsider strategies have historically been able to create a space for 'the polite representations of reasonable [NGOs] [to be] more visible and audible in the corridors of power',[32] and can be an effective way of connecting with actual and potential memberships.[33] Insider strategies target decision-makers directly and involve the exchange of policy-relevant information through formal or informal channels. Groups can and do use both insider and outsider strategies simultaneously.[34] The literature would suggest, however, that outsider strategies can alienate those with whom a group seeks insider relations, although this involves a complex set of dynamics.[35] That mixing insider and outsider strategies comes with some risk and can potentially damage relationships with power-holders was noted by one of our interviewees: 'if you wanna shout loudly in the press and do the kind of public opinion thing, fine, but I don't think you're gonna get those really helpful insider discussions where you can influence guidance and policy documents' (Interviewee 9).

Strategies can be labelled in other ways. Our explanation of insider and outsider strategies in the paragraph above reflects one alternative approach, namely differentiating between 'direct' (insider) strategies and 'indirect' (outsider) strategies. Anne Skorkjaer Binderkrantz, in her study of Danish interest groups, differentiates between administrative and parliamentary strategies (as 'direct' strategies) and media and mobilisation strategies (as 'indirect' strategies).[36] Jan Beyers, in examining EU interest representation, uses the terms 'access' and 'voice' to represent direct participation in the EU decision-making process ('access') and the indirect influence of policy-makers through media attention and political campaigns ('voice').[37]

Regardless of terminology, the literature on interest group strategy recognises that influence can be exerted through different political arenas. Insider strategies exert influence directly through 'the venues where political bargaining takes place' and outsider strategies take place in public spheres 'where the communication among societal interests, policy-makers and citizens becomes visible to a broader audience'.[38]

Whilst it is not a central part of our assessment, it is clear, as we discuss above, that environmental NGOs perceive their actions around Brexit-environment and the Environment Bill as insider-style activities. In our work, we are analysing their approaches in terms of 'lobbying' or 'advocacy'. We provide multiple examples throughout this monograph of environmental NGOs, both individually and collectively through Greener UK, using advocacy to influence post-Brexit environmental law and policy. The precise nature and scope of lobbying varies significantly from one case to another. Interest groups may use different lobbying approaches in different circumstances and will base their exchanges with decision-makers on the expertise and argument that they think will be most effective in achieving their substantive end goals. Our project focuses on the use of a particular form of expertise in lobbying, namely legal expertise. Legal mobilisation is a way of implementing a lobbying strategy.

There are multiple and varied definitions of legal mobilisation in the literature which, according to Emilio Lehoucq and Whitney Taylor, has led to some 'conceptual stretching'.[39] But as we discuss in chapter 1 (page 9), a narrow view of legal mobilisation, namely the defence or development of legal rights through the courts or other formal institutions (and activity associated with such actions[40]) is prevalent in theoretical approaches to legal mobilisation, and dominates empirical investigation of the concept.[41] Much of the literature considers how individuals and groups pursue legal claims to defend or develop legal rights, charting the deployment of litigation strategies in the US, from the court battles by the NAACP Legal Defense Fund to end racial segregation in public schools during the civil rights era.[42] The use of litigation by NGOs to achieve social change is not, however, a uniquely American or recent concept. In the early 1990s, Carol Harlow and Richard Rawlings point to English cases from the mid-eighteenth century, in which the court was used to test the legality of slavery in common law.[43] More contemporary scholarship considers how NGOs have used litigation to advance social change in a range of areas, including environmental protection.[44]

Lehoucq and Taylor wish to reserve the term legal mobilisation for 'the use of law in an explicit, self-conscious way through the invocation of a formal institutional mechanism'.[45] Whilst we have some sympathy for their interest in conceptual clarity, we, as discussed above and in chapter 1, seek to explore the role of legal expertise *beyond* litigation, even broadly defined. We therefore adopt a broader understanding of legal mobilisation which, we argue, reflects the multiple ways in which law and legal expertise can be used to shape and influence outcomes. Our more expansive definition, set out above ('any process by which individuals or collective actors invoke legal norms, discourse or symbols to influence policy or behaviour'[46]) takes as its basis the principle that the law can be mobilised to shape legislation, policy and decision-making outside the courtroom and is fundamentally a way of understanding the world. It allows us to explore the use of law and legal argument in the advocacy activity of NGOs. We return throughout, and especially in chapter 5, to quite what environmental NGOs *do* when they mobilise law.

Explaining and shaping NGO strategies

A number of factors influence the strategies that interest groups pursue when seeking to achieve policy goals. Broadly speaking, these factors can be divided into external and internal influences, although the distinction between the two is not always clear-cut. In this section we consider three factors that can be used to help us understand the strategic choices of interest groups, and which resonate strongly in our case study: legal and political opportunities; resource-based theories; and organisational culture and identity.[47] Some of these factors are also important in explaining group status in policy-making, again emphasising the close link between interest group strategy and interest group status.

The extent to which these (and other) factors can either individually or collectively explain strategic choices is both complex and contested. A diverse body of work, both theoretical and empirical, seeks to better understand why a particular strategy or strategies are (or should be) favoured in any given circumstances. The literature is even divided on whether or not groups actually have a realistic choice of strategy. Kay Lehman Scholzman and John Tierney support the view that there is *some* choice in terms of the approaches adopted:

> .... [A]n organization may have extensive strategic and tactical choices. Although the institutional arena in which political conflict will be waged is sometimes settled in advance by the actions of others, when an organization has a choice, it will try to locate a potential conflict in the setting most likely to produce favourable results. Once strategic matters have been settled, an organized interest still must choose among assorted political tactics.[48]

In contrast, others such as Maloney and colleagues argue that in reality groups have little choice about strategy and that approaches are determined, primarily, by the nature of the interest groups' asks or demands.[49] For example, it is hypothesised that where the desired policy goal leaves room for bargaining and negotiation (as opposed to an 'all or nothing' demand), then groups will look to meet directly with decision-makers. Where this is not the case, group strategies are likely to focus on outsider lobbying approaches to mobilise the public and thereby pressurise decision-makers into adopting a particular position.[50] In addition, where policy goals reflect a narrower interest, it is more likely that groups will use direct strategies whereas broader goals are more likely to be pursued through a combination of direct and indirect (such as media and protest) approaches.[51] Our case study of Brexit-environment is a case in which broad goals about the future of environmental law interact with detailed nitty gritty on how to operationalise those broad goals, and the balance between them varies over the four years of our study. Insider interactions of various types dominate.

Legal and political opportunities

We introduce legal and political opportunities (or opportunity structures)[52] in chapter 1. Political opportunities (such as access to political decision-making bodies and the receptivity of policy-makers) are external factors that 'enhance or inhibit prospects for mobilization, for particular sorts of claims to be advanced rather than others, for particular strategies of influence to be exercised, and for movements to affect mainstream institutional politics and policy'.[53] As discussed further in chapter 3, in the context of the Brexit-environment debate, shifting political opportunities 'really changes the conversation' (Interviewee 2).

Perhaps most obviously, political opportunities refer to the formal institutional structures of the political system and the extent to which they provide (or not) formal access for interest groups.[54] An 'open' state facilitates the use of, for example, lobbying strategies that attempt to talk to those with power, whereas a 'closed' state incentivises the use of other approaches including, potentially, protest and litigation.[55] But these formal institutional structures are only one part of political opportunities. Different authors offer diverse, inter-related dimensions of political opportunity, which can be used to explain differences in the development of, and actions adopted by, social movements.[56] The receptivity of government to particular demands will, for example, influence interest group strategies. If the political environment is clearly conducive to a particular outcome, then insider lobbying strategies can be pursued rigorously, although they may even then be unsuccessful.[57] And of course, government is not a monolith. Pieter Bouwen and Margaret McCown hypothesise that 'increasing deadlock in one branch of government will encourage interest groups more to pursue strategies targeting the other branch' and 'the congruence between an interest group's preferences and that of a branch of government will encourage it to develop influence strategies in that branch rather than the other'.[58] In our study, for example, as noted in chapter 3 we see calls on parliament and government at different times, and receptivity in DEFRA, which is not necessarily matched in the Treasury. The substantive target of lobbying may also be relevant. For example, Page's survey of interest groups found that

55 per cent of respondents agreed with the statement that 'consultation on Statutory Instruments offers groups like ours a better chance to shape legislation than consultation on parliamentary bills'.[59] Perhaps, he argues, the more technical nature of the issues covered in Statutory Instruments (SIs) (relative to Bills) enhances access to government. That would tend to converge with the discussion above (and indeed throughout) about the resources of information and expertise that are sought from NGOs by those making decisions.

A body of work on legal opportunities grew out of the literature on political opportunities. Like the work on legal mobilisation generally, this work focuses on the use of judicial processes by NGOs. Legal opportunities are the important features of the legal, political and social environment that either limit or incentivise the use of litigation by NGOs. Vanhala, who has written extensively on legal mobilisation, identifies, notwithstanding disagreement and discussion, three factors which matter across all jurisdictions and across all policy areas: legal stock (that is the body of substantive law within which NGOs frame their legal arguments); regulations that limit or allow access to the courts (rules of standing); and rules that decide who bears which costs of litigation.[60] These do not exhaust the legal opportunity literature, which also reflects both the resources and organisational identity approaches considered further below.

We discuss our case study in the light of the literature on political and legal opportunities in chapter 3. We argue that the political and bureaucratic state of play gave rise to five sets of overlapping and very specific political opportunities for environmental NGOs during the journey to the post-Brexit Environment Bill, including hybrid political–legal opportunities. However, legal and political opportunity theories cannot provide a full and complete account of interest group strategy-making. Interest group strategy choice is influenced by a multiplicity of factors that consider not only the external political and legal environment but also the internal and social dynamics of the organisations seeking influence. We turn, first, to consider how internal resources can shape interest group strategy.

Resource-based theories

Unlike political and legal opportunity theories, resource mobilisation theories focus on the internal resources of NGOs.[61] These theories are founded on the assumption that movement actors behave rationally and will devise and agree upon mobilisation strategies that make the best use of the resources they have and, conversely, minimise the need for resources which they do not have: 'we make a conscious choice to lean on what we do have very specific expertise in' (Interviewee 9). Our case study speaks strongly to how the availability of legal expertise (as an interest group resource) may constrain or enhance the use of law in advocacy by the environmental NGO sector, and relates the availability of that expertise to financial resources. Economic resources are important and those groups with a sound financial base will generally have greater opportunities around strategy selection. In the words of Florian Weiler and Jonas Reibmann, 'whether an interest group is able to carry out effective lobbying activities is, to a large degree, a question of money'.[62]

Although the extent to which 'lawyers direct [social] movement activity into legal activities' is as yet unclear in the literature, resource mobilisation theories point to the fact that legal mobilisation (the use of law in advocacy) hinges, at least to some extent, on the availability of legal expertise within the organisation.[63] A group with active legal professionals is more likely to turn to the courts than an organisation absent of lawyers.[64] The presence of committed and able lawyers, alongside sources of financing and the presence of organisations dedicated to establishing rights are what Charles Epp terms 'legal support structures'.[65] Similarly, in discussing the use of law in advocacy, one interviewee stated that with relatively less legal resource they were 'probably going to be making those [legal] arguments less' (Interviewee 9). Importantly, this same participant noted that this 'doesn't mean we won't make them, where we feel comfortable doing it, but you know, it's not going to be at the heart of what we're saying, as other things might. And I think that's natural' (Interviewee 9). Chris Hilson notes that the professional and educational background of NGO personnel is important beyond law: 'political lobbying is therefore likely to be a realistic strategy only for those with a professional background: policy-makers are less likely to listen to those from unconventional backgrounds who lack the relevant expertise or who are not used to speaking their language.'[66]

Although one of our interviewees recognised the environmental NGO sector as being 'well tooled up' legally, relative to other NGO sectors (Interviewee 5), 'the absence of lawyers' (Interviewee 1), a lack of legal expertise and capacity, came through strongly in our interviews. One of our interviewees observed that 'a lot of these NGOs don't have an in-house legal expert' (Interviewee 12). For others, 'most NGOs have limited legal capacity: either one or two lawyers, sort of medium-sized organisations' (Interviewee 3) and '... if an organisation has a lawyer, generally they will only have one or two. No-one has a massive team of lawyers I don't really think' (Interviewee 15). One interviewee had a 'sense that [legal capacity has] reduced', partly because of financial cuts within the sector (Interviewee 6).

We are not able straightforwardly to conclude that NGOs are legally poorly resourced; we could equally focus on the very strong pockets of legal expertise within the sector, plus the potential availability of externally commissioned work, including from lawyers who are willing to work pro bono. The difficulty is that legal expertise within environmental NGOs may be spread too thinly to support the use of law in advocacy. As discussed in chapter 5, a considerable amount of legal time is spent on other important work. Lawyers are often 'very stretched. Because you know, there's always more.... Because they'll cover everything from the kind of big strategic stuff ... to case law as well' (Interviewee 2). ClientEarth may be distinctive in this respect: 'other NGO lawyers [...] often [...] would be covering corporate issues and [...] individual policy areas or legal strategies that they might deploy. So just their bandwidth is a lot less' (unattributed).

Cost is clearly an important factor here, demonstrating the important link between financial resource and expertise.[67] A study investigating the use of litigation strategies found lack of access to the courts as the least significant explanation for not using litigation; the high costs associated with, and duration of, litigation were more important.[68] In the context of our work, cost was a constant theme: 'lawyers have been regarded as quite a rare and expensive commodity' (Interviewee 3). As one interviewee told us, 'pesky lawyers asking for more cash' (Interviewee 13). Cost is an even more significant barrier if searching for an experienced lawyer: 'yeah, they did look expensive' (Interviewee 3). Of course, in-house legal expertise is one way in which NGOs can strengthen their ability to mobilise the law in advocacy. In addition, they may seek external legal advice to support their advocacy work. Here, 'I think the biggest barrier to accessing external legal advice is cost' (Interviewee 6). Another interviewee also recognised lack of financial resource as a factor:

> I mean the costs as well. I think if you don't have lawyers working for you, you need to be paying for lawyers. Even the ones who'll do it at cheap rates or low rates, it's been mind-boggling for me in the time I've been at [XXX] to see how much lawyers can charge (Interviewee 7).

We return in chapter 4 to the possibility that the legal community in the environmental sector is relatively inexperienced. A lack of legal expertise at all levels of experience (early career professionals have their own strengths) will weaken the legal expertise available overall. One interviewee raised particular issues around funding legal strategies: funders 'were not going to listen to a twenty-two-year-old or a thirty-two-year-old [...] with rare exceptions' (Interviewee 1).

There are a number of market-based reasons why the sector may struggle to recruit, retain or develop that resource of (experienced) in-house lawyers. Straightforward expense is a factor of the competition on pay from other sectors: 'Lawyers have other career avenues and civil society doesn't pay that well, so civil society is not that attractive' (Interviewee 1), and even for those who want to do public interest work, academic or civil service careers might be more available than in other disciplines. But there may also be questions about the quality of the work, linked also to the attraction of litigation. One interviewee queried whether law in advocacy (rather than litigation) was exciting and interesting enough for high-calibre lawyers to make up for both the lower salary and the more limited career opportunities. So a good case will 'maybe make their reputation, or certainly feel professionally vindicated. They can stand up alongside their peers. And we're all human; this is what motivates' (Interviewee 3). By contrast, other work, 'the sort of day-to-day stuff: oh, you know, quick look at this directive ... it's just less exciting' (Interviewee 3). But the relatively heavy use of law on Brexit may be different:

> And this is a bit more glamorous, and you're in with a lot of community of your peers, other lawyers, you know. They all meet each other a lot. So you're visible in something which is clearly quite significant. And not only that, but other lawyers see it as significant, perhaps most important' (Interviewee 3).

Career opportunities for lawyers inside NGOs may also be somewhat limited: 'in terms of career progression, where you can go especially if you're a small organisation, it's not necessarily obvious how that would happen' (unattributed); 'you can't within the organisation structure move to have more responsibility if you're delivering legal services. You know, you tend to be sort of stuck at a certain level and that's it' (unattributed). One of our participants raised the concern that the sector is 'not bringing on new environmental lawyers' (Interviewee 14). Again,

ClientEarth may be an exception, even if it too has a relatively 'young workforce':

> ClientEarth has attracted some really, really good talent and we're really lucky in that. I would say two things about how we have to recruit and then develop the talent. One is around developing strategic thinking capability, and the ways of understanding an issue and then thinking how we can engage with and what a legal strategy might look like and what might be appropriate to an issue. And, really enabling and empowering people to develop those strategies in quite a dynamic way. And then the second area is also, we do have to be willing to learn new areas of law' (unattributed).

One interviewee queried whether lawyers would be drawn to ClientEarth rather than anywhere else: 'I think the only organisation that doesn't struggle to fill its legal capacity is ClientEarth 'cause, I think if you wanted to work as a lawyer in the green sector where would you go? You'd probably go there, wouldn't you?' (Interviewee 6). We did not hear any suggestions that ClientEarth has weakened legal capacity elsewhere in the sector, but it certainly dominates. Where legal mobilisation strategies are 'owned' by one or two organisations within a particular sector, this may disincentivise others from adopting similar approaches.[69] A small number of our interviewees implicitly acknowledged this when discussing the role of ClientEarth within the environmental NGO sector. For example, making the point that it might be surprising that NGOs are maintaining legal capacity, one interviewee stated that:

> I think at any time, especially with ClientEarth, around [XXX] could have said 'We don't really need to have internal lawyers any more. We can rely on ClientEarth's and go to them and ask, get them to do the things that we need, we think are important' (Interviewee 14).

This resonates with the results of an Environmental Funders Network survey of environmental groups, asking them which skills they thought they needed. Legal skills were low down on the list of priorities, and yet, paradoxically perhaps, ClientEarth was seen as the 'most effective' group in the same review.[70]

We return to ClientEarth in chapters 6 and 8. The purpose of our research has not been to examine ClientEarth, but their place in the environmental legal community is obviously significant. If one accepts that legal expertise is not just a technical service for campaigners, but has a more substantive role to play in understanding and shaping the world, then one might conclude that it is not healthy for a single organisation to dominate the pool of legal expertise in the sector.

Like political and legal opportunity theories, resource-based factors cannot be the sole explanation for the strategy choices of interest groups.[71] The literature raises significant questions about, amongst other things, the extent to which social movements behave with a clean instrumental rationality. Resource mobilisation theories neglect other important factors including, as introduced above and developed in chapter 3, the political context within which interest groups operate, and as discussed below, the self-understanding of an organisation. However, the theory remains an important (and common sense) way of thinking about why social movement organisations adopt one strategy over another.[72]

Organisational culture and identity

Together, opportunity and access, and resource-based theories, can provide a strong account of interest group strategies. However, whether they are the 'primary (or sometimes sole) determinants of strategy choice is questionable'.[73] Organisational culture and identity is important: 'the choice of tactics, and, crucially, how movements stage and pursue them, the roles they play in the development and expression of collective identity at the group level, the meanings they appropriate and give to them, must be accounted for with reference to movement ideas, cultures and traditions.'[74] The strategies that interest groups adopt are rarely neutral constructs but are, rather, expressive of their collective identity, and in turn feed back into that collective identity.[75]

Our interviews confirm that although cost has posed a significant challenge in maintaining sufficient experienced legal experts for advocacy in the sector, it is not the whole story.[76] As suggested above, there may be questions around the quality of work, organisational investment in the development of individual expertise and career progression of lawyers within environmental NGOs. These are linked to the way in which the sector understands the role of law and values legal contributions. An organisation's understanding of themselves, and of law, is likely to be reflected in investment (or not) in law; and in turn, expertise in law reverberates in the understanding of law, in a self-perpetuating cycle. We return to these issues throughout this monograph.

Vanhala, in developing an analytical framework for understanding why interest groups turn to strategic litigation, uses collective framing and identity politics to bring together ad hoc advances in the literature on social movements.[77] Similarly, Hilson considers how identity politics influences the strategies adopted by counter-cultural, sub-cultural and instrumental groups.[78] Using Earth First! as an example, he suggests that counter-cultural groups, who define themselves and develop identity through confrontation, reject the norms that structure traditional political and legal interactions and thereby favour direct action over lobbying and litigation strategies. Instrumental groups will on the other hand pursue strategies that are most likely to deliver the desired substantive outcome. Hilson uses Greenpeace and Friends of the Earth as examples of sub-cultural groups that may favour protest but can and will use other approaches as and when appropriate.

Some participants acknowledged the importance of NGO identity. For example, one interviewee talked about how 'the fundamental thing is probably that [the law is] not in the DNA of those organisations and their approaches' (Interviewee 16). Similarly, another interviewee noted that:

> I mean, it's partly how comfortable the different organisations are. Some, as I said, are, very legalistic in their approach and what they're actually doing, so like [XXX] for example, it's very much at the heart of what they do. They're naturally going to feel very comfortable in that space. And it's part of their cause to use law in that way. It's hard-wired into them (Interviewee 9).

Others bring out the self-perpetuating nature of a lack of legal expertise informing strategic decision-making: 'civil society's understanding of how to drive legal change, and the importance of legal change, was very, very limited. It was very much about litigation. But not about the much broader role of law in society. And how you talk about law, and why law is important' (Interviewee 1). The same participant suggests that environmental NGOs 'tend not to use lawyers, because they haven't identified the need for a lawyer. Or there just aren't enough lawyers there at the right time. And by not understanding at a very deep level' (Interviewee 1).

We have already spoken to the significance of financial resources. The culture that underpins the source of the funding may also be important. One of our interviewees was concerned about the commitment of philanthropy to law:

> you're still driven by a very fickle, almost capricious world. Where they want results now. And policy investments can appear to

generate quick change. And it's also a safe world, where they can make investments without having any unpleasant consequences. If you're campaigning for laws, or you're campaigning using litigation, it's a much harder edged campaign. And the changes that you might win are much more fundamental. So the backlash is equally much more strenuous. And legal campaigns of any nature tend to be longer, harder battles. And philanthropy, it's hard to keep philanthropy engaged in those marches (Interviewee 1).

And those NGOs that get the bulk of their funding from mass membership may face similar cultural challenges using law:

> Just on anecdotal work – sometimes members will write to us and say, 'Why on earth are you spending the organisation's resources on legal resources rather than buying/finding new sites to protect a particular habitat? Your focus should be on protecting habitats rather than suing the government or writing legislation for the government and doing their job for them. Why are you talking to MPs all the time, when you should be shouting at them?' That kind of thing (unattributed).

Conclusions

In this chapter, we set out to introduce and explore some of the key themes of our project. Much of this work is foundational, and we return to it in later chapters. A rich literature seeks to understand the factors that shape both the level of influence enjoyed by interest groups (interest group status) in the law- and policy-making process, and the strategies that they may employ. The literature tells us that both external (for example political and legal opportunities) and internal (for example resources and organisational identity) factors are important in NGO strategic thinking. There are multi-dimensional explanations and understandings of social movements and their actions and strategies, and no single theory can explain the choices that interest groups make in pursuance of their goals. We return to this complex set of influences throughout this book, starting in the next chapter with a detailed insight into the ever-changing political and legal opportunities (and hybrid political–legal opportunities) of the Brexit-environment process.

We are able at this point to offer some preliminary conclusions, based on our interviews, to be explored further in later chapters. First,

Greener UK (and the broader community) has cultivated a trusted insider status, and has favoured insider strategies of advocacy and lobbying when seeking to influence the Brexit-environment landscape. Second, the environmental NGO sector is 'underweight' (Interviewee 3) in legal expertise. This is not a straightforward conclusion, because as we discuss in chapters 4 and 5, we are also able to point to some strong and well-utilised legal expertise in the sector. Nevertheless, with the exception of ClientEarth, legal resource is at least thinly dispersed across the sector. Third, there is a clear link between financial and legal resource, with lawyers and legal expertise viewed as an expensive commodity. But equally, organisational culture ('identity, ideas and values'[79]) is also important, whether legal expertise is in the 'DNA of those organisations and their approaches' (Interviewee 16). We return to these questions in the context of our case study throughout this monograph.

Costs and culture are intrinsically linked, in a loop that we have observed throughout our research between financial resource, legal capacity and organisational culture. Essentially, a relative lack of legal expertise in an organisation might feed into a lack of understanding in that organisation as to what law can 'do'; this in turn limits the financial resource allocated to legal expertise, meaning that legal capacity is not enhanced, and so reinforces a reduced role for law in shaping the cultural identity of the organisation – and on it goes.

Notes

1. See e.g. Revillard 2017 for a discussion of administrative rights enforcement as legal mobilisation.
2. Vanhala and Kinghan 2018, 5. As discussed below, this expansive approach is not without its critics.
3. Either advocacy or lobbying can involve campaigning activities to influence public opinion, as well as direct contact with policy elites, e.g. De Bruycker and Beyers 2019 refers to 'outsider lobbying', 57.
4. Jordan 2009, 371.
5. Hilson 2002, 239 and 240.
6. Page 1999, 206.
7. Department of Environment, Food and Rural Affairs 2018.
8. Maloney et al. 1994, 19.
9. Page 1999 cites earlier work.
10. Grant 1978.
11. Grant 1978, summarised in Grant 2004.
12. Grant 2000, 20.
13. Much of the literature refers to both strategies and tactics. Although in some cases these terms appear to be used interchangeably, there is a distinction between the two: 'strategies are overall approaches to seeking influence, whereas specific activities engaged in can be described as tactics', Binderkrantz and Kroyer 2012, 124.
14. Willis 2020.

15 We return to Wildlife and Countryside Link in chapter 6.
16 https://greeneruk.org/time-now-1 accessed 1 July 2020.
17 Maloney et al. 1994, 17.
18 Maloney et al. 1994, 28.
19 E.g. Grant 1989.
20 Maloney et al. 1994.
21 May and Nugent 1982. Cited in Maloney et al. 1994.
22 Page 1999, 209–10.
23 Truman 1951, 334.
24 Maloney et al. 1994, 36.
25 Jasanoff 1997, 589.
26 Maloney et al. 1994, 19.
27 On conveying legitimacy to policy-makers through a large membership, see e.g. Furlong 1997, 330.
28 Grant 1989, 21. Maloney et al. 1994, 29–30.
29 Marsh et al. 2009.
30 See e.g. May and Nugent 1982, 7.
31 Vanhala 2020.
32 Rootes 2009, 213.
33 For a study of compatibility between different strategies see Binderkrantz 2005.
34 Vanhala 2016 suggests, counter-intuitively, that insider groups with privileged access and influence to state organisations litigate significantly more than those without such access.
35 Marsh et al. 2009, 628.
36 Binderkrantz 2005, 696.
37 Beyers 2004, 213.
38 Beyers 2004; Binderkrantz 2005.
39 See further Lehoucq and Taylor 2020.
40 The literature recognises that the final stage of litigation, when legal claims are considered by judges in a court of law, is just part of a 'larger, complex, dynamic, multistage process of disputing', and that other stages such as the articulation of grievances, settlement, and post-appeal interactions are also significant, McCann 2008, 524.
41 For a brief insight into this literature see Hilson 2013. See also for example Cummings 2018; McCann 2008; Boutcher and McCammon 2019.
42 For a brief summary of the use of litigation strategies in the US see Boutcher and McCammon 2019.
43 Harlow and Rawlings 1992.
44 For a useful overview of the literature see Epp 2008. For a recent example of litigation tactics in the field of environmental protection see Vanhala 2018a.
45 Lehoucq and Taylor 2020, 168. The term 'formal institutional mechanism' is defined broadly to include administrative procedures (e.g. efforts to obtain welfare benefits), quasi-judicial processes and litigation.
46 Vanhala and Kinghan 2018, 5.
47 Much of the literature in this area attempts to explain the emergence, development and structure of social movements, that is groups of people (social movement organisations) that come together to bring about (or at times, resist) change. But these approaches can also help us understand and explain why interest groups choose certain strategies over others and many if not all of these factors are relevant when considering legal mobilisation.
48 Scholzman and Tierney 1986, 169.
49 Maloney et al. 1994, 36.
50 Binderkrantz and Kroyer 2012.
51 Binderkrantz and Kroyer 2012.
52 We refer to legal and political opportunities (rather than opportunity structures) to reflect the fact that whilst some features of the parliamentary and judicial system are structural, others (such as the receptivity of decision-makers) are more contingent, Hilson 2002. Note also Koopmans 1999, who argues that structures are those opportunities that 'cannot be influenced – at least not in the foreseeable future – by collective action', 99.
53 Meyer and Minkoff 2004, 1457–8. Kitschelt 1986, examining the anti-nuclear movement across four European countries, is largely credited with being foundational in the area.

54 Hilson 2002 argues that the openness of the political system should be examined in the context of a particular sub-area, avoiding generalisations. He argues that political opportunities depend very much on the political landscape at the time (e.g. party in power).
55 See e.g. Kriesi et al. 2007.
56 For an excellent summary see Meyer and Minkoff 2004.
57 May and Nugent 1982; Maloney et al. 1994; Walker 1991.
58 Bouwen and McCown 2007, 431.
59 Page 1999, 210.
60 Vanhala 2018a.
61 These theories have a long tradition in law and society scholarship, starting arguably with the work of Marc Galanter 1974.
62 Weiler and Reibmann 2019, 94.
63 Edelman et al. 2010, 663.
64 Epp 1998.
65 Epp 1998. He argues that these structures are crucial in explaining the role of legal mobilisation in the expansion of judicially protected individual rights in the US.
66 Hilson 2002, 240.
67 On access to courts, see e.g. Galanter 1974. Epp 1998 argues that whilst conventional explanations for the growth of the rights movement (such as constitutional guarantees of individual rights) are important, the support structure for legal mobilisation (rights advocacy organisations, rights advocacy lawyers and sources of financing) were essential in shaping the rights revolution. See also Keleman 2003.
68 Keleman 2003; Vanhala 2009.
69 Vanhala 2016. Note also that although when surveyed by the Environmental Funders Network, legal skills were low down on the list of priorities for environmental groups, ClientEarth was seen as the 'most effective' group in the same review, Miller, Cracknell and Williams 2017.
70 Miller, Cracknell and Williams 2017.
71 See e.g. Vanhala's 2016 study of litigation by environmental NGOs in France where there was certainly no clear correlation between financial resource and the use of litigation.
72 Saunders 2013, Chapter 4.
73 Vanhala 2009, 739.
74 Doherty and Hayes 2018, 276.
75 See e.g. Vanhala 2020.
76 Kelemen 2003 studies litigation strategies by 412 interest groups. Of the majority of groups who had not used litigation, only 10.2% indicated that this was due to the various obstacles that prevented its use. Almost 90% of respondents stated that they 'preferred to avoid the use of litigation as it does not fit with our general approach', 232.
77 Vanhala 2011. She later returns to the significance of how organisations shape and frame the idea of law with some organisations more sceptical of what law can offer, and the role of entrepreneurs within the organisation, Vanhala 2016 and 2018a. See also Taylor 2020, for a discussion of how societal actors (including NGOs) contribute to the social construction of individual grievances by helping to frame certain problems through a legal lens.
78 Hilson 2002.
79 Hilson 2002, 239 and 240.

3
Brexit and the journey to the Environment Act – interrupted

Introduction

In the referendum of June 2016, 52 per cent of the UK population voted to leave the EU. This marked the beginning of a tortuous journey: 'a pathological combination of chaos, gridlock, constantly unravelling negotiations, serial failures to find a way forward, and intensely adversarial intra- and inter-party divisions'.[1] Three and a half years later, in January 2020, the UK left the EU. This chapter tells a (not the only possible) story of the process of Brexit, as it relates to environmental protection. Our case study runs from the referendum to the emergence of the Environment Bill, from June 2016 until June 2020. At the time of writing, the Environment Bill has been suspended due to the Covid-19 pandemic, and the timing of its return to Committee is uncertain.

This chapter provides the context for our case study and highlights the political opportunity in which environmental groups operated in this period. It does not – and could not – tell the whole Brexit, or even Brexit-environment, story. Chapter 2 explained how scholars of political opportunity explore the external factors that shape NGO strategies,[2] alongside internal factors including 'resources, identity, ideas and values'.[3] In our outline of the dramatic parliamentary and government context between June 2016 and 2020 (see also figure 1, page xvi), we identify five significant, non-exhaustive, overlapping features that shaped political opportunity, some of which we identify as 'hybrid political–legal opportunity', for environmental NGOs.

First, the relationship between parliament and the executive, and the shifts of power between them, have been extraordinary, and unique in post-war Britain. At times, parliament has been very strong, opening up particular paths to influence for environmental NGOs; at other times, the executive has been dominant. Second, the need for crucial legislation, and colossal amounts of associated government and parliamentary activity, in order to take the UK out of the EU, created a particular set of incentives for NGO approaches to advocacy. Third, the increasing electoral significance of the environment for the governing Conservative Party led to some shared objectives between government (at least DEFRA) and the environmental community. This electoral significance extended also to other political parties, and to parts of parliament. Fourth, the 2017 Government's interest in the environment became the then Secretary of State Michael Gove's 'Green Brexit'. A 'Green Brexit' embraced both an 'equivalence' narrative, and a distinctive 'governance' framing, discussed below. Both of these approaches to Brexit called on legal expertise for implementation. Fifth, the enormous rupture of leaving the EU, which was a technically as well as politically demanding exercise, placed great pressure on government. It provoked an appetite for expertise on the part of government, parliament and NGOs. The ongoing Covid-19 crisis plays through a number of these features of the political context (the relationship between parliament and government; the political salience of environmental protection; the strain on resources) in ways that are yet to develop clearly.

For much of the period of our case study, especially the two and a half years between the 2017 and 2019 General Elections, doors were there to be opened by environmental groups pursuing careful and quiet advocacy with the powerful. A different set of political opportunities and hybrid political–legal opportunities would have led to different results, in terms of what NGOs did, what they achieved, and our findings in the rest of this book. But political opportunity is complex, shifting more subtly and quickly than our five features can convey, with different aspects hampering or enabling environmental groups all at the same time. So this chapter demonstrates how very agile environmental groups need to be. This in turn feeds into questions of resources, and the need for different types of expertise, and different skills.

Before turning to the story of Brexit, the next section of this chapter examines in a little more detail the crucial 'governance' and 'equivalence' framings of Brexit. The governance framing of Brexit-environment understands the environmental impact of Brexit through the institutional architecture that sits over individual environmental rules and standards. These include institutions to render non-compliance with environmental law visible, and to enable those who seek to hold the powerful to account for their environmental performance. The equivalence framing takes seriously the constant reassurance by government that Brexit would not involve any weakening of environmental protections, and that environmental measures would be at least as strong after Brexit as before: 'Brexit will not mean a lowering of environmental standards'.[4] This fed into the governance framing. Frames are ways of seeing the world, and framing signals the intellectual and political labour involved in creating stable ways to see and understand the Brexit-environment issue.[5] It was never inevitable that Brexit would be seen as a legal, let alone governance, problem. The Brexit-environment problem was not a simple fact waiting to be revealed and solved, but emerged in an active and constructive process.

Our attention to governance is not to suggest that environmental NGOs were neglecting other, substantive environmental issues. On the contrary. So for example, active advocacy around substantive sectors of environmental protection pressed for and responded to DEFRA's *25 Year Plan*,[6] and the wider Environment Bill.[7] Nor, as conceded in chapter 1, does the Environment Bill exhaust environmental NGO action on Brexit; even looking only at legislative activity, the environmental community has engaged intensively on the Fisheries, Agriculture and Trade Bills. Also as discussed in chapter 1, we are focusing on the English and UK perspective, from Whitehall and Westminster, although environmental NGOs were active in the other three nations of the UK.[8]

Environmental law: life before and after Brexit

As we discuss in chapter 1, the EU (Withdrawal) Act 2018 introduced the category of 'retained law' to provide some continuity between the UK's legal rule book the day before, and the day after, leaving the EU.[9] But EU law has shaped UK environmental protection much more widely than through the legal provisions 'retained' through the EU (Withdrawal) Act 2018.[10] The broader architecture of obligations and institutions that make those environmental standards meaningful has provided the starting point for the 'governance framing' of Brexit-environment. The 'equivalence' approach to post-Brexit environmental law, positing that levels of protection be at least as good after Brexit as before, feeds into governance as well as into substantive matters of environmental law (and practice).

We outline three 'governance' issues here. First, those aspects of EU law that attempt to enhance the effectiveness of law, in the sense of ensuring that national governments implement EU environmental law. Secondly, UK environmental law and standards have developed and evolved collaboratively as part of the EU. And thirdly, in addition to governance, the environmental principles that have formed part of EU environmental law for many years will not in themselves constitute 'retained law'.[11] For the purposes of our project, we need only comment very briefly on the provisions on each of these matters in the Environment Bill. The overarching concern about the governance and principles provisions of the Bill is the extent to which it leaves discretion and power in the hands of the executive; this is framework legislation, and whilst it could do great things for the next generation of environmental law, it could equally provide a framework for deregulation and environmental regression.

Some of the issues discussed here, especially the European Commission's hard-edged enforcement role, may not fit tidily into an academic understanding of governance,[12] which is often defined by contrast with either 'law' or 'government'. The principles have generally, and properly, been dealt with separately in the debate (principles *and* governance). But governance is a capacious term, and here and in the Brexit-environment debate has generally been used to capture all of the background frameworks, institutions, approaches that make environmental standards and rules work, and understood by contrast with specific environmental standards and rules.

Enforcement and accountability

In a Union of many, diverse Member States, not only the EU institutions but also each Member State has strong incentives to ensure that the laws signed up to are well implemented by all. A range of implementation mechanisms have been developed, which we can broadly divide into direct enforcement, and implementation tools with a less direct impact on legal and political accountability.

The European Commission is famously the 'watchdog' of the EU treaties, with powers to take Member States to the Court of Justice of the European Union (CJEU) for violations of EU law; the Court can impose significant fines in certain cases.[13] The availability of fines does seem to have influenced the UK government, and may have empowered DEFRA in cross-government debates about the resources to be devoted to environmental protection.[14] The CJEU does not accept practical, political or economic difficulties with implementation (unless provided for in the legislation) as a justification for failing to comply with EU law.[15]

This enforcement regime, scrutinising and sanctioning not polluters but their regulators,[16] is probably unique to the EU system. Efforts to provide something similar, to help them to hold government to account after Brexit, has been a major focus of environmental group activity. Whilst we acknowledge that 'success' can mean different things to different groups, the creation of the Office for Environmental Protection (OEP) under the Environment Bill is rightly considered a major victory for the sector. There has been remarkably little open dissent from the 'in principle' benefits of the OEP, although one of our participants expressed some caution: 'you don't have a regulatory body for old times' sake [...] I think it's a legal habit. I think we're used to having a thing called the European Commission. We're used to having this external arbiter of compliance' (Interviewee 1). The political enemies of the OEP are not making public attacks on its existence, but have many other ways to stymie its effectiveness. The OEP is just a distraction (or worse) if it is not adequately independent and resourced (with money, expertise, powers). The lengthy, detailed, technical arguments about the independence, resources and powers of the OEP from environmental NGOs do seem to have had some impact, as discussed in chapters 5 and 7, even if the sector does not have everything it asked for. This ability to divide up issues, as opposed to 'all or nothing' demands, leaves room for bargaining and negotiation, and may in this case have elevated the potential scope and impact of lobbying.[17]

The Commission plus Court enforcement regime is only the most visible part of the EU's efforts to enhance legal implementation. EU law also makes a significant contribution to *legal* accountability within the Member States, relying on 'the vigilance of individuals concerned to protect their rights' as a central part of the supervision of implementation.[18] Direct effect and supremacy mean that much EU environmental legislation can be relied on by individuals (and NGOs) in their national courts, even if a government has implemented it inadequately or not at all; domestic law must in any event be interpreted consistently with EU law whenever possible;[19] and domestic courts are subject to duties to ensure effectiveness of EU law, and to provide adequate remedies if EU law is breached.[20] In addition to these general EU principles, binding rules on access to justice are embedded in certain environmental directives.[21] The Environment Bill does not address these issues. Access to justice remains scattered around domestic legislation, but without the protections offered by its earlier status in EU law; how the courts will develop remedies in the absence of EU law remains to be seen.[22]

Further, banal routines of planning, reporting and reviewing pervade EU environmental law. These can provide an architecture of transparency that sharpens the potential for civil society to hold government *politically* to account, as well as providing information that may lead to legal accountability. Obligations to plan, report and plan again can be found in virtually any piece of EU environmental law.[23] The reports are in principle scrutinised by the European Commission or the European Environment Agency, as well as being available to all Member States, the other EU institutions and the public. Their open publication provides an important opportunity for scrutiny, and external input for improved outcomes. The breach of legislation, and even risk of breach, is rendered visible; lawful derogations and exceptions must also be explicitly acknowledged and explained.

Planning, reporting and reviewing procedures also received some attention during the Brexit process, albeit much less than Commission plus Court enforcement. Analogies have been drawn with the Climate Change Act 2008's architecture, and the provision of scrutiny and advice by the Climate Change Committee under that Act. The value of these mechanisms does seem to have been recognised. The Environment Bill would introduce a planning, monitoring and reviewing framework, for certain areas of environmental protection, with key roles for the OEP and Parliament.[24] They are imperfect, but if well implemented, they enhance the ability of civil society to challenge the environmental performance of government and regulators.

Developing environmental law and standards

For a long time, discussion of the 'governance gap' was backward looking.[25] But Brexit raises significant questions about the future of environmental protection, and how environmental standards and rules will be developed when the UK is no longer part of the EU's expert structures and democratic processes. The EU approach to environmental standard-setting is far from perfect, but it does call on well-developed institutional arrangements, which provide for the pooling of expert knowledge, and some (limited) degree of stakeholder participation.[26]

A target-setting framework appeared for the first time in the Environment Bill published in October 2019. The Bill allows or requires the Secretary of State to set 'long term' ('no less than 15 years'[27]) targets in a range of areas, and 'it is the duty of the Secretary of State to ensure that' those targets are met.[28] Interim targets are to be set in policy (not law). They are subject to a (tardy) framework of monitoring and review, but are not legally enforceable.[29] These provisions are imperfect in many ways, but the key issue is the absence of any protections around their quality. A major source of concern for environmental NGOs has been around 'non-regression', that is a guarantee that environmental standards will not slip after Brexit. The Bill does not require the targets to be set with non-regression in mind,[30] although they are retrospectively reviewed by the Secretary of State according to whether they cumulatively 'significantly improve the natural environment'.[31] Further, the Bill explicitly allows for a weakening of existing standards, if the Secretary of State is 'satisfied' that meeting the target would 'have no significant benefit' or when, 'because of changes in circumstances ... the environmental, social, economic or other costs of meeting it would be disproportionate to the benefits'.[32]

Environmental principles

The Environment Title of the Treaty on the Functioning of the European Union (TFEU) contains four environmental principles (precaution, prevention, rectification at source, polluter pays); the environmental integration principle can be found in Article 11 TFEU. The home of the principles in the Treaty has given them a strong legal role in the development and implementation of environmental law and policy in the EU and its Member States.[33]

The post-Brexit role of 'the' environmental principles has received a considerable amount of attention. The UK environmental community, given its high levels of engagement in nature conservation, was particularly sensitised to the strong interpretation of the precautionary principle for the purposes of the Habitats Directive,[34] but the debate went much further than that. Going beyond the environmental principles contained in the EU Treaty, but still connected to trying to protect the achievements of EU environmental law, NGOs have also (as above) advocated for what was often called a 'non-regression' principle (but was probably closer to a presumption against regression).

Environmental principles are global phenomena. They are diverse and vary according to legal setting and approach. However, a number of general characteristics of environmental principles resonate across different legal and policy contexts, and are also apparent in EU environmental law.[35] They have considerable symbolic power, providing overarching frameworks for environmental policy. They have legal effects, derived in the EU from the Treaties. They guide the making and interpretation of law and policy, and the implementation of law and policy by administrators, shaping the exercise of discretion by public authorities. They inform administrative or judicial review of public decision-making.[36]

The Bill requires the Secretary of State to produce a 'policy statement' on environmental principles 'explaining how the environmental principles should be interpreted and proportionately applied by Ministers of the Crown when making policy' (clause 16). Ministers must 'have due regard' to the policy statement 'when making policy' (clause 18). This approach to principles deprives them of their legal status and enforceability under EU law. Even the weak obligation to 'have due regard to' the policy on principles applies only to Ministers, and only in respect of policy-making, not to all public authorities in all relevant decisions as under EU law. Further, the principles are subject to new major carve outs, for example as to proportionality and with respect to the 'allocation of resources within government', so that they lose their systemic and overarching impact.[37]

The dynamics of political and legal opportunity: parliament and government 2016 to 2020

Theories of political opportunity, as discussed in chapter 2, focus on the external factors that influence NGO strategies. Factors such as internal resources, as well as identity, ideas and values, are equally significant,[38] as also discussed in chapter 2. This chapter outlines and explores the external political context for environmental NGO activity between the Brexit referendum in 2016 and June 2020. It has been a very strange time, which only got stranger with the 'lockdown' introduced as a response to Covid-19.

Entire jurisdictions and political cultures are sometimes ascribed to a category of 'open' or 'closed', 'receptive' or 'non-receptive', to social movement influence. As Chris Hilson argues, this might be useful for comparative work, but a more focused study allows for the exploration of a political landscape as it applies to a particular group or issue, at a particular moment.[39] We take a broad brush to the story of Brexit and the environment in this section, proceeding chronologically. We highlight the dynamics around the five overlapping features of the context outlined in the introduction to this chapter, around which NGO political opportunity coalesced:

1. The relationship and division of power between parliament and the executive, and the extraordinary shifts between them;
2. The crucial legislation, and colossal amounts of government and parliamentary activity, necessary to exit the EU;

3. The political significance of environment and climate change for the governing Conservative Party and others;
4. The promise of a 'Green Brexit', which embraced strong 'equivalence' and 'governance gap' framings;
5. The technically as well as politically complex nature of Brexit.

We do not use these characteristics or features of the political environment to ascribe causal relations between external factors, NGO activity and outcomes, but rather to understand better NGO use and understanding of law and legal expertise. Any of these five issues opens space for advocacy and influence on the environment and sits comfortably in political opportunity theories.[40]

The first feature set out above is the most dramatic. The governing party generally has a majority in the UK Parliament, often a very hefty one. The absence of a significant, or indeed any, parliamentary majority for the Conservative Government between the elections of June 2017 and December 2019 made for an alien experience,[41] and provided a particular moment of political opportunity for environmental NGOs: '… the politics were such and the parliamentary arithmetic was such that it was possible to win stuff in parliament' (Interviewee 16). And, combined with our second characteristic, not only were the parliamentary votes all tight, but some of the legislation was utterly necessary to the Government's key (virtually only) policy agenda:

> if in normal times, if you get a bill that's being held up by a bunch of amendments, you force it through. So parliamentary arithmetic doesn't allow that at the moment. Or you just say, 'Well the bill's gonna fall' and with things like the Withdrawal Bill, it can't fall (Interviewee 13).

That situation changed dramatically after the General Election in 2019, when the Conservative Party won a large parliamentary majority, and easily passed the EU (Withdrawal Agreement) Act 2020, as discussed below. Our third and fourth characteristics were also at their strongest during the strange 2017–19 inter-election period, although there is less of a cliff-edge, as discussed below, in 2020. The complexity of leaving the EU remains constant.

Overall, these five features tend to incentivise an 'insider', advocacy approach to Brexit-environment.[42] Had they been different, we doubt we would be telling the same story about environmental NGOs. Importantly, the external political context faced by NGOs also made particular demands on law and legal expertise. The legal mobilisation literature, as outlined in chapter 2, focuses primarily on the three issues of legal stock (that is the body of substantive law), rules of standing before the court and rules on the costs of litigation.[43] Looking at legal opportunities beyond the court room, as we do here, requires a slightly different approach. Only the first (legal stock) of those three core opportunities is relevant.[44] Additional legal opportunities might be found in phenomena that enhance the role of law in advocating for social and legal change. The intense legislative activity associated with Brexit, the governance and equivalence framings of Brexit and the urgent need for external expertise from Government and Parliament, all created opportunity in this sense. These are perhaps better described as hybrid political–legal opportunity, opening up space for law *and* or *in* politics, reinforced by the high status of law in the Brexit process generally.[45] Importantly, whilst legal opportunity can be an alternative to political opportunity ('a lack of [political opportunity] may influence the adoption of litigation as a strategy in place of lobbying, and that the choice of protest as a strategy may be influenced by poor political and legal opportunities'[46]), this hybrid political–legal opportunity is not. On the contrary, it is part of the political opportunity.

It is important to note that environmental NGOs are not passive victims or beneficiaries of the politics of the moment[47] (although some of these features of the Brexit context are out of their hands). They contribute to shaping opportunity (legal, political or hybrid), for example in our case by becoming trusted and convincing expert interlocutors with government and parliament, by emphasising an equivalence or governance framing. Moreover, much of the governance work by NGOs aims precisely to shape both their legal and political opportunity structure after Brexit.[48] The pressure maintained by environmental NGOs has been an important, understudied part of the Brexit governance story.

We do not use the language of opportunity to suggest that Brexit was welcomed by the sector, or by those we interviewed. On the contrary, almost all of our interviewees referred in one way or another to the opportunity cost of Brexit, which 'squeezes out other areas of possibly more progressive, ambitious work' (Interviewee 15), and has 'sucked up a lot of resource, a lot of people's time and effort' (Interviewee 14). But on the other hand, it may also have reinvigorated the domestic environmental NGO community: 'the Brexit debate, for all its manifest problems, has brought an energy and an expertise back. It has rekindled, you know' (Interviewee 3). The opening of doors through a particular political context has also been recognised by many of our interviewees:

People have never talked about the environment more politically, legally, in campaign terms, have never in my lifetime talked about the environment as much as they are now. So personally, I think it's really exciting. So it comes at a cost, but I think it also comes with huge benefits, huge opportunities, if we don't stuff it up (Interviewee 2).

June 2016 to June 2017: resistance to action on the environment

At the time of the referendum, David Cameron was Prime Minister, and Elizabeth Truss was Secretary of State for EFRA. The Cameron Government that called the referendum[49] had a slim parliamentary majority of twelve seats and followed the first post-war coalition British government (2010–15, Conservative/Liberal Democrat). David Cameron resigned as Prime Minister, and as leader of the Conservative Party, the morning after the referendum. In the UK's parliamentary system it is for the governing party to appoint a new leader, who becomes prime minister.[50] Theresa May became Prime Minister after all other candidates to lead the Conservative Party stepped out of the race. She appointed Andrea Leadsom as Secretary of State for EFRA.

In this period, Government paid very little attention to the environmental impact of Brexit, although Ministers and the Prime Minister continued to repeat the mantra that they would be 'the first generation to leave the environment in a better state than we found it'.[51] The five features of the Brexit context identified above had not really started to develop in a way that provided positive political opportunity for environmental groups. However, the governance and equivalence framings were emerging, and incentivised a particularly lawyerly sort of insider advocacy. Notwithstanding a lack of interest in environmental protection, an equivalence framing of sorts can be found in the emphasis on stability that underpinned the commitment to the EU (Withdrawal) Bill. The Prime Minister's 'Lancaster House' speech in January 2017, for example, assured everyone that 'the same rules and law will apply on the day after Brexit as they did before (sic)'.[52]

The significance of the EU's broader legal architectures (governance) was emphasised by academics (including Maria) during two early inquiries by the Environmental Audit Committee and the House of Lords European Union Select Committee, and was picked up by Parliament, especially the House of Lords report.[53] One of the distinctive things about Brexit may have been the extent to which academics, especially academics in law and political science, involved themselves in the public realm. The engagement was across the board and included environmental issues. The academic contribution seems not to be particularly visible to the NGO community, although at an individual, day-to-day level, contributions are clearly appreciated. This is consistent with our conclusion in chapter 4 that intense specialisation in law may be undervalued, or perhaps more accurately just taken as read, and absorbed into common knowledge.

The Environmental Audit Committee reported on *The Future of the Natural Environment after the EU Referendum* on 4 January 2017. The inquiry was about agriculture and landscape, rather than environmental law more widely.[54] It did, however, begin the governance journey, raising the prospect of 'zombie legislation' to describe EU law that is carried over into UK law, but not updated or enforced. Further, on equivalence and governance:

> The Government should introduce a new Environmental Protection Act to maintain and enforce environmental standards after we leave. This is needed to ensure environmental standards are not weakened when we leave the EU – whether through leaving the Single Market, changes in trading status or through the creation of 'zombie legislation' resulting from our departure from EU governance and enforcement structures.[55]

The House of Lords EU Committee report of February 2017 emphasised the broad framework questions, what we are calling governance, very heavily, although this is not entirely reflected in the recommendations.[56] This report was notable for addressing reporting frameworks, linking them to legal accountability, citing the RSPB's evidence:

> Periodic monitoring and reporting to the European Commission on the implementation of laws such as the Birds and Habitats Directives, combined with robust EU scrutiny enforcement mechanisms, enables progress to be objectively assessed and Member States held to account if necessary.[57]

This report also demonstrated that the Government at this time had no interest in pursuing new mechanisms for accountability, and saw no need to replace EU governance. The report cites (implicitly critically) both the Minister, Therese Coffey, to the effect that 'it is the role of Parliament to hold the Government to account', and the Secretary of State, who said that 'The UK courts are perfectly well able to deal with matters of enforcement. We won't be needing to replace European courts.'[58]

Government's rejection of new approaches to heighten either political ('it is the role of Parliament …') or legal (the courts are 'perfectly well able …') accountability, and more broadly of any overarching 'governance' response, was repeated and emphasised in the responses to both of these reports, and in the papers accompanying the European Union (Withdrawal) Bill.[59] DEFRA repeatedly emphasised what was still being called the 'Great Repeal Bill' (which became the EU (Withdrawal) Act 2018), on the apparent assumption that retaining environmental law would be sufficient to secure environmental protection after Brexit.

A review of the Select Committee submissions, and other public documents, during this period suggests that although they were certainly working with the relevant ideas, environmental NGOs had not yet placed a governance framing at the centre of their work on Brexit. In written submissions to the Environmental Audit Committee inquiry, environmental NGOs expressed some concern about the loss of Commission plus Court enforcement, but were most focused on the potential loss of individual environmental obligations, such as those contained in the Habitats Directive. Greener UK's Manifesto, with its calls for a new Environment Act, 'necessary governance arrangements … for robust implementation and enforcement' and environmental principles, was published in February 2017, a week after the House of Lords report was published.[60] Greener UK's first published briefing picked up the language of the 'governance gap' in August 2017.[61] It addressed monitoring/reviewing/reporting, implementation/compliance/enforcement and transparency, as well as the limitations of existing approaches to judicial review and parliamentary scrutiny.

But the governance gap framing, and its hybrid political–legal opportunity, was emerging even before the Environment Audit Committee and House of Lords Select Committee reports. Oral evidence from environmental groups to the House of Lords Select Committee went further, with more discussion of enforcement and accountability, and some discussion of information and reporting; the RSPB's representative even referred to the 'governance gap' to capture a range of relevant issues. And an internal briefing to the Greener UK Board in October 2016 is concerned with accountability and enforcement.[62] Academics were engaging strongly with the overarching issues in submissions to the inquiries, as suggested above. In summer 2016, Viviane Gravey and colleagues published a blog on the 'governance gap'. It did not focus on the issues set out above, but it did focus on persistently dominant themes that go beyond substantive rules and regulations, most especially devolution.[63]

Of the five overlapping features of the Brexit-environment context introduced above, we see the beginnings of a governance and equivalence framing, creating a hybrid political–legal opportunity that environmental groups are just starting to make use of. The highly (legally) technical character of Brexit is clear, as is the demand for technical and legal expertise in Parliament, if not yet openly so in Government. But the General Election in June 2017 shifts the political opportunity considerably.

June 2017 to January 2018: 'Green Brexit'

The Conservative Party unexpectedly and dramatically lost their overall Parliamentary majority at the General Election of June 2017. Theresa May led a minority Conservative Government with the support of the Democratic Unionist Party until mid-2019.

With obvious simplification, three things happened as a result of the election, each of which fits into our list of the five features of the external environment for NGO advocacy. First, and perhaps most obviously, the influence of Parliament increased, and Government was not able to push through its legislative agenda. Because the legislature is more immediately subject to democratic pressures than the executive, increased capacity for parliament is generally thought to enhance the openness of a political system as a whole.[64] Secondly, younger people had voted in large numbers for the Labour Party,[65] and there was a perception in the Conservative Party that stronger environmental policies would appeal to younger voters.[66] As a result, third, Michael Gove was appointed Secretary of State for EFRA. He was considered a political heavyweight, with considerable influence in cabinet and more broadly. Political opportunity for the environmental community was transformed, and the community (especially Greener UK) stepped into this space.

Michael Gove and DEFRA promised a 'Green Brexit',[67] and accepted that the 'governance gap' was a problem. Michael Gove touched on this in his major speech in summer 2017, describing Brexit as the 'unfrozen moment' when things can be done:

> I know that inside the EU, the European Commission and the ECJ have provided enforcement mechanisms and understandably, some are asking what could or should replace them. My view is that we have an opportunity, outside the EU, to design potentially more effective, more rigorous and more responsive institutions, new means of holding individuals and organisations to account for environmental outcomes.

Michael Gove and his Department engaged energetically with environmental NGOs. His appointment was described as 'critical' (Interviewee 10), 'the primary reason why this has all happened' (Interviewee 11) and it 'definitely made a difference' (Interviewee 3).

The major impact of Brexit on even 'business as usual' DEFRA activity[68] and the large reduction in staff numbers during the 'austerity' period between 2010 and 2016,[69] had left DEFRA under-resourced. An enormous recruitment exercise in DEFRA followed the resurgence of interest in the environment. According to the Institute for Government, in October 2019 DEFRA had 75 per cent more civil servants, amounting to 1,700 new people, than at the time of the referendum, one of the highest increases in departmental staff numbers.[70] Although many of these new DEFRA recruits had high levels of relevant knowledge and experience, many did not. They were learning on the job, about the workings of the civil service[71] and about environmental law and policy and the workings of the EU. What became the Environment Bill is difficult specialist material, building on decades of legislation, case law and culture at EU level. It was a challenging set of issues for people new to the sector to get to grips with.

As discussed in chapter 2, how open a system is to particular interlocutors, and how receptive it is to their arguments, affects the approach that NGOs take. All five of the features set out above enhanced the space for environmental NGOs' insider advocacy during this period. The political interest in the environment, combined with the huge amount of challenging Brexit-related work and considerable recent recruitment to DEFRA, may well have increased access to government officials for well-informed experts of various stripes. From the 2017 election, DEFRA was relatively open to its environmental NGO interlocutors, and receptive to their arguments. And with the embrace of the equivalence and governance framings, it was receptive to the legal expertise of NGOs. Government is not a monolith, however, and whilst DEFRA was receptive, other departments were more resistant. For example, the Treasury and Department of Transport were particularly concerned about the impact of strong environmental governance (or interference as they saw it) on their freedom of action.[72] Whilst 'Brexit' is notoriously difficult to pin down, parts of the pro-Brexit movement were opposed to the EU's strong environmental regulations, perceived as a barrier to economic development. Inter-departmental tensions were present throughout.

The 'unprecedented' nature of the 'access' (Interviewee 6) to DEFRA was well understood by many of our interviewees. This interviewee attributed the access in part to the needs of DEFRA: 'they genuinely need the help and know that they want and aspire towards that challenge as well' (Interviewee 6). S/he also understood that access did not just happen, but was earned by the sector, through different mechanisms including personal attributes ('charm') and personal relationship building, but also having 'the weight of law', as well as other forms of expertise, on their side. As discussed further in chapters 6 and 7, there is a definite perception that the 'disciplined' (Interviewee 3) collaboration helped and that 'it was crucial for civil society to be able to speak with a united voice about what its priorities were in relation to Brexit' (Interviewee 11).

But although some, including some of our interviewees, had good access to the government officials drafting the various iterations of the Environment Bill, much of this was informal and 'by invitation'. This did come up indirectly in some of our interviews, and directly in the following comment from Interviewee 17:

> What there wasn't was a structured process with transparent access. What it generated was, for people who could find themselves in the room, an opportunity to shape and influence. Which I think is better than having nobody shape and influencing it other than civil servants in Whitehall.

It is inevitable that some important voices were excluded from these 'invitation only' discussions.

Nor were our interviewees entirely relaxed about what they were getting out of this intense insider activity, and a number were ambivalent or uneasy about the sector's relationship with politicians in DEFRA.[73] Given that most of our interviewees were directly involved in the Brexit process, and many enjoyed privileged access, it is plausible that we might have seen greater levels of concern among other NGO actors. One of our interviewees saw the DEFRA engagement 'as simply a suckering exercise' (unattributed); similarly, another was concerned that 'a lot of civil society have sunk a lot of investment in a Gove-led Environment Bill, in a context where he ain't going to be Environment Secretary in two weeks' time' (Interviewee 11).

January 2018 to late 2018: consultation and evolution

There were three important governmental/parliamentary occasions for environmental group engagement in the first half of 2018, the most visible elements of intense activity that shaped political opportunities along the five dimensions set out above. First, the *25 Year Plan* was belatedly published by DEFRA, without being preceded by any formal (or apparently much informal) consultation. Second, following up on a number of promises, DEFRA launched its *Consultation on Environmental Principles and Governance After EU Exit* (the *EPG Consultation*).[74] A 'Green Brexit' and equivalence framing were central to government rhetoric for both of these exercises, for example assurances that there will be 'no dilution of the environmental protections that we currently have within the European Union'.[75] Third, the EU (Withdrawal) Act 2018 completed its passage through Parliament, from first reading on 13 July 2017 and Royal Assent in June 2018.

The *25 Year Plan* had been promised in response to a 2014 Report by the Natural Capital Committee and was published in January 2018 after numerous delays.[76] Its origins are obviously unrelated to Brexit, but its publication and development rested in part on the 'Green Brexit' rhetoric. It is wide-ranging, with multiple environmental goals and priority areas. It covers many substantive environmental policy areas, some of which are now in the Environment Bill.[77] The *25 Year Plan* also links tightly to Part 1 (Governance) of the Environment Bill. Clause 7 provides that the *25 Year Plan* is the first Environmental Improvement Plan (EIP) under the Bill; EIPs are to constitute a new English environmental policy programme, reviewed and revised every five years, under the Bill. The wholly aspirational and non-binding nature of the objectives in the *Plan* also laid the ground for advocacy around the targets chapter of the Bill. Finally, the *25 Year Plan* promised that 'Government will launch a consultation in early 2018 on establishing a new, world-leading, independent, statutory body to give the environment a voice, championing and upholding environmental standards as we leave the European Union'.[78] This was the *EPG Consultation*, which ran between May and August. As is apparent from the title, this was framed clearly around principles and governance.

Environmental NGOs engaged vigorously with the *25 Year Plan*, and the *EPG Consultation*. Perhaps surprisingly, given its dry title, NGO membership also rallied around the *EPG Consultation* – there were over 176,000 consultation responses.[79] Two of the primary overarching criticisms of the *25 Year Plan* relate to equivalence. First, many of the targets or aspirations in the *25 Year Plan* either did not exceed or were weaker than existing EU standards; and secondly, the *25 Year Plan* did not commit to legally binding obligations on government. The proposals in the *EPG Consultation* were welcomed in principle, but also strongly criticised. Improvements in the scope and depth of the measures were made when the consultation was developed in the draft Environment (Principles and Governance) Bill, discussed below, although fundamental flaws (capable of severely undermining the provisions) survive to the time of writing. We discuss the progress of principles and governance in more detail in chapter 7.

At the same time as the *EPG Consultation*, the European Union (Withdrawal) Act 2018 was making its way through Parliament. As well as providing for the repeal of the European Communities Act 1972, and creating the new category of 'retained law', discussed in chapter 1, this Act made three other important contributions to our story.

First, it provided for the introduction of secondary legislation to deal with 'any failure of retained EU law to operate effectively', or 'any other deficiency in retained EU law'.[80] This 'tidying up' exercise, designed to address provisions that no longer work once the UK is not a member of the EU (such as a role for EU institutions), was a demanding process for DEFRA civil servants, NGOs and Parliament. It has also provided fertile ground for the use of law and legal expertise, as civil society sought to ensure that government stayed within the powers granted under the legislation. It was:

> literally a case of going through the relevant directives, you know, the European law, as applies to the UK now, regulations. So if they're already directly applicable to us, we'll go through the domestic regulations, look at it and say, 'Okay, if this is maintained ...' going through it line by line (Interviewee 15).

Interviewee 5 suggested that 'the simple proposition is that in some instances, the Government has taken the opportunity – this is the sceptical version of it, obviously, this is the spun version of it – to not just implement but also undermine on the way through'.[81]

This process has arguably brought the insufficiency of NGO legal capacity centre stage, a factor we discuss in chapter 2 when looking at resource mobilisation theories. The sector has 'done its best to cope with the deluge of instruments that Government's put out' (Interviewee 6), but 'I suspect there was a capacity question because people didn't grind their way through the regs' (Interviewee 5); or a broader capacity issue around understanding what law might do (on which see chapter 5): 'I think people maybe didn't *know* to grind their way through the regs' (Interviewee 5 – emphasis added). We should be cautious given the extraordinary extent of the challenge,[82] and both Greener UK and Wildlife and Countryside Link coordinated work on the statutory instruments. This suggests, however, a degree of mutual reinforcement between available legal resource and valuing legal expertise, to which we return in subsequent chapters.

Second, section 13 of the EU (Withdrawal) Act required what became known as a 'meaningful vote' by Parliament on the terms of the UK's withdrawal from the EU. Headed 'Parliamentary approval of the outcome of negotiations by the EU', section 13 provided that a withdrawal agreement with the EU can only be ratified if laid before Parliament and approved by the House of Commons. Whilst obviously not an explicitly environmental provision, this is what brought the four attempts by two Prime Ministers to pass an EU (Withdrawal Agreement) Bill back to Parliament, before finally the fifth attempt became the EU (Withdrawal Agreement) Act 2020. All of these Bills constituted political opportunity, within which the NGO community lobbied Parliament and Government, and all save the fifth attempt involved parliamentary arithmetic that gave the Parliament unusually direct power over whether legislation can pass. Debates were held and promises (or even amendments) were made around the first four bills on issues including deregulation and regression, and the impact of trade negotiations on environmental protection.

Third, and more directly relevant, section 16 of the EU (Withdrawal) Act 2018, headed 'Maintenance of Environmental Principles, etc.', is unprecedented. It provides that the Secretary of State 'must' within six months 'publish a draft Bill', 'consisting of':

(a) a set of environmental principles,
(b) a duty on the Secretary of State to publish a statement of policy in relation to the application and interpretation of those principles in connection with the making and development of policies by Ministers of the Crown,
(c) a duty which ensures that Ministers of the Crown must have regard, in circumstances provided for by or under the Bill, to the statement mentioned in paragraph (b),
(d) provisions for the establishment of a public authority with functions for taking, in circumstances provided for by or under the Bill, proportionate enforcement action (including legal proceedings if necessary) where the authority considers that a Minister of the Crown is not complying with environmental law (as it is defined in the Bill),
[…]

Subsection 2 listed a set of environmental principles. Although imperfect in its substance,[83] introducing this amendment to the legislation tied government down, before its *EPG Consultation* was complete, providing parliament with the opportunity to deliberate on a draft Bill. By keeping environmental governance on the parliamentary agenda when we might have expected the high constitutional and political drama of Brexit to have overwhelmed all else, section 16 was a major achievement for environmental NGOs and their allies who had lobbied intensively around the future of environmental governance and principles post-Brexit. Many of our interviewees referred to the work around the 2018 Act as a key moment. Section 16 indicates the way in which the community (through Greener UK in particular) grasped the opportunity presented by the parliamentary logic, the political significance of the environment, and the existence of a Bill that could be amended. And they used that to create further political opportunity for themselves: the upshot of section 16 was the draft Environment (Principles and Governance) Bill, around which they again worked hard.[84]

Late 2018 to mid-2019: legislative drafts and political turmoil

In November 2018, the UK Government and the European Council reached a draft Withdrawal Agreement and a draft Political Declaration on the future relationship between the EU and the UK.[85] It contained the famous/notorious Northern Ireland 'backstop', more formally the *Protocol on Ireland/Northern Ireland*,[86] which contained a number of significant environmental provisions. The Protocol was to enter into force at the end of the transition period only if not superseded by a trade agreement. Its purpose was to avoid a 'hard' customs border between the Republic of Ireland and Northern Ireland, given the history of violence along that border and the wish to support the peace process institutionalised by the Good Friday Agreement.[87] Reflecting the second and fifth of our Brexit-environment characteristics, the environmental provisions in the Protocol, within a complex draft Treaty and a complex institutional environment, created a space for legal expertise.

Article 6 of the Protocol provided for the continuance of a 'single customs territory' between the UK and the EU. 'With a view to ensuring the maintenance of the level playing field conditions required for the proper functioning' of the single customs territory, it (inter alia) would have given effect to Annex 4 of the Protocol. Part 2 of the Annex contains environmental provisions. It introduces what amounted to a non-regression principle, requiring that 'the level of environmental protection provided by law, regulations and practices is not reduced below the level provided by the common standards applicable within the Union and the United Kingdom' at the end of the transition period. It would have required the respect of four environmental principles: precaution, prevention, source and polluter pays. And it would have required the UK to ensure effective enforcement of those provisions, and to set up 'a transparent system for the effective domestic monitoring, oversight and enforcement of its obligations ... by an independent and adequately resourced body or bodies'.[88] It is easy to see how these provisions provide a 'legal hook' (to quote our participants[89]), an opportunity for legal advocacy. It supported the case for the OEP, essentially providing an argument that these agreed conditions should provide a starting point for the future of environmental law in the UK.[90]

In December 2018, a draft Environment (Principles and Governance) Bill was published for pre-legislative scrutiny.[91] The draft Bill had three main elements: a framework for a set of environmental principles;[92] a requirement on the Secretary of State to prepare an EIP; and provision for a new public body, the OEP.[93] Importantly, the draft Bill was only *part* of a Bill. Substantive environmental provisions were promised, but with no detail on what would be addressed.[94]

The Environmental Audit Committee and the EFRA Committee produced broadly consistent pre-legislative scrutiny reports. The EFRA Committee emphasised equivalence: 'the overwhelming narrative from the evidence to our inquiry is that the draft Bill's provisions for principles and governance are not equivalent to the current environmental protections provided by membership of the EU.'[95] Evidence provided by lawyers (academics, barristers, Parliamentary counsel, NGO lawyers) is most heavily cited in the report. It is clearly not the case that only lawyers can participate; the Environmental Audit Committee cited a wider range of sources, albeit including lawyers.

The approval and implementation of the draft Withdrawal Agreement by the UK Parliament was to be provided for by the EU (Withdrawal Agreement) Bill. This Bill, or versions of it, and hence the 2018 Withdrawal Agreement with the EU, was famously rejected by Parliament three times. As a result of an inability to get her legislative programme through Parliament, and a more general loss of authority, Theresa May resigned from her leadership of the Conservative Party.[96] Boris Johnson was chosen by party members to lead the Conservative Party, and hence became Prime Minister in July 2019. Michael Gove was moved from DEFRA to the position of Chancellor of the Duchy of Lancaster, which notwithstanding its archaic name is a powerful cabinet role giving him oversight of the implementation of government policy. Theresa Villiers was appointed Secretary of State for EFRA. There was no significant shift of approach from the 'Green Brexit' rhetoric.

The next few months were extraordinarily fractious in Parliament and Government; by way of illustration only, 22 MPs resigned the Conservative whip on one day in September 2019; the Party then withdrew the whip from 21 more MPs.[97] Brexit, or leave/remain, had by now become the primary political fault line, within political parties, government and parliament,[98] and arguably also people at large. The environment, especially given the largely cohesive voice of the movement (see chapter 6) may have been a welcome way of speaking across the division. An Environment Bill was laid before Parliament in October 2019. It is important to emphasise the scale of this Bill, with 130 clauses and 17 schedules, covering the governance issues set out above, and a wide range of environmental issues. Its contents are almost identical to the provisions of the Environment Bill 2020.

Prime Minister Boris Johnson and the European Council reached an amended draft Withdrawal Agreement and a draft Political Declaration on the future relationship between the EU and the UK in October 2019. The Northern Ireland 'backstop' was fundamentally changed, such that Northern Ireland will have a very different relationship with the EU from the rest of the UK, tying it more closely to the EU in order to avoid a hard border on the island of Ireland.[99] The 'level playing field' and environmental provisions that had been in the first draft Withdrawal Agreement were removed, removing some of the legal 'hooks' mentioned above. The new EU (Withdrawal Agreement) Bill was rejected by Parliament.

December 2019 to June 2020: getting Brexit done – interrupted

A General Election was called for December 2019, Parliament was dissolved and the Environment Bill fell. The election returned a working majority of 87 parliamentary seats for the Conservative Party.[100] The rollercoaster debate over whether the UK would, after all, leave the EU was over. The executive began to reassert its accustomed dominance (and more[101]) over the legislature, meaning that the first of our political opportunity categories is completely changed, and along with it, the position for those NGOs attempting to influence environmental law and governance. The EU 'equivalence' framing also diminished. From the Government's perspective, Brexit was 'done', and need not be discussed further, and any reference to EU environmental standards was resisted.

This was reflected in environmental NGO publications and behaviour. And Michael Gove had already moved on. The interest of civil servants in engaging with the sector was unabated, however, and environmental protection remained an important political and policy issue.[102] Environmental protection had been unprecedentedly important to voters in the run-up to the 2019 election,[103] and Government rhetoric of high levels of environmental protection persisted.

The utterly changed parliamentary landscape, and its impact on their approach, was recognised by our interviewees. We quoted Interviewee 16 above (page 57) on the role of Parliament before the 2019 election: 'then once the election was called and there was a new composition in Parliament [...] you weren't gonna necessarily win that much in Parliament anyway.' Interviewee 2 also noted that 'the politics of it also have shifted, so obviously now we've a Government with an eighty majority, and so there is a realisation that, you know, getting the bill amended will be very difficult'.

Different approaches to these altered (reduced) political opportunities are contemplated. The 'inside-track approach' may

> become less effective as an approach overall, because of the changing nature of Parliament [...] So you need to then be able to say, 'Okay, we need to switch into a different mode now which is more, let's say, campaign-heavy' (unattributed).

As we note in chapter 2 (page 31), several of our interviewees suggested that 'outsider' campaigning work may be a gap in Greener UK's portfolio. From the perspective of political opportunity theory, our inability to extend our research to explore the sector's activities throughout 2020 may be a limitation. However, alongside a sharp focus on the progress of the Environment Bill, Greener UK (and its members) are considering more 'campaigning' activity, although not necessarily on governance.[104] Others saw insider work as no less significant, just different, for example emphasising Government over Parliament: 'There's a lot more trying to work with Government, you know, obviously you can't try and influence amendments by getting a small number of back bench Tory MPs to side, or to vote with the Labour amendment, for example' (Interviewee 2). But although the ability of Parliament to stop Government pursuing its agenda through legislative votes has more or less gone with the new majority Government, the influence of Parliament does not disappear. Even a parliament in which government has a large majority may enjoy some influence at different policy stages, in behind-the-scenes discussions and in government efforts to anticipate parliamentary reactions.[105] A changing approach to Parliament is recognised by Interviewee 9:

> we shouldn't expect really any amendments to be made frankly. What we need to do is to create an environment where we can persuade the Government of our arguments, if possible, and that can be much more about making sure that the debate is the one that you want to have, rather than the actual accuracy of every specific amendment.

This suggests a continued role for strong and focused insider lobbying, which is clearly also happening.

Some crucial features of political opportunity have closed down for environmental groups since the end of 2019. According to much of the literature, simply put, such a lack of political opportunity might drive a group towards litigation over lobbying. The relationship between political and legal opportunity is less straightforward in our case. Litigation may not be available as a response to the 'governance gap', but more importantly, our hybrid political–legal opportunity is about the role of legal expertise within a political space, and so the closing down of that political space also limits the impact of legal expertise. There will nevertheless be continued engagement with Parliament and Government during the passage of the Environment Bill, as suggested by Interviewee 9 above. Further, in a topic we return to in our final conclusions to chapter 8, Royal Assent to an Act is not the end of the story. Even a perfect Environment Act will require careful scrutiny and attention if it is to do the best work for the environment. Interviewee 16 suggests that 'the lawyers can actually have quite a strong role in trying to make what's there work a lot better'.

The EU (Withdrawal Agreement) Bill returned to Parliament in the days after the election, passed swiftly through Parliament, and the UK left the EU on 31 January 2020. In an indication of the way that concessions made in debate may fail to stick, the Government's parliamentary majority, and largely supportive back benches, meant that the EU (Withdrawal Agreement) Act 2020 differed from the one rejected by Parliament in October 2019. Clause 31 of the earlier version of the Bill, which provided for Parliamentary involvement in the negotiation of the future relationship with the EU, was deleted. Government would have been required to seek approval of its negotiating objectives, and to report on progress every three months. Trade measures can have a very significant impact on the environment, and this space for Parliamentary scrutiny would also have provided political opportunity for the environmental sector. Secondly, in debate on the October 2019 Withdrawal Agreement Bill, the Prime Minister had undertaken to include a legally binding 'non-regression' clause.[106] There was no sign of that in the 2020 Act.

And thirdly, the EU (Withdrawal) Act 2018 provided that decisions of the EU and UK courts would continue to be binding; only the Supreme Court[107] could depart from retained EU case law.[108] Section 26 of the EU (Withdrawal Agreement) Act 2020 inserts a new subsection to the 2018 Act. This allows a minister to make regulations during the Implementation Period, having consulted the senior judiciary, which provide for any relevant court or tribunal not to be bound by retained EU case law, and the test to be applied in such a case. The regulations can also set out the considerations relevant to applying that test. As well as raising broader constitutional questions,[109] this potentially undermines the stability that the 2018 Act aimed for, and allows government to pick and choose the areas of law that it wishes to maintain. It may also limit legal opportunity in the conventional, court-oriented sense, as well as in advocacy – legal stock could become less favourable. And the regulations, which are subject to affirmative procedure in parliament, will make considerable demands on the legal resources of NGOs.

The Environment Bill was published on 30 January 2020, with very few changes from the Bill published in 2019, and had its second reading in the House of Commons on 26 February. The second reading debate was wide-ranging across the issues covered by the Bill. There were very few references to the EU, to Brexit or to equivalence – the process had been more or less entirely domesticated. The Public Bill Committee sat seven times before proceedings were postponed due to the pandemic. It heard oral evidence from witnesses representing business, NGOs, local government and government regulators, in an impressive effort to consider all of the broad topics covered by the Bill, at the obvious cost of depth. The Committee had debated the first six clauses of the 133 clause, 19 schedule Bill when its meetings were suspended. At the time of writing, proceedings are yet to recommence.

Regardless of what happens to the Bill as a result of the response to Covid-19, it is worth thinking about the impact of the virus on political opportunity. There is of course a risk that the economic harm done by the lockdown will trigger a 'recovery at any cost' mentality, in which environmentally progressive measures are postponed and many of those with power are not interested in hearing from environmental groups.

Even if we assume that the Environment Bill, or parts of it, is not openly abandoned or weakened, a rushed and poorly scrutinised Bill is made more likely by the virus, because time and space in Parliament is limited.[110] The quality of formal engagement of civil society with Parliament is uncertain, and informal contacts with parliamentarians and staff may be even more difficult. DEFRA is working remotely, with its own challenges around engagement. Many of the civil servants engaged on the Bill have been transferred to Covid-19 work, amplifying existing resource issues in government. And the lockdown is likely to hit environmental groups (along with almost every other sector of the economy) rather hard. The world is very uncertain:

> I think we all thought, well this'll be a stable parliament, there'll be stable timetables, we'll know kind of how everything will work now. And obviously the current world events have thrown everything up in the air again and thrown it all out the window [...] we are in extraordinary, new extraordinary times (Interviewee 2).

Conclusions

Public life in the UK has been divided and fractious since the run-up to the 2016 Brexit referendum. In this chapter, we have explored the features of our case study through the lens of political opportunity. Our case study confirms the literature's emphasis on external political opportunity for shaping NGO activities and success, and we are confident that the story we tell would have been different had the external context been different. However, political opportunity is not determinative, and we return also to the internal organisational context throughout this book, especially resources (including expertise), identity, ideas and values.[111]

Although some of our interviewees observed that the drama made working life difficult for many, for the two and a half years between the General Elections of 2017 and 2019 the political opportunities were highly receptive to the insider, expert approach pursued by the sector. Brexit has brought the demand for expertise to the centre of power, with government and parliament both highly receptive, or even demanding, of expertise. And some aspects of the external context, what we have called hybrid political–legal opportunity, emphasise *legal* expertise. So although the public drama of Brexit illustrates the complexity and dynamism of the circumstances in which environmental NGO advocacy takes place and highlights the difficulties of making generalisations about NGO advocacy, it has illuminated the ways and circumstances in which environmental NGOs use law and legal expertise.

Political opportunity is dynamic and its shifts and changes are difficult to pin down or represent. Environmental groups experience open and closed, receptive and unreceptive, political features all at the same time. They need to be agile and quick to respond. This in turn feeds back into questions of group resources.

Notes

1. See McConnell and Tormey 2019.
2. E.g. Meyer and Minkoff 2004.
3. Hilson 2002, 239 and 240.
4. May 2018.
5. We use the term framing, the subject of a large literature, relatively loosely. See e.g. Bradshaw 2020 for a discussion of the literature; Hilson 2015.
6. HM Government 2018.
7. These broader demands are in principle Brexit-independent, although the way Brexit developed provided a significant opportunity for their advocacy.
8. The Scottish Government has published the UK Withdrawal from the EU (Legal Continuity) Bill. The Bill includes a power to make regulations to 'keep pace' with EU law in devolved areas; would give the environmental principles legal status; and introduce Environmental Standards Scotland to monitor compliance and implementation. See Reid 2020b. The Welsh Government is also promising legislation, Welsh Government 2020, but is continuing to consult. Both governments are delayed by Covid-19. The Environment Bill contains the option for provisions on the OEP to be extended to Northern Ireland; Northern Ireland will be in a different position from the rest of the UK because of the Northern Ireland Protocol, Weatherill 2020.
9. Note that EU law continued to apply in the UK during the transition or implementation period running from EU exit on 31 January 2020 until 31 December 2020.
10. Maria's involvement in the phenomenon being studied is discussed in our methodology, Chapter 1. The following draws on her work, in particular Lee and Fisher 2016; Lee 2018a, 2018b, 2019a, 2019b; Lee and Scotford 2019.
11. EU judicial interpretations of law (including those that used the principles) would have been retained law under the EU (Withdrawal) Act 2018, but section 26 of the EU (Withdrawal Agreement) Act 2020 amends the provisions on retained case law (see page 73).
12. There is a vast literature on governance. See e.g. Levi-Faur 2012; Enderlein, Walti and Zurn 2010; in environmental law Gunningham 2009; de Búrca and Scott 2006.
13. Articles 258–260 TFEU.
14. House of Lords European Union Select Committee 2017, 24.
15. Case C-68/11 *Commission v Italy (air quality)* ECLI:EU:C:2012:815 (also discussing the limits of force majeure in EU law); Case C-56/90 *Commission v UK (bathing waters)* [1993] ECR I-4109. We might contrast the High Court's concern about 'serious political and economic questions' arising in *R (on the application of ClientEarth) v Secretary of State for Environment, Food and Rural Affairs* [2012] Env LR 18, para 15, with the approach taken under EU law.
16. In the person of the Member State.
17. As discussed in Chapter 2, Binderkrantz, Skorkjaer and Kroyer 2012, 120.
18. Case 26/62 *Van Gend en Loos* [1963] ECR 1, 13.
19. Case C-106/89 *Marleasing* [1990] ECR I-4135.
20. Articles 4(3) (principle of sincere cooperation) and 19 (effective legal protection) TEU, developed and applied by the Court, including in Case C-404/13 *R (on the application of ClientEarth) v Secretary of State for the Environment, Food and Rural Affairs* [2015] 1 CMLR 55.

21 Directive 2010/75/EU on industrial emissions (integrated pollution prevention and control) [2010] OJ L 334/17; Directive 2011/92/EU on the assessment of the effects of certain public and private projects on the environment [2012] OJ L 26/1.
22 Access to justice is one of the three pillars of the Aarhus Convention on Access to Information, Public Participation in Decision-Making and Access to Justice in Environmental Matters 1998. The compliance mechanisms under the Aarhus Convention is stronger than most international treaties, but not as strong as in EU law.
23 Directive 2000/60/EC establishing a framework for Community action in the field of water policy [2000] OJ L 327/1, Article 15.
24 The Secretary of State reports to Parliament on the targets set under clauses 1 and 2 (clause 5), and provides annual reports to Parliament on Environmental Improvement Plans (EIPs) (clause 8). The OEP must 'monitor progress' on the current EIP and on targets (clause 25(1)); it must prepare a progress report for each EIP annual reporting period (clause 25(2)). The OEP must monitor, and may report on, the implementation of environmental law (clause 26).
25 Raised by Jordan, Burns and Gravey 2017.
26 See e.g. Abbot and Lee 2015.
27 Clause 1(6).
28 On the complexities of these sorts of obligations, see Reid 2012.
29 They are set in EIPs (clause 13).
30 Note clause 19, which requires a Minister introducing a Bill to Parliament to make a statement on whether it will 'have the effect of reducing the level of environmental protection provided for by any existing environmental law'. This is not even a good procedural protection for non-regression, because it applies only to primary legislation, and only to primary legislation that 'is mainly concerned with environmental protection'. Regression is much more likely to take place in non-environmental legislation, in secondary legislation or guidance, or in failure to enforce.
31 Clause 6. The weaknesses of this 'test' are in the absence of clear criteria, independent assessment or consequences. It is also a cumulative test, creating the risk that deterioration in one area may be discounted because of improvement in another. See Lee 2019b.
32 Clause 3.
33 Scotford 2017.
34 C-127/02 *Landelijke Vereniging tot Behoud van de Waddenzee* v *Staatssecretaris van Landbouw (Waddenzee)* [2004] ECR I-7405.
35 Scotford 2017.
36 Lee and Scotford 2019.
37 Lee and Scotford 2019.
38 Hilson 2002; Vanhala 2018a discusses framing and the logic of appropriateness, and the role of strategic entrepreneurs within NGOs.
39 Hilson 2002; also Meyer and Minkoff 2004.
40 Although we note Meyer and Minkoff's 2004 concerns that the extensive capacity of 'political opportunity' creates the potential for the term to mean different things in different contexts.
41 For context, see Prosser 2018.
42 Meyer and Minkoff 2004 urge us to distinguish 'opportunities for policy reform from those for political mobilization', 1462.
43 Vanhala 2018a.
44 The legal stock may provide 'hooks' for advocacy, as discussed below. Chichowski 2007 conceptualises the expansion and hardening of EU environmental law as providing political opportunity, there being no opportunity to litigate. We might also conceptualise legal guarantees of access to political fora (e.g. rights around consultation), as similar to standing before the courts.
45 Exemplified by e.g. *R (on the application of Miller)* v *Secretary of State for Exiting the EU* [2017] UKSC 5; [2017] 2 WLR 583. *R (on the application of Miller)* v *The Prime Minister* [2019] UKSC 41; [2019] 3 WLR 589.
46 Hilson 2002, 239. Hilson emphasises that this is not a straightforwardly deterministic relationship, and see Vanhala 2016.
47 Vanhala 2018b.
48 Parliament has also emphasised the mechanisms that allow it best to exercise its political accountability role.

49 The referendum was carried out under the European Union Referendum Act 2015. There is a whole other story to be told about the journey to the referendum: for different perspectives, see e.g. Thompson 2017; Saunders 2016.
50 The Prime Minister must then retain the 'confidence' of the House of Commons.
51 Conservative Party 2015, 54.
52 May 2017.
53 Environmental Audit Committee 2017; House of Lords European Union Select Committee 2017.
54 Its earlier report (Environmental Audit Committee 2016), published before the referendum and before our case study, had been more wide-ranging. In perhaps an early public signal of how law-heavy Brexit would be, this report was almost entirely limited to law and legislation, focusing on substantive law.
55 Recommendation 5. Andy Jordan referred to zombie legislation in evidence to a House of Lords Select Committee in July 2016, see http://data.parliament.uk/writtenevidence/committeeevidence.svc/evidencedocument/eu-energy-and-environment-subcommittee/The-potential-implications-of-Brexit-on-environmental-policy/oral/35297.pdf, accessed 1 July 2020.
56 Again, we should note caution around Maria's involvement in the phenomenon being studied; Maria is cited in this report for the governance and broader legal framework issues.
57 House of Lords European Union Select Committee 2017, para 67.
58 House of Lords European Union Select Committee 2017, para 80, quoting evidence given to the Environmental Audit Committee.
59 Department for Exiting the EU 2017, in 'Frequently Asked Questions'.
60 Greener UK 2017.
61 Baldock 2017.
62 Personal communication.
63 It focused on skills in government, international law and devolution, Gravey, Jordan and Burns 2016.
64 Kitschelt 1986.
65 Curtis 2017.
66 Bright Blue 2017; Politico 2018.
67 See e.g. Gove 2017a; Department for Environment, Food and Rural Affairs 2018, Executive Summary.
68 The National Audit Office 2017–19 singled out DEFRA's 'unprecedented management challenge' both in managing exit through legislation and negotiation, and also in the need to prepare to provide new services and functions after Brexit; 'approximately 80% of Defra's areas of responsibility are currently framed by EU legislation', 5.
69 According to the Institute for Government, the number of civil servants in 2016 was at the lowest level since the Second World War, Lloyd 2019, 13.
70 Freeguard et al. 2020, 29.
71 E.g. Chambers 2019.
72 E.g. 'it is clear where the competing interests of different Departments have influenced the drafting of the Bill, which weakens its effectiveness', Environmental Audit Committee 2019, 3.
73 The promise of a dramatic improvement to the Common Agricultural Policy gave the 'green' tag a little more plausibility.
74 E.g. Department for Environment, Food and Rural Affairs 2018.
75 Environmental Audit Committee 2018, para 12, quoting the Secretary of State, who is citing the Prime Minister.
76 See House of Commons Library 2018.
77 E.g. conservation covenants, nature recovery networks.
78 HM Government 2018, 139.
79 https://www.gov.uk/government/consultations/environment-developing-environmental-principles-and-accountability accessed 1 July 2020.
80 Section 8(1).
81 See the unsuccessful challenge in *R (On The Application Of (1) ClientEarth (2) Marine Conservation Society v Secretary of State for Environment, Food And Rural Affairs* [2019] EWHC 2682 (Admin).
82 The number of corrections to SIs issued indicates that this was also a challenging process for DEFRA. Sinclair and Tomlinson 2020 is a useful review.

83 In particular, the list of 'environmental principles' was both over- (including what are currently rights rather than principles of participation) and under- (not including a non-regression principle) inclusive; and the obligation to 'have regard to' the policy statement has dogged the principles ever since.
84 Section 16 was repealed by the EU (Withdrawal Agreement) Act 2020.
85 See Craig 2020.
86 See Weatherill 2020.
87 Northern Ireland Office, Agreement Reached in the Multi-Party Negotiations (1998).
88 Protocol, Annex 4, Article 3.
89 Chapter 5, section 4.
90 It was referred to in several submissions to the pre-legislative scrutiny committees.
91 On pre-legislative scrutiny, designed to improve the quality of legislation, see Kennon 2004.
92 See Lee and Scotford 2019.
93 See Lee 2019a.
94 Note the disquiet of the Environmental Audit Committee 2019 at not being able to scrutinise the whole of the Bill.
95 Environment, Food and Rural Affairs Committee 2019, Summary.
96 Lloyd 2019.
97 See the discussion of Parliament in Freeguard et al. 2020.
98 E.g. Lloyd 2019.
99 Weatherill 2020 describes the Protocol in terms of 'intellectual intrigue and dismal duplicity'.
100 Speaker and deputy speakers do not vote and Sinn Fein representatives do not attend.
101 House of Lords Select Committee on the Constitution 2019–21. Of the early literature on the impact of the coronavirus on executive/parliament relations, see Ewing 2020.
102 Extinction Rebellion and the school strikes in spring 2019 had been part of a surge of public attention, and one of Theresa May's last acts as Prime Minister was to introduce regulations to legislate for a net zero 2050 carbon emissions target, The Climate Change Act 2008 (2050 Target Amendment Order 2019 No 1056).
103 Carter and Pearson 2020.
104 Personal communications. See also the virtual lobby of Parliament on 30 June 2020.
105 Russell and Cowley 2016. (Note that they are consciously recalibrating the scholarship.)
106 *Hansard*, 22 October 2019 Volume 666, Column 831, Prime Minister in response to an intervention from Caroline Flint MP.
107 And the High Court of Judiciary in Scotland in certain circumstances.
108 Applying 'the same test as it would apply in deciding whether to depart from its own case law', Section 6(4).
109 See Reid 2020a and Ekins 2020 for criticism from very different perspectives.
110 Chambers 2020.
111 Hilson 2002.

4
Law and legal expertise

Introduction

Our aim in this project is to enhance understanding of the use of 'law' and 'legal expertise' by environmental groups. We start from the observation that something recognisably composed of 'legal expertise' *is* sometimes called on by environmental groups (and others) when they advocate social, policy or legal change.

We begin this chapter by discussing some very well-known challenges to and critiques of expertise as a mode of decision-making, which we suggest apply as much to legal expertise as to the areas of regulatory science that are the focus of the legally-oriented science and technology studies (STS) literature. Starting from the proposition that expertise alone provides a problematic basis for decision-making, we are concerned in particular that over-emphasising technical legal debate might render crucial normative disagreement inaccessible, bracketing or postponing the underlying debate.

This discussion complicates our central analytical category of 'legal expertise', drawing on rich and diverse literatures. Legal scholars of many stripes are interested in what is special about the knowledge and practice of law; scholars from a range of disciplines have paid attention to who or what constitutes an 'expert' or 'expertise'; the making and nature of knowledge are central concerns of STS. We do not attempt to synthesise or summarise the diverse literature, but bearing in mind the purpose of our project, exploring the complexity and contestedness of 'legal expertise' is crucial. We leave to one side the jurisprudentially interesting and complex question of what 'law' is. The diversity of laws, sources, actors, methods and materials is crucial to our discussion in this chapter. For the purposes of identifying the *use* of law by environmental groups, however, in this and the next chapter, we focus on formal state, EU and international law. We do recognise that the line between soft and hard law is blurred, and that legal material may embrace policy in interesting ways. Exercising legal expertise may involve more than 'using' formal law.

We then turn to the identification of 'expertise'. Legal expertise is a complex phenomenon. The literature suggests that what legal expertise is, who holds it and is entitled to speak on it, is constructed during the process, by both the expert and the broader community, ideally openly and deliberatively. An abstract a priori definition of expertise would be unhelpful (if it is even possible), not just for the reasons discussed below, but also because we are as interested in how our participants understand and use legal expertise as we are in an abstract idea of what it 'is'. But as a starting point, which is not inconsistent with even the contesting positions discussed in this chapter, we understand expertise, with Liz Fisher, as a matter of sufficient 'knowledge, skills and experience'.[1] These three interlocking criteria are neither decisive nor final, and other constructions are possible.[2] They do however provide a useful analytical starting point for the final section of this chapter, in which we draw on our interviews to explore how the environmental NGO sector understands legal expertise. As should be clear from our discussion in this and following chapters, there is considerable legal expertise in the environmental NGO community, which has been impressively marshalled and deployed in response to the shape of political–legal opportunity during the Brexit process. However, we conclude here that the relative scarcity of legal resource discussed in chapter 2 is matched by a weak understanding of the complexity and diversity of legal expertise, and even a little complacency about how well equipped the sector really is.

The fragility of expertise

Categories we use to make sense of the world, such as fact/value (or expertise/politics, or science/society, or knowledge/power) are partially socially and politically constructed. Nor are they neatly severable. Any tendency to assume that the first of each of these pairs can be extracted in a neutral, objective way from the world, and simply inserted into the second, is convincingly challenged by decades of work stressing the social context and commitments of experts and expertise, and rejecting the autonomy of 'facts' from society. As Yvonne Rydin puts it, the consensus that bright lines can be drawn between nature and society, and that knowledge (or expertise or science) will hold a mirror to nature for the benefit of society, no longer holds.[3] Our understanding of our physical and social worlds are thickly entwined. And just as 'the facts' cannot be taken for granted, as something that exists independently of society, 'out there' and waiting to be discovered, nor can 'the social'. Society (or value, politics, power) is also partially constructed by 'facts', by what and how we know about the world.[4] These binaries are blurred.

Our understanding of law is not innocent of values and politics. Although we may assert propositions of law, law is also an element of social life and an instrument or representation of power. Law is not 'a datum, a fact, unproblematic and one-dimensional';[5] the meaning and role of law is constructed rather than found. The challenges that this poses to the 'truth' of legal propositions are well represented in legal scholarship, with considerable scrutiny of objective presentations of law.[6] That law is partially constructed as a result of exogenous forces (rather than entirely autonomous and self-contained) is, with varying emphases, commonplace, alongside an openly normative and critical approach to law's persistent autonomy and influence.[7] Law itself can construct meaning, establishing facts about the way the world works.

As well as this scholarly take, as academics we experience the contestedness of law in unrealistic or simplistic external expectations of us as 'lawyers', when we are sometimes expected 'to identify "the law", stripped of complexity and preferably in the form of a rule of obligation that is specific to a limited social setting'.[8] Beyond the academy, legal experts might be more inclined than others to recognise (if only implicitly) the contingent and contested nature of legal arguments.[9] Further, legal professionalism's claims may be 'precarious'[10] in a way reminiscent of the broader fragility of expertise. In practice and in scholarship, what the law 'is' is contestable: 'an applicable legal norm on anything but the most banal question is like to be complex, nuanced and contested'.[11]

Scholarship on expertise highlights the elusiveness of 'objectivity', either in the sense of legal understandings that simply exist and can be relied upon by all people everywhere regardless of their position or interests, or in the sense of an utterly disinterested state of mind.[12] While discussing our project, we heard from one legal practitioner (not an interviewee) that legal arguments from NGO lawyers in the Brexit debate (in Select Committees and the like) cannot be taken particularly seriously because of the lawyers' commitment to the cause. To an extent, this is a version of the 'only the left have politics' school of thought (is it true that those who are uncommitted to environmental protection are neutral or objective?).[13] The concern about disinterestedness or objectivity is interestingly paradoxical, however, because the last thing practising lawyers expect is even-handedness; on the contrary, partisanship is demanded of lawyers, whatever their personal beliefs, when representing clients in our adversarial system.[14] But there is something in it. Although practising lawyers are expected to commit professionally to their clients' agenda, irrespective of its ethics,[15] there is also an associated expectation of 'affective neutrality', an 'emotional distance from clients',[16] perhaps enabling 'neutral' advice.[17] One of our interviewees suggested that as a lawyer 'even if you're part of a campaign group and your morals and your goals are there, you've got to be detached [...] and be realistic and not read into things' (Interviewee 10). NGO lawyers, or other lawyers committed to environmental values (including us), might be perceived to breach this norm of detachment.[18]

Our practitioner may have been alluding to different expectations as to partisanship in different settings, including appearing as an 'expert' before a Select Committee or in discussions with government. But if the partisan legal expert may, when engaging in policy-making, be expected to 'check her clients at the door', the idea that we could leave behind our 'conceptual frameworks', our whole way of understanding the world, just takes us back to the elusiveness of objective expertise.[19] Nevertheless, an expectation that experts (including legal experts) should be even-handed and open-minded is more plausible than the suggestion that we should be 'objective'. It speaks to behaviour as much as to knowledge, skills and experience, in a gloss on our tripartite division of expertise above.[20] Sheila Jasanoff's discussion of objectivity as a hard-won social achievement is not intended as a criticism (or indeed as praise).[21] It describes the social labour involved in producing something (knowledge) that is good enough, and socially sensitive enough, for the purposes it is required.[22]

And our practitioner's concern about commitedness speaks also to credibility in these fora, which in fact resonates with a number of our interviewees: 'mostly if you get something from barristers it's because you want to be absolutely certain about the credibility of it' (Interviewee 14); see also chapter 5. If the recipients of expert contributions simply think 'Well, they would say that, wouldn't they?' (Interviewee 10), that contribution is not going to be helpful. A number of interviewees shared a tactical understanding that advice from an 'establishment' (Interviewee 5) barrister who is not associated with the environmental movement would be more effective than advice from the usual suspects.[23]

The elusiveness of value-free arguments leads to multiple insights on the fragility of legal expertise as uniquely influential in decision-making. Another longstanding tenet of STS emphasises the importance of deciding which facts matter: the salience of factual propositions is a social question.[24] Scientific risk assessment's facts about 'safety' might close down arguments by underestimating or underemphasising its normative underpinnings, and presenting certain outcomes as inevitable:[25] the safety of (for example) chlorine-washed chicken may not be the most publicly salient issue; the concern could equally be with animal welfare, the survival of valued forms of farming or associated broader environmental pollution.

This is not new to lawyers, whose concerns about juridification or excessive legalisation are longstanding.[26] It speaks somewhat to the ways in which propositions about law, for example in the debate on the environmental principles discussed below, might close down political arguments, in just the same way as propositions about 'safety'. A legal way of seeing the world may be similarly self-perpetuating: 'strategic legal action expresses, reflects, and often deepens reliance on legal frames of meaning-making'.[27] As we suggest throughout this book, the availability of legal expertise contributes to the perceived need for legal expertise. The description of litigation as 'a careless way to do politics' (which we understand as replacing 'is it right?' with 'is it lawful?') by one of the participants in Lisa Vanhala's study of environmental litigation, may reflect recognition of this phenomenon in the environmental NGO community.[28]

This raises significant questions for the role of law in advocacy around the environmental implications of Brexit. Prolonged disagreement over whether the EU 'environmental principles' are binding on administrative actors in routine administrative decision-making illustrates some of the issues. EU and domestic case law galore provides authority for the proposition that the principles must be applied by administrative decision-makers in all relevant cases.[29] Government, however, has insisted that the principles are not binding in EU law,[30] and that hence its limited vision for the principles is 'equivalent' to the EU regime.[31] Perhaps the disagreement is in the more subtle question of what we mean by 'binding':[32] although they must be applied, the environmental principles do not dictate a single answer in all (or possibly any) cases. Perhaps the difficulty is that (our) expertise contradicts lived experience: on occasion we were told that people working in relevant areas have never heard of certain of the principles – so how can they possibly have been bound by them all along?[33] Or perhaps government is emphasising doubt in order to avoid acknowledging a diminution in environmental protection.

This may be a fairly simple, if troubling, case of expert disagreement, or even a deliberate manipulation of ambiguity. Regardless of the authenticity of the 'technical' disagreement, the 'legal' argument might simply be too narrow a framing. Is this really a discussion about the (apparently objective, expert) question of whether the post-Brexit statutory arrangements on environmental principles have a similar legal impact to existing EU provisions? Or is it really about the normative question: are environmental principles a positive addition to the legal landscape, and if so, should they look more or less as they do now? Interviewee 7 agreed:

> But actually the argument, for example, of equivalence with the Commission or the principles working equivalently, that's more a political and a policy argument than a legal argument. There's no reason why the UK has to do things the same. So I think it's actually kind of more useful to be clear that what you're making is a political argument rather than trying to sort of wrap it by saying, you know, pretending it's a legal argument when it's not.

More fundamentally, the legal argument takes Brexit for granted, never engaging with the rights and wrongs of leaving the EU, or the process that brought us here: 'there's a lot of effort working on Brexit but not spending that effort to oppose Brexit' (unattributed). It also takes for granted the persistence of formal regulation and environmental protection measures in a post-Brexit UK. A focus on legal equivalence postponed[34] engagement with the possibility that opposition to the EU in some cases opposes precisely the EU's legal institutions, including its environmental rules and regulations, and domestic government's accountability. And indeed it brackets all of the longstanding concerns about the quality and effectiveness of EU environmental protection measures. Arguing from law occupies the space in which some might have argued against Brexit, and others might have argued for or against the regulatory state. It may be part of an effort (conscious or unconscious) to close down the deeper questions.

The closing down of the discussion of reasons and deeper objectives is problematic, especially if it means that government decisions or actions (like dismantling environmental protection), which should be subject to debate, are done by stealth. But we do not suggest that it is always to be denigrated. It was an understandable response of a bruised NGO community, who probably saw little alternative to engaging with a Secretary of State and Prime Minister who, as discussed in chapter 3, from mid-2017 were promising so much. Large parts of the NGO community were also keen to maintain 'neutrality' on Brexit, in part because of concern about lawfulness under charities law,[35] but also because of concern about alienating NGO members. This came up in a number of interviews: 'Almost certainly half of the environment groups' membership voted leave. Because it's broadly representative of where the public's at' (Interviewee 11). Put in this context, the legal focus by NGOs may be an effort to step back from political controversy, on the basis of putatively and provisionally shared values of lawfulness and high levels of environmental protection. A valuing of lawfulness may underpin and strengthen the use of legal expertise in advocacy: 'people hate to see the law broken' (Interviewee 2).

As discussed in chapter 3, the equivalence framing was driven by the concern that Brexit would reduce environment protection, and by a response to that concern through 'Green Brexit' Government rhetoric. Fear about the loss of EU environmental rules and standards, but also about the erosion of the broader architecture of EU environmental law discussed in chapter 3 (the governance gap), took centre stage. Law also had a high status in the broader debate about how to leave the EU, exemplified perhaps by the two Supreme Court *Miller* judgements,[36] and the associated sensitivity of political actors and the public to legal ways of thinking about Brexit.

The focus on governance, equivalence and law by environmental NGOs was a legitimate (if contestable) decision. Non-legal approaches to equivalence would have been possible, for example by focusing on equivalence of outcomes or policy rather than law. Once the debate had been framed as primarily about equivalence, and equivalence as about legal standards, policy- and law-makers, but also media and the environmental NGO community itself, became hungry for legal expertise.

Identifying expertise

In this section, we ask what we mean by 'legal expertise'.[37] What law is, what lawyers do and should do, their role in society, is, as one might expect, addressed in a range of academic legal work; arguably virtually the whole of legal scholarship. For example, in environmental law specifically, Liz Fisher characterises environmental law scholarship as 'a form of expertise'.[38] She is primarily preoccupied with scholarly self-reflection, the skills and approaches needed in the complex, plural and dynamic field of environmental law. Fisher positions legal scholarship within Richard Sennett's idea of craft as care for the thing in itself, for quality.[39]

An emphasis on the significance of the social context for expertise pervades otherwise distinctive approaches (in law and beyond).[40] Expertise is conceptualised as a practice, as a social process,[41] as 'sociable'.[42] 'Tacit' knowledge[43] or expertise ('the taken for granted, the unspoken, the unspeakable'[44]) can only be acquired, and is created and exercised, within a community.[45] Expertise is not a 'thing' that exists in isolation, but speaks only from and within a community. Closely linked to this is an emphasis on institutional context: for example, Jasanoff emphasises the institutions of the state and of administration for 'regulatory science';[46] Fisher, the institutions of and surrounding universities.[47] The set of institutions are part of what sustains expertise as a meaningful category. Gil Eyal finds 'expertise' not in individuals or specific institutions, but in a more diffuse network, which 'produces, reproduces and disseminates expert statements or performances', so that attention must be paid to 'the mechanisms that secure the cooperation of ... other parties involved'.[48] Eyal blurs the boundaries between producers and users, which is also apparent in our case study: the NGO community is not simply a producer of expertise, but also an avid recipient of expertise from academics and practitioners (who in turn learn from NGO expertise);[49] policy and law-makers are not simply recipients of expertise, but are also holders of relevant expertise. All share in the production, development and use of expertise.

Expertise is frequently presented as relational, that is related to a third party, who is often the lay or novice 'other'.[50] This allows a pared-down approach to experts, as being people who know (a lot) more about a relevant issue than non-experts. It also turns attention to the function of expertise in any particular context (better at what than whom?).[51] The relation however might also be with peers, that is being addressed as an expert by other experts.[52] Harry Collins and Robert Evans' 'normative theory of expertise',[53] which Sergio Sismondo also calls 'realist' (by contrast with a constructionist approach),[54] depends not on recognition by the lay other, but on those who are expert in assessing that expertise, a 'meta expertise'. As suggested above, expertise on this approach has an objective core, and that core is capable of being defined and policed by meta-experts, who in our case may include the community of legal experts.[55] Collins and Evans have been criticised for their evasion of some of the key conclusions in STS: for reifying the distinction between facts and values (seeing the technical dimension and the political dimension as self-evidently severable), and for glossing the difficulty of identifying the publicly salient questions for which expertise purports to provide the answer.[56] As discussed above, expertise can only do any work in the world if accepted by the relevant audience as reliable and relevant or socially useful, and to that extent it must be relational. Placing the validating role with other experts only, so that the expert community is the sole place for identifying and policing expertise,[57] can only be contingently helpful. Nevertheless, a 'common sense' insistence on the distinctiveness of expertise can be helpful, and certainly resonates with our interviewees, who in most cases simply assume that they will know an expert when they see one.

From any of these perspectives, the role of the professions in defining legal expertise might be a short cut to identifying expertise: a qualified/practising solicitor or barrister embodies expertise. From a social or institutional perspective, the professions create and sustain expertise; the legal profession's formal (expert) gatekeeping might be a form of meta expertise. Professions are commonly understood as being organised predominantly around abstract knowledge, 'a particular body of esoteric knowledge',[58] in some cases by contrast with 'craft' as technique,[59] although skills and experience (and technique) are also significant for the professional gatekeepers. The professions are also differentiated from other occupations by reference to their obligations and commitment to the public interest, 'the *public* good, rather than lawyers' self-interests, or the interests of government, or [...] private interests such as powerful clients'.[60]

Ideas of professionalism in law are complex, contested and constructed,[61] from the conceptual and practical questions as to 'which' knowledge, skills and experience suffice for entry,[62] to how seriously lawyers take the (anyway contested) public interest.[63] We do not seek to add to the rich literature on the role, ethicality or competence of the legal profession, valuable as it would be to examine NGO lawyers from that perspective.[64] It is however clear that, unless one takes a very thin realist perspective, a reliance on professional (or for that matter academic) credentials simply displaces the debate, from what constitutes 'expertise' to what criteria must be satisfied for professional or academic accreditation, and whether our 'expert' possesses them.

Looking to professional identity may nevertheless, as suggested above, be a common-sense short cut as to 'good enough' legal expertise on some occasions, and is referred to by a small number of our interviewees. When commissioning external assistance, professional credentialing (specifically 'QC-ness', so high status[65]) seems to be important, as suggested above; the advice of a QC can be reassuring, 'to check that I've not, like there's not some sort of secret lawyer thing that I've missed' (unattributed).

But this high-status professional qualification is clearly not perceived by our participants as the only way of being an expert or demonstrating expertise, and we agree. We, and some of our interviewees, observed individuals who had become experts in areas (either law or areas of law) in which they were not trained.[66] Interviewee 13 asserted strongly that non-lawyers have lawyerly skills: 'It's policy folk and advocates trying to engage in legal process and I'm not necessarily saying that practising lawyers or legally trained academics are any better at it'. A number of NGO actors with a legal background, whom we have clearly seen treated as legal experts by others within the community, do not have professional or academic legal qualifications. When we pressed one such individual, whom we thought to be highly legally expert (and who was talking expertly about legal issues at the time), s/he clarified: 'I wouldn't describe myself as a legal expert. I might, if I were feeling bold, describe myself as a constitutional expert on a good day' (unattributed). S/he was not the only interviewee whom we considered to be extremely skilled users of law, but who (somewhat to our surprise) had no formal legal qualifications, and we witnessed what we interpreted as an unnecessary reluctance to claim legal expertise on a number of occasions.[67] Institutionalisation and socialisation in law, within the NGO community, seems to be at least as significant as external qualifications.

Formal professional or academic accreditation only takes us so far theoretically and is far from decisive in practice. Importantly, we have not come across any public challenging of individuals' or groups' 'expert' credentials; qualifications and experience are not significantly questioned, even while what is said (the content of the expertise) may be strongly challenged, internally (within the NGO community) as well as publicly: 'I think it was important to have enough pockets [of legal expertise] that they could disagree with each other as well and have a proper debate' (Interviewee 8). Nor have we witnessed any serious questioning of self-identification as being equipped to talk expertly about law. Norms of professional etiquette (or basic politeness) seem to allow performances of lawyerliness to 'stick' in political debate, by stark contrast with the challenging of the embodiment of expertise in courts and public inquiries.[68] Although some do emphasise the importance of different types of practical experience (perhaps a very gentle challenge to our academic expertise), as discussed below, what boundary work[69] we see in our empirical material is largely consensual and not easily perceived.

There may however be some complacency among our interviewees about how easy it is to pick up requisite legal expertise. Interviewee

13's quotation above hints at this. One of our interviewees, a very experienced EU and domestic lawyer, clearly had something of an internal organisational battle to be allowed to speak for the organisation on Brexit. This perception is reinforced by the possible undervaluing of legal specialisation, discussed in the next section. Contributions based on lengthy specialisation seem to be largely taken for granted, simply appropriated into a (sometimes simplified) 'common knowledge'.[70] Those whom we refer to above as non-lawyer experts had years of immersion in different legal environments.

Knowledge, skills and experience

Our tripartite gloss on 'expertise' is not decisive or complete, but it is a useful way of delving more deeply into our participants' understanding of legal expertise. Knowledge, skills and experience are intertwined, and their relative importance will vary according to context.

In terms of knowledge, the diversity of the 'legal' adds to the complexity of expertise. Knowledge and expertise are not synonyms, but we do not intend to draw sharp lines between them: both are contestable and complex, both are constructed rather than found, and both shape, as well as being shaped by, society.[71] Complicated as 'knowledge' might be, a simple list of things a legal expert might need to know about for the Brexit/environment debate immediately brings out the conditionality of any claims to expertise in 'law'.

Environmental law itself is a large and diverse category, from soil contamination to air pollution, plastics to neonicotinoids. Jurisdictionally, EU, UK and devolved environmental law are most obviously relevant, and already diverse. International environmental law is also significant. There has been a recurring assumption that international law is what will be 'left' in terms of external commitments once the UK leaves the EU,[72] and an insistence that the UK should comply with international law, even if not strictly bound to do so by domestic law.[73] Further, 'discourses of diffusion'[74] from one jurisdiction to another pervade environmental law in general and Brexit-environment in particular, bringing potentially *any* other jurisdiction into the debate. The preoccupation of civil servants, legislators and environmental groups with successful working examples from other jurisdictions or areas of law (the 'discourses of diffusion') risks trivialising expertise, calling for a quick search and shallow understanding of somewhat random cases. Whilst this has manifested most commonly in behind-the-scenes communications between civil servants and environmental groups,[75] we also see it publicly. For example, DEFRA's *Consultation on Environmental Principles and Governance After EU Exit* outlines domestic and international or foreign governance arrangements.[76] It may be helpful and well-intended as 'evidence based' policy-making, and can be a useful tool of persuasion,[77] but it is often superficial.

And environmental law is only the start of the story. The condition of the environment and the effectiveness of environmental measures are fundamentally linked to the institutions that surround environmental law, including the governance issues introduced in chapter 3. The intricacies of trade law (EU and WTO as well as bilateral treaties), and their relationship to environmental protection have been recurring themes, as have EU and UK constitutional and administrative law.

The subtleties of what 'law' involves are sometimes lost in political advocacy, but they can assume considerable importance as debates get more detailed, and some may be left behind. In our interviews, we heard very little engagement with this breadth and diversity of legal knowledge, and indeed a certain dismissiveness of legal specialisation. On occasion gaps in expertise were raised, most often trade,[78] and looking beyond Brexit, Interviewee 17 suggested that NGOs 'need a few regulatory specialists, who worry about regulation, not litigation. About regulatory design'. S/he was 'really surprised' at 'how disinterested NGOs were with the construction, the intervention choices, the construction of law, whether it would be effective. Whether it had any chance of delivering environmental outcomes'. Interviewee 17 was talking about the world beyond Brexit, and we might note that this question of the construction and effectiveness of law has been precisely (although at a high level) what has driven much NGO activity around Brexit. This suggests that when sufficiently roused, when the issue is put straight in front of decision-makers, resources of expertise can be found.

As might be expected, those few who did engage in a meaningful way with the complexity of legal expertise were experienced and sophisticated users of law. Interviewee 1 was critical:

> NGOs tend to recruit in a much more willy-nilly way [than universities or businesses]. So a policy crisis or political crisis like Brexit will suddenly flare up, and they won't look around themselves and say, 'Hmm, we need to have particular people to help us to win this battle.' That is not how the sector organises [...] So they just drift into these situations. And rather than saying, 'Okay, who are the best people in our sector in the UK, to get around the table to

really help us to think this through?' That conversation I suspect never occurred.

This is sweeping. Several of our interviews suggest that Greener UK thoughtfully sought skills in, for example, parliamentary affairs, and in 'law' generally, including at Board level.[79] But it does resonate: discussions with those of our interviewees working in environmental NGOs on Brexit did seem to confirm an ad hoc approach to the allocation of human (expert) resources to Brexit. We were struck in particular by how few NGO actors working on Brexit seemed to have much prior expertise in EU law. When asked, only two volunteered EU experience as a reason for their identification to work on Brexit, with one additional interviewee conceding some EU expertise when pressed. Again, Interviewee 1 expressed surprise that one particular NGO 'didn't put a much more senior Europeanist and UK-ist into that setting ... their choice of lawyer, to assist the most senior people thinking on this, was the wrong person'. This also resonates with Maria's ad hoc, but lengthy and on occasion intense, involvement with Greener UK's Brexit Scenarios Group (see chapter 1); it seems to have been helpful, and a more formal invitation/ relationship would probably not have been appealing, but it was not a strategic use of academic pro bono effort.

It strikes us that NGO lawyers are expected to be generalists who can turn their hand to specialising in almost anything,[80] and it is rarely appreciated how difficult it is for a generalist to engage in some of the more specialist debates at the right level. One interviewee expressed mixed feelings about specialist legal knowledge or training; 'I think it's often an advantage [not to have] a traditional legal background in lots of ways. Because it means that, sometimes I feel that lawyers have been trained in a certain way, think that things are immutable which I don't think are' (Interviewee 7). This is just the clearest example of a widespread ambivalence towards intense legal specialisation.[81] Our sense that legal specialisation is undervalued was reinforced by the way in which many of our NGO participants talked about Wildlife and Countryside Link's deep expertise in substantive environmental policy areas. This policy and scientific expertise was presented as inaccessible to generalists, necessary and distinctive – by contrast with the way our interviewees talked about legal specialisation.

However, Interviewee 7 later acknowledged that: 'I think sometimes for the team doing some of the more kind of nitty gritty work, I think, actually, a deeper understanding of the, specifically EU law, would be valuable. But I mean you can't have everything.' We discussed resources in chapter 2; here, resources are not just a practical limit on what expertise is available, but also spill into the very understanding of what constitutes expertise. This is reinforced by Interviewee 16 in particular, who commented that expanding legal resource allows an expansion into more 'niche' areas. And the expertise available, in turn, shapes not only what NGOs do, but what they think they ought to do, and hence what resources they think they need, in the circle between NGO resources and NGO culture that pervades our monograph.

More specifically, there is much truth in the idea that all sorts of people and types of knowledge (and skills and experience) can contribute usefully to this debate. Certainly, a legal NGO Brexit community composed entirely of EU environmental lawyers would have provided a very thin form of expertise. This size and the scope of knowledge required not only further destabilises any vision of legal expertise as monolithic or easily defined, but also emphasises the importance of collaboration, and of an ecosystem of knowledge within a social or institutional framework for expertise, as discussed in chapters 6 and 7. Bringing together legal experts otherwise spread thinly around different organisations can generate more than the sum of its parts, as they discuss, debate and learn, deepening their knowledge and skills, as well as sharing specialisation. Non-specialist perspectives can be helpful, and expertise can be acquired by those not trained in an area, who can facilitate 'a richer, discursive' process.[82] But this requires what Collins and Evans call 'interactional expertise', sufficient expertise for meaningful communication with experts in an area, for example so that trade and constitutional law experts, environmental law experts and experts from other disciplines can work together. This is not a trivial form of expertise, and the challenge of attaining it may be underestimated in the sector.

Further, we are not just concerned with different bodies of knowledge. There may be different skills associated with different areas of law, such as reading cases from different jurisdictions. Varied skills in written and oral communication for different purposes and audiences are part of the 'expertise' of law, and came up a lot in our interviews.[83] Legal experts are often expected to be skilled with words, so both written and oral communication might be part of the legal repertoire. This might be in drafting skills, where 'presentation' can be persuasive: 'so the language is right, the way that it cross-referenced was right, detail was shoved into a schedule [...] I felt that we'd be taken more seriously' (Interviewee 12). This comment is about draft legislation, but legal drafting of other documents might be equally relevant to being taken 'seriously' (and see chapter 5 on the perceived 'authority' of law).

Oral communication might also be important. Some of the literature characterises lobbying as essentially adversarial, but consensus-seeking approaches are also significant, depending in part on institutional context.[84] Legal skills might be helpful in either case: lawyers' expertise might include skills in putting arguments in the strongest adversarial form, or in managing disagreement in a collaborative way, or both simultaneously. One interviewee commented that 'lawyers with litigation backgrounds understand how to structure that kind of confrontation so that it's not sort of shouty and you know, it's more meaningful' (unattributed). S/he also went on to say that legal training 'makes you very rigorous about how you analyse material … How you combine that with evidence … And then how you construct arguments'. This is an important role for law, although maybe only lawyers see it as a uniquely legal skill. Another participant makes the point that science can also provide a 'quite rigorous sort of way of thinking about things which I actually think helps when you're thinking about campaigning or lobbying or influencing, 'cause a lot of it is down to the discipline of how you do it' (unattributed).

Experience is also significant and is linked to the gaining of both knowledge and skills. Experience reverberates in two different ways: first, experience in terms of the length of time an individual has spent developing their expertise; secondly, experience in terms of practical hands-on experience, by contrast with academic or theoretical expertise.

We are struck by how relatively early career (to use the academic label) many of those working in the sector are.[85] Among many of our interviewees, there is a perception that, overall, the sector lacks experience: 'if we were to some kind of review of the sector, if you did like a SWOT [strengths, weaknesses, opportunities, threats] analysis or something, experience would be something that was scored quite lowly' (Interviewee 6). Interviewee 1 observed that 'Most people working in NGOs are very young.'

We explored some of the possible reasons for the relative lack of experience in chapter 2 (page 41). The significance of experience is made clear by Interviewee 3: in discussion with public bodies, 'if we had a lawyer, they had to be quite a high-calibre lawyer. It was no good having a junior'. Interviewee 1 is concerned by 'a lack of historical perspective. That huge … that what we have experienced in the last seventy years or sixty years are potentially an aberration.' Whilst this comment might seem distant from our topic, it may reflect a concern about the ways in which the sector understands Brexit. On the other hand, one interviewee also recognised that although 'maybe lessons aren't being digested as well', a young sector can bring benefits: 'You know, they will have weathered fewer attempts at this. [...] perhaps fewer people who are jaded and you know, defensive about what's gone before' (Interviewee 9). Further, and interestingly, as Interviewee 2 pointed out: 'No-one has expertise in leaving the EU ... so all of us have sort of weirdly fallen into this role and have become experts, I guess, as much as you can be, as it's happened.'

And on that, 'Brexit' has now been going on for rather a long time. We have observed at a personal level that some individuals who were fairly inexperienced at the beginning have developed into very accomplished NGO actors. Our reading of submissions to Select Committees, discussed in chapter 5, suggests that the role of law has increased as the Brexit process has advanced, with noticeably more sophisticated legal analysis feeding into advocacy. There are various possible explanations. The community may be learning more about the law of Brexit, or the debate might have been increasingly framed as a legal debate, rather than a political or policy debate. It might also be that as we have moved closer to legislation, it has seemed self-evident to those making strategic decisions in NGOs that law has a role. (Although on that, importantly, it is perfectly possible, as we see in the next chapter, to engage in the scrutiny of a draft Bill from a policy rather than legal perspective.)

Several of our interviewees pointed to the value of experience of working in the legal system, and whilst acknowledging that much can be learned from speaking with experts and reading texts, emphasised the importance of practical experience of law:

> unless you've been through one, or five or seven [judicial reviews] or whatever, or at least sat in a court or read the documents beforehand, so seen the type of submissions, but I think more importantly sat in the court and seen some High Court judges falling asleep, others asking terrifying questions, others asking questions where you realise they've not read anything before that day ...' (unattributed).

Another participant emphasised that hands-on experience in how law works can enhance understanding of what legal demands might actually achieve in operation: 'So I've been in rooms where ministers have been discussing, for example, what their legal duties are, how that should translate to their actions now' (unattributed).

As suggested above, we sense a naivety or dismissiveness in the sector about the highly specialised nature of diverse areas of legal expertise. This is partly self-perpetuating, as a community of generalists muddle through (that is not supposed to be denigrating) specialised areas, without having the space to reflect on what more they might do, or how differently another specialisation might see a problem, and possible solutions. It may also be related to the sometimes unrealistic expectations of law that we referred to earlier, an expectation from those on the outside that there are simple answers to legal questions, a trivialisation of legal expertise that is reinforced through the discourses of diffusion also mentioned above.

We do not suggest that legal arguments are necessarily more important than arguments based on other forms of expertise. We share with our interviewees the view that other areas of expertise, from economics to parliamentary procedure to relationship building, are also crucial. We are however concerned that the sector seems to have neglected the space for legal expertise, at least until very recently, other than in judicial or quasi-judicial fora.

Conclusions

This is a necessarily untidy part of our work. We have complicated one of our central analytical categories: leaning on a vast and important literature on expertise, we hope that it can at least be taken as read that we do not take our discussion of 'law and legal expertise' to be unproblematic. To be clear, the point is not that 'anything goes' – 'we're all experts now' or 'it's all politics anyway'.[86] But neither the literature nor our interviews provide a settled abstract expectation of what constitutes 'good enough' expertise.

The legal expertise that is relevant for Brexit is expansive and diverse, most obviously in the sorts of knowledge at stake, but also in skills and experience. There are pockets of impressive legal expertise in the sector, which have, as is discussed further in the next chapter, been well used in the Brexit debate. But there are gaps and weaknesses in the appreciation of the complexity of law, and what it can do, and sometimes a superficial understanding of what is at stake. Legal expertise is generally understood in a fairly broad-brush manner. The amount of expertise in the sector is partly shaped by resource constraints, but the expertise that *is* to hand in turn shapes the understanding of what legal expertise is and what legal resources the sector needs in the area. This emphasises the significance of the NGO community that surrounds those using law, and the recipients of the expertise; categories that overlap in our case. We return to these issues in chapters 6 and 7.

Our argument in this book is not that law *should* be privileged as a source of argument about social change. We are especially concerned that legal expertise, like other forms of expertise, may 'inadvertently' (or advertently presumably) '[suppress] full-fledged expression of normative questions, political values and democratic aspirations'.[87] Some of our participants seem to implicitly or explicitly recognise the possible dangers of using law to settle debates, and many acknowledge the importance of other expertise. However, legal expertise certainly has a role to play in advocacy. Foreshadowing our discussion in the next chapter of the 'equalising' potential of legal expertise, environmental groups' interlocutors and antagonists do have access to legal expertise.

Notes

1. Fisher 2012, 48.
2. Ericsson 2006 refers to expertise as 'the characteristics, skills and knowledge that distinguish experts from novices and less experienced people'.
3. Rydin 2007, 58, citing Latour 1999.
4. Jasanoff 2004; Weimer and de Ruijter 2017.
5. McCrudden 2006, 648.
6. There is a large literature, see the discussions in e.g. Lang 2015 and Shaffer 2013.
7. Tomlins 2000.
8. McCrudden 2006, 648.
9. Valverde 2005 observes that in Parliamentary inquiries, non-lawyers 'treated legal categories in a more black letter manner' than lawyers, 421.
10. Moorhead 2014.
11. McCrudden 2006, 648.
12. E.g. Jasanoff 2005.
13. See Boukalas 2013, arguing that a separate category of 'cause lawyering' risks ignoring the politics and ideology of *all* lawyers.
14. Boon 2004.
15. There is a huge literature on 'role morality' and professional ethics; see Vaughan and Oakley 2016; note also their observation that the 'zealous lawyer paradigm' seems to extend to transactional lawyers.
16. Boon 2004, 261.
17. Moorhead, Vaughan and Godinho 2019.
18. Although note that Boon 2004 observes that there is no evidence that 'cause lawyers' pose any additional threat to ethical paradigms.
19. Rubin 1993, 749, 753.
20. With thanks to Steven Vaughan for this observation.
21. Jasanoff 2011.
22. Jasanoff 2011.
23. This resonates with Moorhead, Vaughan and Godinho 2019's 'tournament of influence', discussed further in chapter 5.
24. There is a large literature; see e.g. Oreskes 2004; Wynne 2002; Jasanoff and Simmet 2017.
25. Wynne 2006.
26. The strong position of law in the EU, and in EU polity-building, has long raised concerns about its potential to hollow out critical debate. For the classic tale of how political and legal processes came together in the expansion of competences, see Weiler 1991. In the US, see

Hirschl 2008, on 'the spread of legal discourse, jargon, rules and procedures into the political sphere and policy-making fora and processes', 121.
27 McCann 2008, citing Silverstein 1996.
28 Vanhala 2018a, 402.
29 Lee and Scotford 2019.
30 See e.g. Department for Environment, Food and Rural Affairs 2018, para 23; the Explanatory Notes to the Environment (Principles and Governance) Bill 2018, para 19. These paragraphs were not repeated in these terms in later documents, presumably at least in part because of the response to them, but Maria (alone and with others) had a number of exchanges on this subject up to the time of the 2019 version of the Bill.
31 Although as discussed in chapter 3, the 'equivalence' rhetoric diminished during Boris Johnson's premiership.
32 Lee and Scotford 2019.
33 That could simply mean that the principles are rarely relevant, or genuinely intuitive, or that stakeholders have not pressed their relevance in many cases.
34 There was more public critique of government environmental policy after Boris Johnson's summer 2019 cabinet reshuffle, see e.g. Spiers 2019.
35 See Miller, Cracknell and Williams 2017.
36 *R (on the application of Miller)* v *Secretary of State for Exiting the EU* [2017] UKSC 5; [2017] 2 WLR 583. *R (on the application of Miller)* v *The Prime Minister* [2019] UKSC 41; [2019] 3 WLR 589.
37 We leave aside expert 'performance' as an observable criterion (as when an expert chess player is expected to beat a recreational chess player), e.g. Ericsson 2006 and Evetts, Mieg and Felt 2006. A 'better' lawyer in our context would be contested and difficult to observe.
38 Fisher 2018; also 2012.
39 Especially Fisher 2018; Sennett 2008.
40 Evett et al. 2006 note that a psychological approach does not need context.
41 Latour and Woolgar 1979, Collins and Evans 2007.
42 Fisher 2013.
43 Polanyi 1966.
44 Collins 2007.
45 Collins 2007.
46 E.g. Jasanoff 1998.
47 Fisher 2018.
48 Eyal 2013, 875.
49 See also the discussion of collaboration beyond the community in chapter 6.
50 Evetts et al. 2006.
51 Mieg 2006; although note that Mieg defines 'function' more narrowly, as 'what would be paid for', 743.
52 Chi 2006.
53 Collins and Evans 2003.
54 Collins and Evans 2009; 2002.
55 Collins and Evans 2007; Collins 2014.
56 Jasanoff 2003; Wynne 2003.
57 Eyal 2013.
58 Moorhead, Vaughan and Godinho 2019, 44–5.
59 Eyal 2013.
60 Moorhead, Vaughan and Godinho 2019, 15.
61 Moorhead 2014.
62 Think of the lengthy debate over the Solicitors' Qualifying Examination.
63 E.g. Vaughan and Oakley 2016; Moorhead, Vaughan and Godinho 2019.
64 Lawyers in-house with environmental groups clearly do potentially face ethical dilemmas, most obviously, for example, recent scandals in charities and the potential tension between the interests of vulnerable communities/individuals and environmental objectives. Lawyers in the third sector are represented in the research by Moorhead, Vaughan and Gordino 2019 in more or less the same proportion as in the in-house community (Table 2.3), although the purpose of that research was not to explore the distinctiveness of NGO lawyering.
65 Although that might be the nature of our project; perhaps QCs were the most appropriate choice for Brexit work.

66 Shapiro 2015. Enright et al. 2021 discuss 'feminist law work' by 'non-lawyer activists'.
67 As an aside, we suspect that the ease with which our interviewees were willing to assert legal expertise, or indeed any expertise, was at least somewhat gendered and at least somewhat related to seniority; our approach has not however been designed to speak authoritatively on that. We do not think that in the context of our interviews, reluctance to claim 'legal expertise' reflected concern about regulatory obligations related to describing oneself as, for example, a solicitor or barrister, although that might be relevant in other contexts.
68 E.g. Lynch 2004.
69 The STS concept of 'boundary work' sees categories (such as 'legal') as conceptual resources, rather than a fixed line, requiring effort to maintain. See Gieryn 1999; Lynch 2004; Irwin 2008. Boundary work is often effortful, an insistence, not always successful, that certain matters are subject to expert assessment and decision.
70 We are not suggesting that this appropriation was wrong.
71 Rydin 2007.
72 On international law in the Withdrawal Agreement, see Cremona 2020.
73 See Affolder 2006, in the Canadian context.
74 Affolder 2019.
75 Experienced by Maria in her membership of Greener UK's Brexit Scenario Group.
76 Department for Environment, Food and Rural Affairs 2018. Annex D is headed 'Oversight and accountability bodies in other areas of policy'; Annex E, 'Examples of environmental governance arrangements in international law and other countries'. Annex E cites UKELA and other sources (including Wikipedia).
77 Jasanoff 1997.
78 Note that trade and finance are considered 'Cinderella' issues in terms of funding, Miller, Cracknell and Williams 2017.
79 See chapter 5 (page 105).
80 See also chapter 5 on the breadth of work by NGO lawyers.
81 Moorhead, Vaughan and Godinho 2019 suggest that in-house work may more generally have the effect of 'blunting technical specialisation', 190.
82 Shapiro 2015, 1099.
83 We may be in the 'craft' of expertise, Shapiro 2015.
84 Woll 2012 attributes the much discussed difference between 'aggressive' US styles of lobbying versus 'soft spoken' EU styles to the extent to which institutions incentivise/demand consensus.
85 Note also that many of the recipients of NGO legal expertise are also relatively inexperienced in the field; see chapter 3 on DEFRA recruitment.
86 Collins 2014.
87 Expert Group on Science and Governance 2007, 11.

5
Mobilising law in practice

Introduction

In this chapter, we explore what it means to mobilise law in advocacy, and why law might be mobilised: what do NGOs do with law or legal expertise, and why? As discussed in chapter 2, whilst there is a considerable literature on NGO use of litigation, broadly defined,[1] the literature on the role of law in lobbying and advocacy is limited:[2] 'studies of legal mobilization in social reform struggles almost always involve litigation campaigns'.[3] Indeed, by comparison with other areas of legal practice, there is little work on what environmental NGO lawyers 'do'.[4] Law is, however, a significant part of our social and political world, and as discussed in chapter 3, the Brexit process provided a number of hybrid political–legal opportunities for environmental NGOs, creating spaces within which law can be used to argue for change. Legal expertise may sometimes be in a strong position to influence policy:

> law is a critical discipline. […] it's whole economy, it's enduring, it's adaptable. It holds the consensus, it reflects the consensus, it drives the consensus, it mobilises every part of the state, every part of society. It is a mirror back to society. It's just, it's endemic (Interviewee 1).

We begin this chapter by looking at the range of legal activities undertaken by and in NGOs. We are struck by the amount and variety of legal work in environmental groups; advocacy is not a priority for legal experts. We think it is significant that legal expertise seems to have a limited leadership or strategic role in most UK environmental groups, and we pursue that a little further in the following section. Richard Moorhead and colleagues describe the jockeying for position between lawyers and others in their organisation as 'a tournament of influence which in-house lawyers sometimes (perhaps often) expect to lose'.[5] We conclude that environmental NGO legal experts only occasionally even participate in that tournament.

We then explore more literally what legal mobilisation looks like in advocacy, relying heavily on our analysis of submissions to Select Committees and the Environment Bill Committee. Environmental groups take four key approaches to legal expertise in these highly formal fora. Law is used as a path to credibility and authority; 'legal hooks' are used to provide evidence for arguments; the manifestation of government promises or commitments are assessed within broader legal architecture and frameworks; and government promises or commitments are compared with the best from elsewhere. Part of the role of legal expertise, and one of the challenges with its use in advocacy, revolves around communication, which we touched on in chapter 4 (pages 92–93), and now turn to separately.

In this and earlier chapters, we have observed weak and patchy engagement in environmental groups with the potential of legal expertise. However, there has been significant legal input into the public debate on Brexit-environment. We conclude from this that there is some sense, if underdeveloped, of the importance of legal expertise, enabling the community to grasp hybrid political–legal opportunity at a time of crisis. Finally in this chapter, we discuss the possible value of law and legal expertise in the Brexit-environment debate, including the perceived power and authority of law among our interviewees. We share the sense of many of our interviewees that legal expertise had considerable, if not uniquely significant, influence in the playing out of the Brexit-environment debate. Combining the heavy use of law that we discuss in this chapter with the sector's influence as discussed in chapter 7 reinforces this conclusion.

NGO lawyering

The purpose of this chapter is to explore what environmental groups *do* when they 'mobilise' law. The legal mobilisation literature developed to explore the role of law in social movements and social change. As discussed in chapter 2, 'legal mobilisation' means different things to different scholars. Although we often see expansive definitions of 'legal mobilisation',[6] empirical work and theoretical analysis in the area focuses almost entirely on litigation (broadly defined[7]). Much of the literature addresses what prompts or incentivises social movements' turn to law. Chapters 2 and 3 on the internal and external shaping of NGO activities around Brexit, and the following chapters, build on this literature.[8] Whilst some urge a narrow conceptualisation and definition of 'legal mobilisation',[9] it is important to explore the broader use of legal expertise by environmental groups to achieve their objectives.[10] Legal mobilisation embraces 'any process by which individuals or collective actors invoke legal norms, discourse or symbols to influence policy or behaviour'.[11] We explore the mobilisation of legal expertise by environmental groups in their advocacy or lobbying, to shape environmental law and policy after Brexit.

'Corporate work' (Interviewee 3) and 'case work' (Interviewee 12) seem to take up a considerable amount of legal time. Corporate work involves looking after the organisation's affairs, such as employment, property, charity law. Case work might include legal work associated with managing sites and complying with regulatory and contractual obligations, responding to planning and licensing applications, ensuring compliance by others with their legal obligations or using the law to defend protest and protestors. It is important not to overemphasise the lines between different types of legal work.[12] Some case work will be closely connected with either litigation or lobbying/advocacy. Scrutiny of others' compliance, for example, might carry an implicit or explicit threat of litigation. Equally, as noted by one of our interviewees:

> Understanding actually whether governments are exercising their discretion correctly when there's policy or law is quite important. Because you might not want to litigate about that, but you might actually want to go and talk to government and say, 'We don't think you're carrying out your role in the way that you ought to' (Interviewee 14).

If differing views on 'good' implementation are not subject to judicial resolution, scrutiny of compliance could be used to create a demand for action, through communication with government, agencies, media, membership and general publics.

The breadth of activity is striking when we listen to NGO lawyers talk about their work. This reflects in-house lawyers' general experience of 'a more embedded, varied role; less legally specialised, but involving a broader set of skills'.[13] It is also clear how stretched they are. As Rosie Sutherland of the RSPB put it at our closing event, they spend a lot of time in a 'firefighting role'.[14]

In different contexts, different legal activities, such as engaging in committees setting regulatory standards,[15] will be appropriate. ClientEarth has not been a specific subject of our research, but its range of activities gives a useful perspective on what legal expertise might contribute to advocacy. For example, it tries to influence financial and corporate decision-making by taking an activist approach to the legal frameworks around pension schemes, insurance, banking and investing.[16] It seeks to shape and then exploit disclosure obligations, to influence the understanding of climate 'risk' in the financial sector. Again, this could fall within a broad definition of litigation, in the sense that there may be an unspoken threat of legal action. But it can also be considered as an advocacy mechanism by which the law is used to shape stakeholders' understandings of legal obligations, influencing expectations of what compliance looks like. In more general terms, Lisa Vanhala and Jacqui Kinghan also identify a range of 'legal tactics' for NGOs, including:

> providing expert legal advice; developing and coordinating legal research and strategy; providing financing or aid in finding sources of financing for use of the law; sponsoring or coordinating non-legal research that may support particular legal claims; providing publicity about legal issues and developments; and developing or participating in legal networks and facilitating the exchange of ideas.[17]

Although begging the question as to the line between law and non-law (for example when does 'research' become 'legal research'?) this reinforces the breadth of work for legal expertise.

Leadership and strategy

The possibility that legal expertise might play a role in leadership and strategy-making within an organisation or the sector was rarely mentioned by our participants. In chapter 2, we discuss the importance of the culture and 'fit' of a strategy within an NGO. The inclusion of legal expertise[18] in leadership would shape the way the organisation engages with law in all of its activities. Opportunities and challenges may be visible to those with legal expertise that may otherwise not be visible. Its absence may affect an organisation's general understanding of itself.

Our sense is that generally, legal expertise makes at most limited contributions to strategy within NGOs. For one interviewee, this relates to the positioning of lawyers within interest group governance structures:

'if I showed you the [organogram] they have, the lawyers are so buried under the massive edifice of policy people, they have no influence' (Interviewee 1). For another, 'leaders of NGOs and culture-setters at NGOs in the UK – and this is fairly true in the rest of Europe, in my experience – are not lawyers. And they're more communicators, political animals, scientists, for the most part' (Interviewee 3). One interviewee described NGOs as not necessarily understanding 'the value of having legal advice and structure, as part of their advocacy thinking' (Interviewee 14).

Beyond our own participants, the late Phil Michaels, legal lead at Friends of the Earth, when interviewed about ClientEarth by Martin Goodman, said that he was more comfortable with the campaigner-led approach, in which 'campaigners ask lawyers what they can contribute to the wider objective'.[19] He said that it was 'the right call' for Friends of the Earth's campaign on the Climate Change Act 2008 to be campaigner led.[20] We do have some sympathy for any concern that law can overwhelm other ways of thinking about the world, as noted in chapter 1 (page 10), and we recognise the critique that the use of law may be inherently conservative, inherently status quo preserving. Although law can be activist or radical,[21] law tends to the pragmatic and incremental. But Michaels' concern that lawyers can slow things down is a fairly limited objection, and starts from the assumption that lawyers are serving rather than leading.

An educational role for NGO lawyers was raised by Interviewee 10, in which they 'kind of educate [campaigners] when to ask a legal question, […] thinking, "Look, I'm now entering a period where actually some legal questions …"'. Education could imply a sort of leadership, and certainly has the potential to shape the ways in which an organisation understands the world. But it seems to be understood as a more supportive and instrumental role, in the sense of taking legal expertise to deliver objectives that have been set elsewhere, rather than contributing to those objectives. This may be apparent in Interviewee 15's description of NGO lawyers' role as 'translators' in the passage of the Environment Bill:

> when you actually go through the Bill […] actually having a legal mind look at it and translate it […] it's very useful for other teams across organisations who work more just on the ecology side of things to understand what the implications are, and then they can say what the problems are.

We do not wish to suggest that this instrumental, supportive role is anything less than crucial. But from the perspective of our work, an absence of legal expertise in the leadership of environmental groups means that a relatively shallow engagement with what law might do is hardly surprising. Less legal expertise in the strategic brain of NGOs links with some of our other observations in a mutually reinforcing loop. It both contributes to *and* reflects a relative absence of individuals with long legal NGO experience (contributing to strategy is a long game[22]), as well as a certain flatness in appreciating the complexity and diversity of legal expertise: it sees legal expertise as purely technical (chapter 4). The same non-linear relationship may apply to the availability of legal resources (chapter 2), where over-stretched legal capacity may be both the result of and contribute to a relatively weak engagement with the strategic need or potential for legal expertise. And as above, the place of legal expertise in leadership is also closely connected to the discussion in chapter 2 (pages 43–45) of whether using law is 'in the DNA' (Interviewee 16) of an organisation, or 'part of their cause' (Interviewee 9).

Whilst the caveats below are significant, the relative silence from our participants on legal expertise in leaders is surprising. This is a sophisticated and well-resourced sector (relative to other public interests), whose area of interest is utterly dominated by complex regulation. Our concern at the outset had been that our interviewees, because of their involvement with Brexit, might be *more* sensitive than the sector as a whole to the significance and complexity of legal expertise. So the limitations we see here are likely to be more acute elsewhere.[23]

But there are three caveats, which give us pause for thought. First, there are exceptions, including NGOs with lawyers in senior organisational positions, outside lawyers who are 'embedded in [NGO] thinking'[24] (Interviewee 5) and 'examples of […] lawyers having played quite pivotal roles in advancing some of the strategies of their organisation' (Interviewee 16). Interviewee 1 would even nuance the idea that the Climate Change Act campaign was without law:

> Friends of the Earth called for a Climate Act without all being a team of lawyers, but the fact that Friends of the Earth already had, at the time they went into the Climate Act campaign, they had a very strong legal unit, was no accident, I suspect. It was endemic to how they thought (Interviewee 1).

Second, Brexit was probably an exception, due to the particular opportunity context discussed in chapter 3. Legal expertise became a central (although not the only) feature of the sector's response. The 'governance gap', whilst not accessible only to lawyers, was packed with legal questions and legal knowledge, and a level of expertise (knowledge, skills, experience) was necessary to identify and allow the sector to make the most of the governance (and equivalence) framing. Nor is it simply a question of rules that could (prior to a learning process) be looked up by anyone with a basic legal competence: Todd Aagaard's observation that 'law operates first and foremost within a legal system' may seem a little self-evident, but this is an example of what it might mean.[25] Not only do we see complex legal issues raised in Select Committee submissions, as discussed below, but we see a certain insistence and repetition, educating parliament and government as well as the environmental NGO sector itself.

Focusing so much resource on lawyerly issues after the referendum was a strategic issue for the sector. Law 'was sort of embedded in the strategy and so, in a way, that was very nice […] that was a big change I think, was to see, for the law, for the lawyer to have a seat at the strategy table' (Interviewee 16). Throughout much of the Brexit-environment process, legal expertise does seem to have been relatively well embedded in the Greener UK Board.[26] Whether this was coincidental, or someone noted that legal expertise was necessary at a senior level, is not clear. Amy Mount, former Head of Greener UK, suggested at our closing event that it had been a 'pivotal decision for Greener UK to have a space on the Board for a legal brain'.[27] In either case, it is at least consistent with the proposition that legal expertise in strategy-making and an understanding of the significance and complexity of legal expertise may go along with a considered and sophisticated use of legal expertise in advocacy. A central role for legal expertise was not necessarily recognised by all organisations, or at all stages. We mentioned in chapter 4 (page 89) that one of our very experienced lawyer participants had to persuade colleagues that s/he was the right person for Brexit; it might be that s/he could see how lawyerly this was going to be, before colleagues.

Third, ClientEarth is of course an outlier. ClientEarth has been around for a while now, but did introduce a new way of thinking about and doing law when it arrived in the UK. To really get to the bottom of what ClientEarth does, and how that affects the sector, would require an additional research project. But ClientEarth:

> built up the programmes and then the lawyers in those areas get the space to figure out what a legal strategy could be and what ClientEarth could offer, what they could offer really, as a public interest lawyer in that space (unattributed).

ClientEarth's work also suggests that some funders of UK environmental groups (although the extent to which ClientEarth considers itself UK is open to question) are thinking strategically about law.[28]

Again, we are not arguing that lawyer-led is necessarily superior: 'you have to kind of remember that the law's only one tool in the box' (Interviewee 11). Law does though have something to offer.

Mobilising law in advocacy

The previous two sections look at the range of legal work in and for environmental NGOs. Our focus is on what Interviewee 12 calls 'policy advocacy legal advice', and Interviewee 14 'the legal advocacy side of things', both speaking generally rather than just about Brexit (although we should note that we introduced our project to interviewees in terms of 'advocacy' by contrast with 'litigation'). This is closely related to leadership and strategy: whether law is invited into advocacy, shapes advocacy or is absent from advocacy is in part determined by leadership. And our discussion of NGO lawyering above includes some of the legal activities that might form part of an advocacy campaign.

We found that many of our NGO interviewees struggled to explain literally what they do with law, even if they said that they use law or legal expertise in their work, or we witnessed their high legal accomplishment. That is hardly a criticism, since our interviewees are not interested in conceptualising expertise, but in influencing outcomes. Policing precisely what is legal work and what is not would anyway require some tricky boundary work, and a sharp line between law and politics is hard to maintain.[29] But the absence of reflection on what they do with law does reinforce a sense that law may not be well appreciated, and brings out that self-perpetuating nature of a lack of legal expertise informing the understanding of legal expertise: 'civil society's understanding of how to drive legal change, and the importance of legal change, was very, very limited. It was very much about litigation. But not about the much broader role of law in society. And how you talk about law, and why law is important' (Interviewee 1).

When asked about what they do with law, many of our interviewees began by talking about law and legal change as an output of their campaigning. When turned towards legal expertise as an input, they instinctively thought about courts, compliance and litigation, reflecting the sorts of bias towards 'cases' discussed in chapter 1 (page 9): a 'natural tendency to equate the functioning of the legal system as being purely, if you like, enforcement' (Interviewee 4). One of the consequences of a focus on litigation may be that law is understood as antagonistic and adversarial,[30] when it need not be. This may in turn mean that law is under-valued as a whole because of a 'fear of losing their fluffier membership base' by being adversarial (Interviewee 13).

When we emphasised our non-court room context, some attention was paid to the use of law to frame submissions on and amendments to legislation. Most of our participants did not elaborate. Interviewee 3 described 'the shaping of amendments, the debating of them, the legitimacy of them, you know, the technical integrity of them etc'. Amending legislation is we think seen as technical support for campaigners, rather than a particularly central element of an NGO's objectives. Many interviewees, for example, saw the role of legal expertise on the 'monster' (Interviewee 3) Environment Bill's 'substantive' policy elements (water, waste, etc.) as being to respond to the needs of the policy experts. This does not engage with the centrality of law to much of the Bill's content, for example the way 'net gain' fits into and potentially shapes and is shaped by the planning system and property law more broadly.

We do interpret Interviewee 2's approach as recognising a more significant role for legal expertise in legislative work: legal expertise is used 'to point to safeguards' that are needed for the Bill to work, avoiding '[leaving] too much to secondary legislation, or to policy, then obviously you're leaving an awful lot to government intent'. In the context of the Environment Bill, Interviewee 16 went further:

> The question of architecture that I mentioned before ['the overarching framework of the bill, the legal architecture around the design of targets and how it would all fit together'], thinking that through. The other would be sort of a pure, in a drafting context, thinking about amendments and language. And then there will also be the types of issues that lawyers typically get into around enforceability of some of the provisions and how effective are they... You know, I think that some of pieces of the Environment Bill were pretty ambiguous or waffly.

Another interviewee recalled a group of lawyers, through Wildlife and Countryside Link (Link), drafting 'a whole Marine Act because the government at the time was saying that they couldn't introduce a Marine

Act ... that dealt with all of the different sectoral issues that came up', which was then used 'as a tool to go to government, and say, "Here, here it is"' (Interviewee 14).

More generally, when pressed on what NGOs do with law, discussion turned to law's detail, perhaps reflecting a cliché about law and lawyers. The use of legal expertise involves 'a lot of textual study, a lot of textual analysis' (Interviewee 3). Law has clearly been used in the study and analysis of both domestic and EU legal texts, with a view to developing the 'legal baseline ... for what would be lost from the EU' (Interviewee 6). Further:

> ... a lot of work looking in detail at, both at case law from the EU as to how influential the exercise of discretion has been, and how much is about judicial culture versus the letter of the law. And domestically looking at some, you know, well-trodden but important questions around procedural versus substantive aspects of judicial review (Interviewee 13).

This is not trivial. As Aagaard puts it, 'lawyers can look at a legal principle or piece of statutory or regulatory text and see things – ambiguities, contingencies, interdependencies, implications – that others will not see'.[31] There was little in our interviews, however, on the way that legal expertise can open up the big picture, how individual rules and regulations function as part of a system. The crucial ways in which law shapes the rules of the game seems not to be much appreciated within the community. Interviewee 17 suggested that NGOs should 'have a more open mind to looking at the system as a whole. And the intervention, design and the reason for failures in systems'.

Several of our participants offered a 'fact checking' (Interviewee 15) function for legal expertise. This may sound a little dismissive, and whether its complexity and significance was fully appreciated in the sector is open to question. 'Fact checking' might be in part about 'the kind of intellectual demands' of the work on Brexit, which means that people want 'the confidence of having that access to lawyers' (Interviewee 3), the worry about the 'secret lawyer thing' (unattributed). It goes beyond that, to establishing the accuracy of statements made by politicians and others (Interviewee 15), which resonates with the perception of the power and authority of law, discussed below. More generally, and perhaps hinting at the discussion in chapter 4 (pages 80–85) about distance and objectivity, arguments in law can also be seen as a sort of evidence base, 'Saying "No, we're not just having a whinge, here are all the reasons, here's all the evidence, here are all the details as to what we're worried about, concerned about, complaining about"' (Interviewee 7). This resonates with Boukalas' suggestion that law, including arguments based on underpinning legal principles or ideals, can be used to legitimise demands.[32] This is articulated by two of our interviewees as 'legal hooks'. 'We talk about hooks all the time. We look for what the hooks are for us to achieve our objectives' (Interviewee 7); environmental groups look for 'legal hooks and legal arguments, either from international or European law, to justify our policy asks, where we feel that domestic legislation isn't good enough' (Interviewee 12).

The purpose of our analysis of submissions to Select Committee inquiries and the Public Bill Committee is to provide some additional insight into the use of law and legal expertise in advocacy. As discussed in chapter 1, we explored environmental NGO submissions to four Select Committee inquiries (one of which was a joint inquiry, leading to separate reports from the Environmental Audit Committee and the EFRA Committee), plus the Environment Bill Committee, as follows:

- Environmental Audit Committee, *The Future of the Natural Environment after the EU Referendum* 6th Report of Session 2016–17 HC 599;[33]
- House of Lords European Union Select Committee, *Brexit: Environment and Climate Change*, 12th Report of Session 2016–17 HL Paper 109;[34]
- Environmental Audit Committee, *The Government's 25 Year Plan for the Environment* 8th Report of 2017–19 HC 803;[35]
- Joint call for evidence, Environment, Food and Rural Affairs Committee, *Pre-Legislative Scrutiny of the Draft Environment (Principles and Governance) Bill*, 14th Report of 2017–19 HC 1893;[36]
- Environmental Audit Committee, *Scrutiny of the Draft Environment (Principles and Governance) Bill* 18th Report of 2017–19 HC 1951;[37]
- Written and oral evidence submitted to the House of Commons Public Bill Committee on the Environment Bill.[38]

Given the purpose of our analysis of Select Committee submissions, it might be objected that the terms of reference for these Select Committee inquiries tend towards the legal and technical in any event, or that inquiries into legislation or steps on the road to legislation self-evidently require legal expertise. It is true that these inquiries bring out the lawyerly contribution, and so allow us to explore the role of legal expertise in NGO advocacy more easily than normal. But the inquiries' terms of reference were not all focused on law and did not necessarily invite particularly lawyerly responses. Even the inquiries about the draft Environment (Principles and Governance) Bill[39] received submissions with little or no legal content; the same applied to the Public Bill Committee, albeit to a lesser extent. It is perfectly possible to respond from a wholly policy-focused perspective, arguing about what should happen rather than legally how it should be done. It is not even necessary to refer directly to the draft Bill; some responses refer to what others say about it (including the Government itself in the Explanatory Notes), and only a handful analyse the draft clauses in detail. The existing legal situation can be referred to in a general way, if at all. So it is certainly not the case that because the public debate is about legislation, a law-heavy approach will necessarily be taken; there is nothing tautologous about querying the use of law in advocacy around legislation. But of course, many of the NGO respondents do engage in detailed analysis of law or proposed law.

Our analysis of the submissions to the inquiries turned around environmental group advocacy. We excluded a number of categories of submissions from our analysis: government/NDPB/advisory or statutory bodies, such as Natural England or National Parks;[40] trade groups and professional representative bodies; individual businesses and 'business' coalitions (including those focusing on the environment, such as the Aldersgate Group); individuals submitting evidence in their own names; academic bodies or organisations, such as Brexit & Environment;[41] NGOs who do not specialise in environmental matters, such as 38 Degrees; and local NGOs, such as the Devon Hedge Trust.[42] We fully analysed only written submissions, with two exceptions: the House of Lords inquiry, which did not make a call for written evidence, but invited oral evidence; and the Public Bill Committee, to get a broader sense of input at this crucial stage.

We analysed over 130 written submissions, which amounted to several hundred pages of material, going beyond the organisations represented by our interviewees, and beyond England. Reading the submissions, we identified explicit references to laws, and considered the level of detail and apparent sophistication of those references (ranging from simple lists to very refined analysis), explicit assessments and analyses of existing or proposed law, explicit calls on broad legal frameworks and understandings, as well as discussions where a profound understanding of the law seemed to be implicit. The contribution made by legal expertise, the level of legal sophistication in submissions, increases over time. We suggested in chapter 4 (page 94) that this may be in part because the community has learned more about the 'law of Brexit', and we refer to the possible educational role of NGO lawyers above. Moving closer to legislation may also have meant the role of legal expertise has become more evident to those making strategic decisions in the sector; the instinctive expectation as above that *this* is what lawyers do.

Turning back to the submissions to our committees, we see four main approaches to law, all of which are explored further below: law is used as a path to credibility and authority; 'legal hooks' are used to provide evidence for arguments; the manifestation of government promises or commitments are assessed within broader legal architecture and frameworks; and government promises or commitments are compared with the best from elsewhere. There may be a certain amount of collaboration in the construction of environmental NGO submissions to Select Committees. Many of those involved in writing the submissions of individual organisations will have discussed the issues at length in Greener UK (especially), Link and other spaces such as workshops and conferences. Although we do not believe that individual NGOs consulted each other in detail on their submissions (we cannot rule it out), Greener UK certainly shared its submissions with its member organisations.

First, many submissions begin with, or include somewhere, an explanation of the legal context as background.[43] This may be as much about establishing credibility as providing information and, when read in bulk, these parts of the submissions have a certain throat-clearing quality.[44] The necessity of credibility for achieving 'insider group' status is discussed in chapter 2. Environmental groups or collaborations get legitimacy from their large memberships. 'But you also get legitimacy through the sort of whether you're competent, whether you're plausible, whether you actually understand what's going on' (Interviewee 3). The rehearsal of legal context reinforces the message that interest group access provides law- and policy-makers with valuable expertise. It may also relate to the perceived authority of law and lawyers, to which we return below.

Second, simple references to one or more from a very long list of existing legal provisions is extremely common. The terms of reference for the Environmental Audit Committee *Future of the Natural Environment* Inquiry[45] turned around agriculture and the Common Agricultural Policy (CAP), rather than broader environmental law. But submissions from environmental NGOs consistently referred to and discussed EU environmental legislation, making it clear that the CAP, and any opportunities from leaving the CAP, sit in a framework of protective EU law. The Habitats and Birds Directives were most frequently referred to, rightly given both their significance for agriculture, and the fact that compliance with the nature conservation legislation was at that point considered to be the least likely to form part of a post-Brexit trade deal.[46] But in addition, many of our environmental NGOs are especially interested in the nature conservation legislation, managing sites or seeking the protection of particular species or habitats. This reinforces our argument that the type of expertise available to an organisation does not simply *reflect* what the organisation thinks it needs; it also, in the mutual reinforcement mentioned above, partly *drives* what it thinks it needs. In some respects this is simply a sensible use of resources. As Interviewee 9 puts it, 'our overall approach to advocacy and one that we try to do within ourselves is we try to make use of our expertise ... What is our area of knowledge, what have we got direct experience of, and what is specific to our cause' (Interviewee 9). But it also means that the expertise in the sector influences what gets attention and the nature of the debate. It is plausible therefore that the fact that many of our environmental groups manage nature conservation on the ground leads to a focus of advocacy and campaigning on conservation issues, and a neglect of (as suggested in chapter 4) 'Cinderella' issues such as trade,[47] or chemicals.

Turning to 'legal hooks', simply mentioning relevant legislation, as many submissions do, demonstrates a fairly thin expertise (if it can be called expertise at all).[48] Legislation is sometimes referred to in a way that suggests that although the respondent's expertise lies elsewhere, they feel an obligation of some sort to make a legal contribution – the credibility point above.[49] More often, there is at least a general sense of the value or otherwise of the legislation, and sometimes a very detailed analysis, referring to particular legal provisions and arrangements. We see 'legal hooks' being called on in Select Committee submissions, most often with EU law and equivalence-based arguments, but going beyond that to argue that certain things must be done for a lawful system of environmental protection. For example, the draft Withdrawal Agreement 2018 (which in the end was never ratified) would have required 'effective, proportionate and dissuasive' sanctions for failure to comply with environmental law; this was used to argue that there was a gap in the draft Environment (Principles and Governance) Bill.[50] Case law (surprisingly given its starring role generally[51]) is only occasionally mentioned, and rarely discussed in any detail. The focus for case law is often limited to litigation that the organisation itself had been involved in. The ClientEarth air pollution litigation is an exception, raised on a number of occasions in written submissions and by our interviewees. It was mainly used as a recent cause célèbre, rather than as a perfect example of the significance of broader EU systems and structure for the implementation of environmental law,[52] suggesting a relatively shallow approach to its legal significance.

As to our third approach to the use of law in advocacy, we see consultation respondents referencing 'bigger' legal frameworks and institutions, most commonly in the discussion of enforcement. Again, this runs from the broadest of statements about the very well-known Commission-plus-Court enforcement regime,[53] to extremely careful assessment of tricky legal questions. A good example is the detailed discussion of judicial review in some NGO submissions to the *Environmental Principles and Governance (EPG)* element of the *25 Year Plan* inquiry.[54] A number of submissions were underpinned by serious knowledge of, for example, costs, remedies and procedural issues, some going so far as a comparison between the intensity of review by the Court of Justice of the EU relative to domestic judicial review.[55] There were many examples of these sophisticated approaches to legal regimes. In its critique of the definition of environmental law, Greener UK explained how the OEP could engage with international law, without undermining the UK's 'dualist' system. WWF's explanation of the necessity of an overarching objective if the proportionality obligations in the draft are to function effectively, is another useful example.[56]

When the NGO community uses references to individual legal provisions, or bigger overarching frameworks, the purpose seems to be to highlight what could be lost in Brexit, and how to avoid that. This is in many cases supplemented by a vision of what the world could look like. At this point, we are as likely to see a substantive environmental vision as a legal one. But a legal prescription of what should be done is not unusual, for example WWF's submissions on a due diligence obligation for public and private bodies.[57] This certainly gets stronger the closer we get to legislation, unsurprisingly, from general calls for legislation in the early inquiries, to detailed proposed clauses towards the end, alongside less lawyerly narratives of the work law must do.

Fourth, and running through the other three points, comparison is a very frequent tool of appraisal, which can call on detailed and careful representations, but can also be a degraded form of expertise, as discussed in chapter 4 (page 89), a quick and random reference to different systems. Comparison is made to EU law (most obviously through the 'equivalence' approach), international law or other jurisdictions' domestic law. Recurrent government rhetoric that its environmental laws will be 'world leading' provides a lever for comparison with any progressive approach,[58] including perhaps most powerfully, the situation that existed in the UK at the time, before leaving the EU. Domestic approaches in other areas are also important, and the UK's Climate Change Act 2008 is frequently discussed in Select Committees and broader debate.[59] Its target-setting, monitoring and reviewing process, with the significant roles for the Climate Change Committee and Parliament in holding Government *politically* accountable, and binding targets for (possibly[60]) legal accountability provides a model of sorts. Again, it can be referred to in the most generic way, but the benefits and limitations of this regime can be thoroughly brought out with the assistance of legal expertise. Interviewee 2 provides a good overview of how this sort of comparison works:

> it's extraordinary to me the government would point to new world-leading piece of legislation that doesn't have those existing [Climate Change Act] safeguards in it, to the point that when we were pulling together amendments around what advisory functions would look like, we pulled the 'comply or explain' model from the Climate Change Act to point to it, to say, 'This is not unusual, it's not an unusual ask, you know, for government, there is legal drafting we can point to, there is a law, you already comply with it, it's not a problem'.

The Government's claim to be taking a 'world-leading' approach to the environment was taken seriously, expanding political opportunity, which is taken up by environmental groups, and also legal opportunity, such as the legal stock[61] provided by the Climate Change Act. This is a further dimension of the hybrid political–legal opportunity, a political space for legal argument, discussed in chapter 3.

Although these four approaches stand out, there is no formulaic approach to the use of law in advocacy. Even groups that share some important characteristics may use law in different ways and at different times. It is worth comparing a small number of submissions in a little more detail: submissions from UK Environmental Law Association (UKELA) and ClientEarth, which both see environmental law as their raison d'être, and from RSPB and WWF. We make these comparisons simply to emphasise that there are many ways to use legal expertise and to craft an argument with legal expertise. The availability of legal capacity does not dictate the same response, or a highly legal response at all.

We introduced ClientEarth, a well-resourced campaigning organisation with law at its heart, in chapter 1 (page 4). UKELA is a group composed of lawyers from other bodies (academics, private practice, NGOs) whose stated 'aim' is specifically 'to improve understanding and awareness of environmental law – to make better law for the environment'.[62] Whilst the use of 'strategic, focused and influential interventions that promote dialogue and have identifiable impacts on UK environmental law'[63] is one of its core aims, UKELA does not have a campaigning arm. Its activities revolve around reports and seminars, rather than litigation or public campaigns. Both UKELA and ClientEarth have considerable resources of legal expertise.

UKELA's written submissions to Select Committee Brexit-environment inquiries are surprisingly non-committal and lacking in detail. They tell inquiries that they have not yet formalised a position or approach to Brexit, or particular parts of the story. By contrast, ClientEarth provided consistently careful, detailed submissions that are highly legally oriented and legally sophisticated. They are very focused on precisely what should be done (legally), frequently using their own more detailed reports as references and authority. ClientEarth display and perform their legal expertise, and expect to be taken seriously. It is possible that the UKELA response to inquiries are a little ad hoc compared to more formalised and resourced groups, because they depend on someone being available on a voluntary basis.[64] It is also likely that UKELA's big investment in Brexit was in the highly detailed and authoritative reports produced by its Brexit Task Force,[65] rather than responses to the many consultations that Brexit stimulated. UKELA officers are frequently invited to give oral evidence to Select Committees, either in their own capacity or as UKELA officers, when they are much fuller.

The RSPB and WWF submissions to pre-legislative scrutiny make another interesting comparison.[66] Neither is explicitly a 'legal' organisation, both are well resourced and expert, both have some in-house legal resource. Both produce extremely knowledgeable, thorough, detailed and compelling submissions. They make compatible and broadly similar points, but they are different in tone. WWF's submission is much more direct, for example including more detailed analysis of draft clauses and proposed changes. RSPB's submission spends a little less time on the draft clauses, and on what should be done legally, and more on generally what law needs to achieve. However, both organisations respond to the 'is there anything else' question with their own priorities: RSPB focuses on nature and biodiversity, WWF on global footprint and due diligence.

Our exploration of Select Committee submissions in this section is necessarily impressionistic, because we were deliberately not looking for a simple set of 'legal' criteria. And notwithstanding what we have said about the relative lack of legal expertise in the sector, some very sophisticated legal expertise is apparent in the responses to Select Committees, and increasingly so as time progressed.

Law and communication

As discussed in chapter 4, legal experts are often expected to be skilled with words, in both written and oral communication. Legal presentation might be helpful in being 'taken more seriously' (Interviewee 12). Legal communication skills might be helpful in both facing up to and defusing conflict, and might help with being 'very rigorous about how you analyse material … [H]ow you combine that with evidence … And then how you construct arguments' (unattributed).

Several of our interviewees talked about the sensitivity 'of communicating to different audiences' (Interviewee 8). Government (ministers and civil servants) and legislators (Members of Parliament and parliamentary staff) are key interlocutors for NGOs. Some interviewees differentiated between government officials and MPs, arguing that the latter may be more strongly influenced by the political than the legal argument. Interviewee 7, for example, suggested that:

> If you're talking to some government officials for example, you might want to start talking about compliance with international law and talking about the requirements that are out there […] But actually with MPs, obviously, a much more political argument is, tend to be, and you know, it's not that clear cut. So it's about saying, 'Well, here's what we think is the best thing to be doing.' Whether that's for thinking about what the UK's place in the world is or the government has promised or the sort of world we want to, you know, society will be building, etc.

As discussed above, however, the legal dimension was very strong in Select Committee submissions, albeit not to the exclusion of political arguments.

The use of law to communicate with the public (including NGO members) was a dominant theme in our interviews: 'there's a difference between talking to parliamentarians versus talking to the general public, very much so' (Interviewee 8). One interviewee emphasised the effectiveness of legal argument when communicating to their broad-based membership:

And so actually communicating what we stand to lose in terms of that, I think, was really important. Because I think for our membership [...] they understand the importance of protected sites. But the reason why they understand they're so important is because they're legally protected. [...] we used [the Withdrawal Bill] in advocacy quite a lot. And I think, it was weird because it's obviously a piece of procedural legislation, but actually I think, because it was in the press so often, people talked about it quite a lot. So we used that, we engaged with that from kind of legal point of view (unattributed).

The same interviewee discussed the use of 'legal challenges that we had been involved in', and went on to say of law that:

It's ultimately the way that you can unlock quite a lot of stuff. [...] I think is really snappy and punchy. And they get it – people hate to see the law broken; it doesn't matter who's breaking it, you know. I think it talks to them in that way.

This perception that law can be a powerful way of speaking to memberships and broader publics is perhaps borne out by the press briefings, blogs and other public communications by membership groups such as the WWF, the National Trust and the RSPB,[67] and by the surprisingly large public response (over 176,000 responses[68]) to the unpromisingly titled DEFRA *Consultation on Environmental Principles and Governance*,[69] our 'geeky lawyer issue'[70] (Interviewee 16).

However, most of our interviewees saw the communication challenges posed by 'the pretty impenetrable language and institutions that surround law' (Interviewee 7) as one of the key limitations on the use of law by NGOs. 'It has to be understandable in a jiffy' (Interviewee 13), but law is 'complicated and not many people understand when you talk about the law' (Interviewee 6). This will be a particular challenge for membership organisations who are seeking to use their membership base to promote legal change, and to fund their activities: 'I think it's dry, it's hard to make it exciting. There's a whole vocabulary that doesn't make sense to most people. [...] I think it's a big challenge for us to make salient what we're campaigning on' (Interviewee 8). Philanthropy may have its own blind spots, and although philanthropy does support law (not least ClientEarth[71]), 'selling the word governance to philanthropy was like selling something incomprehensible to an audience with the attention span of a gnat' (Interviewee 1).

The impact of legal expertise

Assessing whether particular arguments (for our purposes, those based on legal expertise) are impactful, in the sense of attributing clear causal links, is even more difficult than looking at NGO influence generally, and it is simply not attempted in the literature.[72] We do not purport to make such a direct assessment. We do, however, attribute influence in the Brexit-environment debate and influence on the existence and shape of the Environment Bill to the sector generally, and Greener UK in particular, in chapter 7. Given the role of law and legal expertise in the debate about Brexit, and the way that the strange political and political–legal opportunities of the Brexit process made legal arguments particularly visible, this provides some indirect evidence of the influence of law and legal expertise. Further, our interview data, albeit necessarily speaking to perceived rather than proven influence, suggests that arguments based on law and legal expertise had *some* impact on politicians and civil servants.

Most of our participants thought that the role of Michael Gove as Secretary of State was central to the Government's acceptance of 'the governance gap', although without generally tracing his appointment back to the 2017 General Election, as discussed in chapter 3. But they also saw legal expertise as making a contribution, especially on the governance gap: '[O]ur sort of geeky lawyer issue was actually recognised not only by our colleagues, but also, in the sector, by the Secretary of State and the Government. So that was sort of, yes, the lawyers did play a role in that' (Interviewee 16). One participant, whilst acknowledging the difficulty in 'measuring' the impact of legal argument suggested, in the context of the governance gap, 'I don't think it was as simple as saying, "Well these lawyers say we need to do this, so therefore it should happen." [...] But I think it must have cumulatively had some input' (Interviewee 10). Legal arguments were 'necessary but not sufficient' (Interviewee 8) and were part of a broader package of submissions made and tactics employed by NGOs throughout the process:

> I think [arguments based in law] played a central role but they weren't the only role ... But that wasn't the only thing that we did to win that [equivalence] argument so I think, with all of this I'd say that, you know, the legal mobilisation is a huge part of what we've done and how we've achieved it, but it's only a part and it's part of

a package and if you get the whole package, then you're more likely to succeed and win those legal arguments (Interviewee 6).

Interviewee 2's comments emphasise the way in which the legal and political combine, when s/he says of the Climate Change Act arguments discussed above that Government 'kinda get the legal argument because obviously they still point to that piece of legislation as being world-leading climate legislation'.

Several of our interviewees pick up the significance of context to the appropriateness and persuasiveness of law. The use of law in argument had impact '… in different amounts in different areas' (Interviewee 13). With respect to the OEP, this interviewee suggests that arguments based in law have the biggest impact on questions relating to litigation mechanisms and remedies (as opposed to the funding and independence of the OEP):

> But there law has played a much greater role and has been a lot of work looking at, in detail both at case law from the EU as to how influential the exercise of discretion has been, and how much is about judicial culture versus the letter of the law. And domestically looking at some, you know, well-trodden but important questions around procedural versus substantive aspects of judicial review (Interviewee 13).

We raised the disagreement over the EU legal approach to the environmental principles, with Government insisting that its approach to principles does not involve a reduction in their role or strength, in chapter 4 (page 83). This argument was carried out in legal terms, around the very complicated question of the status and role of the principles in EU law. The environmental sector, and this heavily legal approach, succeeded in getting principles into the Bill, certainly got principles into the debate, and convinced sections of parliament, particularly the two Select Committees which carried out pre-legislative scrutiny of the draft Environment (Principles and Governance) Bill.[73] But the detailed legal approach failed to get any meaningful concessions on the future place of the principles in UK law.

Reinforcing our thoughts on credibility above, the power and persuasiveness of law is a strong theme in our interviews. Law has 'a certain authority' and 'mystique' (Interviewee 10); NGOs can use 'legal skills to lay into some fairly sort of soft political stuff' (Interviewee 3);

'you know, if you've got legal arguments behind you, you're kind of more likely to succeed' (Interviewee 6); 'a more powerful bargaining tool, if you like' (Interviewee 6). The value of legal expertise did seem generally to be accepted in the broadest terms. Only one of our participants gave a hint of scepticism about law and lawyers generally. Of course our sample, dominated by those working on Brexit including lawyers, and our presence as interviewers, might limit what we draw from that.

Consistent with our findings in chapter 4 that legal expertise, its significance and its complexity are understood in a broad-brush way, where the power of law comes from is unarticulated. Further, the lawyer and the law were more or less interchangeable in the observations made by our participants; getting a lawyer into the debate was seen as a powerful step however. Revealingly, two of our interviewees talked about law as being their strongest option for making a difference: 'I guess I wanted to save the world. So I thought, "Okay, how do I do that?" Thought about it and talked to people about it and realised that law would probably be quite a thing' (unattributed). The phrase 'saving the world' was offered knowingly, but certainly not facetiously. Along similar lines, another participant 'didn't become a lawyer to become a lawyer; I became a lawyer to do that kind of law' (unattributed).

Given these assumptions about the potency of law, the idea of NGO law being a question of equalising arms permeates the interviews, specifically with respect to government. Interviewee 2, for example, suggests that government can sometimes bring a lawyer in to try to close down debate, and the NGO brings a lawyer 'to try and level an argument or level a disagreement'. At our closing event in June 2020, Kierra Box of Friends of the Earth suggested that lawyers provide 'a kind of organisational confidence', in the same way as a chief scientist or a chief economist would.

The nature of our research (and perhaps of Brexit, where the environment versus economy discourse has not so far been especially strong) means that equality of arms with corporate lobbyists was not raised in our interviews.[74] But the ability to match corporate legal input may also be significant,[75] and the inclusion of the perspective of environmental groups on as equal a footing as possible is crucial.[76] Understanding both the detailed implications of law, and the overarching frameworks and institutions that govern outcomes, can provide a different way of seeing the world, and a different way of changing the world. Law and legal experts play a significant role in shaping the rules of the social and economic game, in determining the way things get done. Environmental NGOs need to be part of that debate.

Conclusions

We reach two ostensibly conflicting conclusions in this chapter. On the one hand, we see an underdeveloped and variable engagement with the potential of legal expertise, including legal expertise in leadership. But on the other hand, we see significant legal input into the public debate on Brexit-environment, employing the hybrid political–legal opportunity that we identified in chapter 2. We conclude from this that there is some sense, if underdeveloped, of the importance of legal expertise and that the sector was impressively able to round up their thinly spread capacity at a moment of crisis. Collaboration in the sector played a major role in bringing out legal expertise, a subject we pursue in the following two chapters.

When asked about legal expertise and law, our interviewees from NGOs all began by talking about law, or legal change, as an output of their activities. When asked what legal expertise can contribute to their objectives, most talked instinctively about litigation and courts. When pressed beyond litigation, most had relatively little to add. Our sample is especially sensitised to the role of law, since it is composed of lawyers and others working on Brexit, and we have explored the highly professionalised end of the sector, focusing on big organisations. Moreover, the environmental arena is dominated by regulation. So we were surprised not to see more pervasive and far-reaching reflection on legal expertise trickling through our interviews. We conclude that there is limited consideration of what legal expertise can do in argument, with at best a patchy and ad hoc involvement of legal expertise in strategic thinking. Given the nature of our sample, we suspect that we could safely extend these findings further into the sector.[77]

Whilst we do not attempt to claim clear causal links between the use of legal expertise in argument and outcomes or effects, we should note that other types of expertise more conventionally used (and assumed to be useful) by environmental NGOs (policy expertise, science) would be equally difficult to isolate for the purposes of assessing influence. There is certainly plenty of work for law to do, and we have explored some of the roles for law in this chapter. For Brexit, legal expertise was needed to take the first steps in pulling apart and articulating the ways that systems and structures enhance environmental measures, and later to provide the necessary detailed analysis of how parts of the system fit together.

Our argument is not that lawyers should take over and determine the strategic direction of environmental NGOs, in the 'tournament of influence'[78] within an organisation. We are sympathetic to the concern that law may stifle other approaches, and in some cases may be unduly conservative and incremental; although in the disruptive context of Brexit, law's stabilising approach may have been especially appropriate. However, especially in the environmental sector, it is a significant way of understanding the world and how to change it, and it is one of the approaches available to convince influential audiences. Without wishing to see an arms race, if government and economic actors are 'tooled up' in law (Interviewee 5), then environmental NGOs need to be.

Notes

1. Galanter 1974 includes 'the presentation of claims to be decided by courts (or court-like agencies) and the whole penumbra of threats, feints, and so forth, surrounding such presentation', 165.
2. McCann 2008 and Cummings 2018. Boukalas 2013 explores non-court work, although he explicitly attributes an advocacy approach to the unavailability or failure of litigation and street protest, 413–14; Ghose 2005 offers a practical guide; Goodman and Thornton 2017 is an interesting history of ClientEarth. At a more detailed level, see e.g. Hilson 2009, 999 on 'citizens' weapons inspections'; Enright et al. 2021 on abortion rights in Ireland.
3. McCann 2008, 532.
4. The literature on 'cause lawyering', e.g. Boon 2004 and Boukalas 2013, provides some insights into NGO lawyers. Lawyers in the third sector are represented in the research by Moorhead, Vaughan and Gordino 2019 in more or less the same proportion as in the in-house community (Table 2.3), although the purpose of that research is not to explore the distinctiveness of NGO lawyering.
5. Moorhead, Vaughan, Gordino 2019, 243.
6. Lehoucq and Taylor 2020.
7. See the discussion of e.g. welfare claims in Lehoucq and Taylor 2020.
8. E.g. Boutcher and McCammon 2019.
9. Lehoucq and Taylor 2020 define legal mobilisation as 'the use of law in an explicit, self-conscious way through the invocation of a formal institutional mechanism', 168. The term 'formal institutional mechanism' is defined broadly to include administrative procedures, quasi-judicial processes and litigation.
10. Lehoucq and Taylor 2020 put other uses of law into 'framing' ('the use of law in an explicit, self-conscious way to give meaning to an event') or 'legal consciousness' ('the implicit, nonarticulated use of law to give meaning to an event'), 179.
11. Vanhala and Kinghan 2018, 5.
12. Kinghan and Vanhala 2019 link litigation with what we might call advocacy, including engaging in consultation before litigation, and litigation's 'legacy' of implementation work. Legislation also has a legacy. The framework for mitigation introduced by the Climate Change Act 2008 requires constant scrutiny, for example; Fuchs 2009 tells the story of how many NGOs, having mobilised energetically for the development of EU chemicals regulation, moved on to other things once the legislation had been passed; see also our discussion of the future Environment Act in chapter 8 (page 181).
13. Moorhead, Vaughan, Gordino 2019, 240.
14. 24 June 2020.
15. See e.g. Abbot and Lee 2015.
16. See also ClientEarth's work on directors' duties post Paris Agreement discussed in Thornton and Goodman 2017, chapter 7.
17. Vanhala and Kinghan 2018, 5–6.
18. Which does not simply mean in-house lawyers, but also those with legal expertise who are not lawyers.

19 Goodman and Thornton 2017, 82. Also Gordon 2007.
20 Goodman and Thornton 2017, 82.
21 Consider e.g. Stone 1972, McAuslan 1980, or ecocide law put forward by Polly Higgins, https://ecocidelaw.com/ accessed 1 July 2020.
22 Moorhead, Vaughan and Gordino 2019.
23 Flyvberg 2006.
24 Although outside lawyers in private practice may have a litigation perspective, given that is when they are 'brought in'.
25 Aagaard 2018, 13. See also the quotation from Interviewee 17 (page 108).
26 https://greeneruk.org/about/board accessed 1 July 2020. Until recently, two of the senior people who represented their organisations were legally qualified (ClientEarth and WWF) and one of the two advisors (David Baldock) has strong legal expertise and is a former Director of the Institute for European Environmental Policy. Interestingly, in May 2020 ClientEarth's representative on the Board was replaced by their Director of Public Affairs and Campaigning, a non-lawyer.
27 24 June 2020.
28 Goodman and Thornton 2017; see also e.g. Foundation for International Law for the Environment, https://filefoundation.org/home accessed 1 July 2020. Even if the funders' emphasis is ultimately on litigation, as we have said several times, that cannot easily be separated from other legal activities.
29 Boukalas 2013.
30 Boukalas 2013.
31 Aagaard 2018.
32 Boukalas 2013; see also Hilson 2009.
33 Environmental Audit Committee 2017.
34 House of Lords European Union Select Committee 2017.
35 Environmental Audit Committee 2018.
36 Environment, Food and Rural Affairs Committee 2019.
37 Environmental Audit Committee 2019.
38 https://services.parliament.uk/Bills/2019-21/environment/committees/houseofcommons publicbillcommitteeontheenvironmentbill201921.html accessed 1 July 2020.
39 Environmental Audit Committee 2019; Environment, Food and Rural Affairs Committee 2019.
40 We included the National Trust, which does have statutory status, but is not a government or official body.
41 https://www.brexitenvironment.co.uk/ accessed 1 July 2020.
42 We did read many of these submissions. Given that we are not attempting a comparison of different 'types' of organisation, in order to get a reasonably coherent body of material for analysis, we have focused on NGOs operating at the national level. We recognise, as suggested above, that this has limitations.
43 Especially e.g. Environmental Audit Committee 2017.
44 See Yong et al. 2019 on the way select committees use legal advice for authority and influence. Although she is focusing on courts, Ann Southworth's discussion of 'the conservative legal movement' in the US identifies the challenge of 'developing and disseminating intellectually respectable arguments' and 'developing credibility', 'well before lawyers take their cases to court', Southworth 2018, 1705.
45 Environmental Audit Committee 2017.
46 The nature of the future relationship with the EU was at that point very uncertain, and membership of the European Economic Area (EEA) was still being discussed. EEA membership requires compliance with much EU environmental law. The nature conservation legislation is not binding on non-EU members of the EEA, although that would always have been a matter for negotiation between the EU and the UK.
47 Miller, Cracknell and Williams 2017.
48 Nearly all relevant submissions to the Environmental Audit Committee 2017 mention the Habitats and Birds Directives (Council Directive 92/43/EEC on the conservation of natural habitats and of wild fauna and flora [1992] OJ L 206/7; Directive 2009/147/EC on the conservation of wild birds [2009] OJ L 20/7). Contrast this with e.g. Buglife's submission, which although very concise, provides legal expertise on the EU pesticides regime, mentioned in far fewer submissions.

49 E.g. PlantLife's reference to the 'Public Participation, Human Rights Directives' in its submission to the Environmental Audit Committee 2017.
50 See e.g. the Greener UK and RSPB evidence.
51 Chapter 1 (page 9) of this book, Duxbury 2012.
52 See e.g. Maria Lee's written and oral evidence to Environmental Audit Committee 2016; Alan Andrews, giving evidence on behalf of ClientEarth to House of Lords EU Select Committee 2017, does make the point that the cases are not only based on EU air quality law, but also on the EU right to go to court to enforce that law.
53 This starts very early, and is clearly in the mind of environmental groups as a major impact of Brexit.
54 Environmental Audit Committee 2018.
55 e.g. Wildlife and Countryside Link.
56 Environmental Audit Committee 2019 and Environment, Food and Rural Affairs Select Committee 2019. See also Wildlife and Countryside Link's submission, although here the discussion is briefer.
57 Submission to the Environmental Audit Committee and Environment, Food and Rural Affairs Select Committee 2019.
58 See e.g. ClientEarth's reference to the French approach to non-regression in its response to the Environmental Audit Committee 2019 and Environment, Food and Rural Affairs Select Committee 2019, citing a Greener UK publication prepared by a ClientEarth lawyer, West 2018.
59 Of many examples, see WWF's response to the Environmental Audit Committee 2018.
60 E.g. McHarg 2011; Reid 2012.
61 Vanhala 2018a.
62 UKELA. 'What We Do: About Us'. https://www.ukela.org/UKELA/About_Us/What-we-do/UKELA/About-Us/What-we-do.aspx?hkey=4e0ff2dc-d41d-4b29-997f-1014c3fb1a7a accessed 7 December 2020.
63 UKELA no date.
64 Surprisingly, given that it was less obviously 'legal' than some of the other inquiries, its submission to the broader *25 Year Plan* inquiry was the most detailed of its submissions to the four inquiries we explored. More detail was provided for pre-legislative scrutiny, but other groups had also upped their legal game by this point.
65 Eight reports were published between July 2017 and February 2018, https://www.ukela.org/UKELA/Reading-Room/Brexit/UKELA-work-on-Brexit/UKELA/ReadingRoom/Brexit/UKELAsworkonbrexit.aspx?hkey=7cffd471-5434-4efb-97b2-c87fac9500f3 accessed 1 July 2020.
66 Environmental Audit Committee 2019 and Environment, Food and Rural Affairs Select Committee 2019.
67 See e.g. on the draft Environment (Principles and Governance) Bill https://wwf.org.uk/updates/much-do-strengthening-new-environment-laws; https://ntplanning.wordpress.com/2018/12/20/a-draft-environment-bill-national-trust-initial-reaction/; https://community.rspb.org.uk/ourwork/b/martinharper/posts/thoughts-on-the-draft-environment-bill, accessed 1 July 2020.
68 https://www.gov.uk/government/consultations/environment-developing-environmental-principles-and-accountability accessed 1 July 2020.
69 Department of Environment, Food and Rural Affairs 2018.
70 Speaking of 'governance' rather than the public consultation itself.
71 Goodman and Thornton 2017.
72 Resource-based exchange theories tend to assume that expertise (generally) is impactful and affects the status of the NGO. See chapter 2 and Maloney et al. 1994.
73 Environmental Audit Committee 2019, Environment, Food and Rural Affairs Committee 2019.
74 Interestingly, there is a similar focus on government in Goodman and Thornton 2017.
75 A lobbying 'public policy' practice is now common in corporate law firms, Rubin 1993. Galanter 1974's analysis of 'why the haves come out ahead' remains a powerful reminder of the uneven distribution of the capacity to engage in legal mobilisation.
76 Abbot and Lee 2015.
77 Flyvberg 2006.
78 Moorhead, Vaughan and Gordino 2019.

6
Lobbying in coalition

Introduction

The lobbying literature frequently depicts a competitive, cut-throat environment in which interest groups, even those who share similar concerns, seek to protect their organisation and compete against each other to claim credit for success with members and interested publics.[1] This extends to the environmental sector: 'there's ferocious territoriality between NGOs. And that gets in the way of a lot of conversations' (Interviewee 1). There are also plenty of opportunities for NGOs to act on their own and lobby successfully, and parliamentary work might even be 'much easier to do if you're just doing it in a single organisation' (Interviewee 3). It is perhaps surprising then that NGOs would act together in the public interest at all.[2] But groups do choose to lobby in coalition, and the strength and quality of collaboration on Brexit (especially through Greener UK) emerged as an absolutely core theme of our interviews.

An interesting body of theoretical and empirical work considers the why, when and how of interest group collaboration.[3] This literature identifies a complex and interrelated set of push and pull factors that may influence NGO decisions on whether to lobby as a single interest group or to join other NGOs and lobby in coalition. Drawing on both the literature on interest group coalitions and our interview data, we seek in this chapter to understand the opportunities and challenges for collaboration around Brexit-environment. By contrast with most of the literature, we are not seeking to explain *why* individual groups choose to collaborate or not, or *how* individual groups contribute to the collaboration. The intense collaboration that developed around Brexit-environment is explored to help us understand the role of coalitions in advocacy by the environmental

NGO sector, and their contribution to the use of law and legal expertise in that advocacy.

We begin by considering the characteristics of coalitions, using examples from the English environmental sector to illustrate the diversity of coalition groups. A coalition is, in essence, an agreement 'between two or more autonomous groups to collaborate in advocating for a common policy position.'[4] But we mean something more than simply taking the same position on an issue; collaboration involves 'the conscious exchange of resources and information, some division of labor, or the coordination of advocacy efforts with the aim of influencing policy outcomes.'[5] We occasionally refer to less formal and more ad hoc approaches to collaboration, but our interest in this chapter is really formal coalition working. Our Brexit-environment case study also provides us with a rare opportunity to observe 'grand coalitions', coalition groups working with other coalition groups to achieve shared goals.

We then turn to the challenges and rewards of collaboration.[6] Although it is difficult to separate out the 'swings and roundabouts' (Interviewee 14), we begin with the positive reasons for collaboration, and the value that our participants experienced in collaborating around Brexit. Here, we can see the power of collective resource. Collaboration has enhanced the efficiency and effectiveness of lobbying and has strengthened the role of law in advocacy through the pooling of legal expertise. It has also deepened that expertise by creating a space for reflection and deliberation. Greener UK's work with other coalitions emphasises the potential for joint working to enhance collective resource, notwithstanding the difficulties of forming such alliances.

We then explore the costs and challenges of collaboration, including as experienced by our participants. Deciding whether or not to collaborate is clearly difficult, and building a successful coalition is challenging. The literature and our case study tell us that shared goals, necessitating compromise and concession, are important if collaboration is to work. The seismic nature of Brexit has led to a set of shared goals around principles and governance, overcoming pressure to maintain individual organisation identity. Interests would also seem to be more or less aligned around the broader substantive aspects of the Environment Bill, although more compromise has been necessary, and certain areas such as environmental targets have been more problematic.

Much environmental group advocacy in the aftermath of the referendum was channelled through the Greener UK coalition, and Greener UK was consistently raised, unprompted, in our empirical work. Many, although not all, of our interviewees were involved, in some cases heavily, with Greener UK. That should be borne in mind when considering our conclusions in this and the following chapters (although we expect that we would have heard any concerns and complaints loud and clear). However difficult it is to identify success, and however incomplete and imperfect the outcome is, at the time of writing, collaboration was generally agreed to be 'an absolute bright side of what's going on' (Interviewee 13). We assess Greener UK's profound influence on the Brexit process and the Environment Bill, along with the factors that made it successful as a collaborative enterprise, in chapter 7.

Collaboration and environmental groups

There is a strong history of collaboration between environmental groups,[7] and the result of the referendum on leaving the EU seems to have intensified coalition working across the sector.[8] Coalitions come in different shapes and sizes. They may be long-lived or short term. They may be realised through formal institutional structures or may revolve instead around more informal understandings in which 'we kind of recognise each other's unique areas of expertise and skill' (Interviewee 9). This same interviewee noted that this informal way of working in coalition 'makes us stronger altogether if we can, you know, complement each other quite consciously'.

There are a number of significant coalitions in the environmental area, some of which have been set up with the explicit purpose of working on Brexit. Greener UK, a coalition of environmental interest groups set up to work on the environmental impact of Brexit, has featured heavily in this book so far, and we explore its impact and successes in chapter 7. Green Alliance, which hosts Greener UK, was a suitable home for a formal collaborative arrangement that would focus on leveraging influence through advocacy; they were 'very well placed at Westminster to lobby on broad, strategic issues rather than maybe the very specific kind of policy ones that we'd been working on before' (Interviewee 2).

Other than Greener UK, Wildlife and Countryside Link (in England[9]) was mentioned by some of our participants as an important coalition of environmental groups. Much of Link's governance work has taken place in its specialist Legal Strategy Group. Although that work was largely channelled through Greener UK, Link made independent contributions to the debate. In some cases (for example in written evidence on the pre-legislative scrutiny of the draft *Environment (Principles and*

Governance) Bill[10]) that evidence explicitly complements Greener UK submissions. Other specialist Link groups, such as Blueprint for Water, have provided the central collaborative framework for some of the sectoral environmental (waste and resources, water, nature and biodiversity, etc.) parts of the Environment Bill, building on work they were doing in these areas before 2016, including in preparation for the *25 Year Plan* (see chapter 3).[11]

The Brexit-environment debate has provided fertile ground for coalitions to work with other coalitions. These 'coalitions of coalitions' include, perhaps most significantly for our purposes, Greener UK's relationship with Link.[12] This relationship has led to the pooling of complementary areas of expertise. Although it brought with it some tensions and challenges, discussed further below, the relationship has been described by Ruth Chambers of Greener UK as 'a genuine and deep partnership'.[13] It has intensified over our period of study into something of a 'conjoined grand coalition' (Interviewee 6), with Link groups now working closely with Greener UK on the Environment Bill.

In the words of one of our interviewees, Greener UK 'had to be different to Link, otherwise what was the point of it?' (Interviewee 6). Both groups are coalitions of environmental NGOs. Greener UK was established specifically to consider environmental protection post-Brexit, whilst Link is longer-standing and focuses on nature and wildlife. Twelve of the thirteen Greener UK member organisations are also members of Link. Link has 57 members comprised of large and small NGOs who have environmental and animal welfare considerations at their core.[14] Link is therefore a much bigger and broader coalition than Greener UK: part of its purpose 'is to bring together all of these relatively small specialist groups. You know some of them quite species-specific. Trying to make a big tent and to bring everybody together for that purpose' (Interviewee 3). This provides it with a very deep expertise on particular policy issues.

Some coalitions are more heterogeneous in nature and bring together both NGOs and business groups who share common interests in a policy area. A coalition comprised of diverse organisations with different characteristics can be beneficial, because it 'potentially relies on a wide range of constituencies and therefore mobilizes a varied set of political resources and expert knowledge that enable it to address a broader set of policymakers'.[15] When we asked our interviewees about collaboration beyond the environmental NGO sector, both the Aldersgate Group[16] and Broadway Initiative[17] were frequently mentioned as relevant business–environment coalitions, with whom the sector has worked.[18]

Greener UK and individual NGOs have also worked with others including academics and research institutions. We return to these 'new, unusual partnership' (Interviewee 2) ways of working below. All of these working partnerships (formal or informal) have enriched the environmental sector's discussion around Brexit-environment. In the words of one of our interviewees, 'our ability to be able to draw on legal experts, on academics, on business and really shape some quite crucial and helpful arguments has been, I think, a real benefit' (Interviewee 2).

Given that we are concerned primarily with law and legal expertise, it is worth pausing for a word on ClientEarth, and its revealing place in collaboration in the sector. We have not studied ClientEarth in particular, and claim no specific conclusions as to its approach or role. But ClientEarth was raised unprompted in our empirical work, and some of the comments made do point up the challenges of collaborating, the importance of context, and the intensity of the Greener UK collaboration.

As outlined in chapter 1 (page 4), ClientEarth is a relatively recent addition to the UK/European NGO community, set up in 2007. Its approach was also innovative, 'not a wholly new approach, but a new approach at scale and with a kind of slightly different idea about how to strategically use the law for the environment and how that could work with the environmental movement' (Interviewee 16). This new beast clearly created:

> quite a lot of angst amongst the rest of the green sector [...] they kind of were caricatured at the beginning. Which was like basically a bunch of gung-ho American lawyers who didn't really get all the sensitivities around all the political context, political strategies, who were just going to sue everything that moved (Interviewee 11).

Apparently the tension came from both sides, in the sense of both resistance to ClientEarth from the established NGOs, and the approach by ClientEarth to the rest of the sector. Interviewee 1, for example, told us that s/he was surprised that the arrival of ClientEarth on to the UK/European scene was met with 'suspicion, extraordinary turf jealousy, very sharp elbows', and also remarked on the deliberate exclusion of ClientEarth from some key decision-making fora: 'they just simply would not let ClientEarth into that conversation. And to ClientEarth's great credit, they just said, "Well okay. Sod it, we'll just do our own thing"'. But it was clearly not one-sided: 'Now it wasn't helped, it has to be said

[...] by ClientEarth's way of interacting with other NGOs. [...] Not collaborative, unwilling to attribute shared effort to achieved outcomes' (Interviewee 1). Both sides of this dynamic come out more generally in several of the interviews,[19] and although we exclude some of the more salacious tales we heard, 'I have to be honest, the start of that relationship was really, really tricky' (Interviewee 12).

For current purposes, it is interesting and important that the role of ClientEarth in collaboration around the Brexit/Environment Bill process seems to have been far more positive, with ClientEarth clearly seen as 'a very valuable partner' in that effort (Interviewee 16, plus personal observations). Using their legal expertise in law-making to 'kind of shape things, even before and ever you get to [the litigation] kind of space, I think that they've probably learnt that this is a very productive space to be in' (Interviewee 6). ClientEarth has been heavily involved in the legal element of the Brexit work, both in the Greener UK groups and on the Board.[20] Without referring to ClientEarth or Brexit specifically, Interviewee 11 suggested that 'I think you've seen a bit of a shift in how the legal groups work in the sector, interact with the rest of the sector, as they increasingly work with the grain of the rest of the [sector]'. One of our interviewees from ClientEarth noted 'the opportunity [provided by Brexit] to work in a different way with the other UK environmental organisations has been really incredibly valuable' (unattributed). Although this participant and others highlight Brexit, it is clear that Interviewee 11 does not attribute the 'high level of collaboration and working now' to Brexit specifically. Other things might be going on. Most obviously, as ClientEarth has evolved, not only have their personnel changed and different personalities come to the fore, but the rest of the sector has grown accustomed to the lawyers. And the recognition of the legal complexity of Brexit, and ClientEarth's visible ability (along with others) to make a contribution, does seem to have contributed to change.

Collaboration as an opportunity: individual v collective resource

The literature on NGO coalition-building reveals a multitude of reasons for NGO collaboration around shared goals. Much of the literature assumes that by working together in coalition, interest groups enjoy greater access and influence.[21] In the words of one of our interviewees, 'the most effective way to kind of get the voice of the environment heard would be to work in coalition' (Interviewee 2). Coalitions enhance the impact and efficiency of lobbying through the sharing of information, expertise, access to power-holders and other resources (including financial and human). They will also 'send a credible signal that their policy views enjoy broad support'.[22] For some, especially smaller groups, collaboration may be the only way in which they can survive and maintain some degree of influence in a growing, competitive environment.[23] For others, working in coalition can enhance the impact and efficiency of lobbying and may move NGOs into areas of interest that are 'not necessarily their natural home' (Interviewee 15). In this section, we focus on the power of collective resource with a particular emphasis on law and legal expertise.

As discussed in chapter 2, resources (people, money, information, expertise, etc.) are 'highly interrelated and indispensable for successful advocacy efforts'[24] and are a key factor in determining NGO status, strategy and influence. Influence itself is a crucial resource, and agreement across the sector can contribute very powerfully to that influence. Jan Beyers and Iskender De Bruycker suggest that 'advocates bundle their political weight and signal to policymakers that their views enjoy political support beyond their own organization'.[25] External observers will attach significance to the membership of a coalition.[26] This influence may be especially strong in heterogeneous coalitions of business and environmental groups where 'there is something extremely powerful, particularly for the current Government in showing that industry and business are of a like mind to the environment sector' (Interviewee 9). This same interviewee points to the role of such coalitions in promoting their cause to both publics and the media. S/he also commented on the way that working with broader business/interest group coalitions has provided additional political opportunities and greater political reach, as did Interviewee 2:

> So we've been able to go to meetings with Treasury for example, as a united voice calling for the same thing. And it's been much harder for kind of government to say, 'We hear you green NGOs, but business are telling us something else.' Because we've been singing from the same hymn sheet.

With respect to more homogenous groups, and Greener UK in particular, some of our interviewees explained how speaking with a single voice makes life simpler and more efficient for those they are seeking to influence. For example:

> I think sometimes there's a tendency within government to do stakeholder engagement in quite a lazy way. So they do it in a fairly kind of lowest common denominator, 'let's have a group, let's have a group of groups so that we don't need to talk to everyone'. [...] that's how DEFRA likes to work (Interviewee 6).

Similarly:

> And there's clearly a demand on the DEFRA side in particular, I think less so in other government departments, to engage with a representative group from the NGOs. And of course that could get to be a more influential factor than it should be over time, you know, it could become a bit of a lazy short cut for ... instead of dealing with a whole panoply of stakeholders in the sort of optimal way, you could say, 'Well let's just talk to Greener UK and people who we know and see all the time' (Interviewee 3).

This sense from two interviewees that a call on the coalition alone is a 'lazy' approach speaks to a real dilemma for individual organisations trying to maintain their own profile, as explored below.

Working in coalition can also be more efficient and effective for its member organisations, because at a practical level, lobbying is an expensive strategy, and 'coalition formation enables participants to share those lobbying expenses'.[27] All NGOs, large and small, face resource constraints.[28] One of the most powerful arguments in favour of collaboration therefore is that it enables groups to pool their resources, thus enhancing the likely effectiveness and efficiency of lobbying. This collective resource can be important in a number of ways. First, lobbying will be most effective when groups have 'relevant and detailed knowledge about the legislative process surrounding the issue targeted by a group's advocacy efforts'.[29] Possessing this type of political (and procedural) intelligence at the right time provides groups with a strategic advantage but is difficult to gather, especially for smaller groups. Collaboration can address access and skills, as well as resource deficits in this respect:

> And also having just one contact – XXX – with MPs. It means that each organisation didn't have to duplicate public affairs work as well. So it meant that I could do my [...] job, without necessarily having to get dedicated resource from public affairs [...] Because there's already that dedicated resource from Greener UK (Interviewee 15).

Similarly, '[T]here's no point five of us having meetings with XXX, when we can just go with XXX and have that, that single stand-alone meeting' (Interviewee 12).

And practically, 'It meant there was no duplication of work. I mean, for one lawyer to draft all the amendments necessary ... along with the actual day to day workload as well. [...] To share it out that way has been very useful' (Interviewee 15). Collaboration, especially under an umbrella coalition that dedicates specific resources to working in partnership (such as Greener UK), can maximise the efficiency of lobbying activities, facilitate the sharing of workload and avoid duplication of effort.

We saw this also in Greener UK's work with Link. Broadly speaking, Greener UK has been leading work on the first part of the Bill around the OEP, governance, principles and the target-setting framework, with Link focusing on the sectoral (waste, water, nature, etc.) elements of the Bill. Greener UK's leadership on the governance elements of the Bill was widely acknowledged by the time the sectoral elements of the Bill were revealed by Government, and Greener UK had distinctive expertise in the necessary strategic political activity. Link's broad-based membership brings with it some distinctive strengths. Several interviewees emphasised Link's detailed policy expertise: 'it has got lots of the kind of really experienced, fabulous techie, nerdy people who have been working on this stuff for years' (Interviewee 12); 'within Link, the expertise in certain policy areas really runs very deep' (Interviewee 16). By working together in this way, Greener UK and Link could play to their strengths in terms of expertise. This collective resource was clearly important, especially given the 'monster' scale of the Bill (Interviewee 3). Further, 'there was a sense, especially because there's a big overlap in membership, that you needed to make the two coalitions sort of work together at key points' (Interviewee 16).

By working in coalition (and with other coalitions), groups can pool their expertise in any given areas and thereby enhance the advocacy efforts of the collective.[30] This resource exchange approach has arguably been especially powerful with respect to law and legal expertise during Brexit. As discussed in chapter 3, the post-Brexit governance debate was framed for a lengthy period as largely about 'equivalence', which in turn was framed largely as *legal* equivalence, making political and other actors hungry for legal expertise. Furthermore, this expertise is (with the exception of ClientEarth) dispersed thinly across the NGO sector, especially if one considers how diverse and specialist the relevant legal expertise can be (chapter 4). Our interview data points strongly to the fact that one of the positive consequences of collaboration, which was probably not anticipated when Greener UK was set up, has indeed been the pooling of legal expertise: 'being able to draw on the pockets of expertise across the sector was very important ...' (Interviewee 8). Collaboration makes legal expertise available to the sector, as a service or resource. In Link for example, 'the idea is that that Legal Strategy Group does its own policy area [...] but also is a resource for the working groups' (Interviewee 12); and of ClientEarth: 'we try not to be a service provider in that sense, because we do have our own strategy and we're not sort of taking instructions from others. And we can't do that but we do, you know ... the work does serve the wider coalition' (unattributed).

This extends to making particular specialisation available, for example, the relatively limited trade law expertise in the sector. One of our interviewees said that 'I think there needs to be more sort of pooling of resources. Because there's no sense in [XXX] hiring trade experts and sort of keeping them to themselves or whatever. So it should be an organisation like Greener UK then gets in someone like that' (Interviewee 15). This, however, obviously clashes with organisational competition, discussed below; if there is money available for, and recognition available from, trade expertise, NGOs may well want to 'own' it.

As well as pooling expertise, collaboration can also deepen that expertise. Bringing a number of otherwise dispersed legal experts together to discuss and debate proposals and ways forward, seems, both intuitively and according to our interview data, to have more potential than individual lawyers working independently. It is not only more efficient; the result is more than the sum of its parts, because combining legal capacity may shape a more deliberative forum in which lawyers have the 'opportunity to sort of actually bounce these things around, if you like' (Interviewee 15). This can enrich debate and discussion:

> I mean it's brought together lawyers from different organisations who, yes, would have talked together and worked together before. But certainly in my view, in order to get your head around a lot of this stuff, you need to have a sensible conversation with someone who's actually thought about it a bit and you can talk about it (unattributed).

We would argue that this can only improve the quality of legal argument in advocacy: 'I think it was important to have enough pockets that [lawyers] could disagree with each other as well and have a proper debate. I think I would have been nervous if it was just one person and that's an advantage of pooling' (Interviewee 8).

We can also point to a number of ways in which collaboration can indirectly strengthen the place of law and legal expertise in advocacy, both in the short and longer term. Deeper and broader legal capacity may strengthen the perceived value of legal argument both within and across environmental NGOs. For example, one interviewee noted that it 'sort of raises the profile [of law] within organisations' (Interviewee 15):

> [F]or one lawyer to raise an issue in an organisation like XXX, it's a bit of an uphill struggle, because you've got a team of ten people working on species, a team of ten people working on fresh water, and then one lawyer, it's very difficult to actually drive the direction and the agenda in an organisation like that. So when everyone came together for Greener UK, even though actually within each organisation it might have been two or three people who are practically engaged with Greener UK, because you've got that umbrella organisation, that has all the logos attached, even within XXX, it raises the profile of the work you're doing. And draws other people into it as well (Interviewee 15).

It is of course too soon to say, but it is plausible that this may, in time, influence the culture and identity of interest groups, placing legal expertise closer to the forefront of NGO action,[31] in the loop between resources of expertise and culture discussed throughout this book.

Of course, collective resource benefits are not limited to legal expertise. Collaboration through Greener UK has promoted cross-disciplinary working where there is 'actually quite a nice combination of lawyers and non-lawyers sort of working together very much, where there's a bit more interplay between, between the two. And I think that doesn't happen quite so much in my experience' (Interviewee 3). And a depth and breadth of expertise can be enabled in collaboration that may not be possible in a single organisation. For example, 'and actually through this Brexit process I think a lot more organisations have got to grips with [using parliamentary processes] and have become adept at using those procedures to get what they want, which is a very welcome development actually' (Interviewee 13).

One other point is worth making. In using this 'resource exchange' approach, it could be argued (perhaps intuitively) that large, resource-rich groups are less likely to work in coalition with others. After all, they have the resource (money, expertise, etc.) to lobby as an individual organisation and, in turn, will have neither the need nor desire to share the credit for any lobbying success.[32] However, empirical evidence indicates that as groups grow in capacity, they are more likely to pursue lobbying coalitions.[33] This could be because bigger groups are more regularly invited to join coalitions, and better resourced groups are more able to absorb the additional costs of collaboration. Both possibilities could be applied to the Greener UK coalition, whose members, on paper at least, appear to have considerable resources of expertise.

Collaboration as a challenge

There are clearly multiple benefits to interest groups working together in coalition, and we return in more detail to the attributes of Greener UK that enhanced these benefits in the next chapter. In this section, we seek to understand the quite significant risks and challenges of collaborative working. We consider these under two broad and interconnected headings: alignment of interests and compromise; and profile, competition and identity. Both of these challenges are felt more acutely, perhaps, when small and large organisations work together in collaboration. When talking about Link, for example, one of our interviewees noted that there is:

> some tension between the big organisations, you know, the WWFs and the RSPBs and the little ones, if you like. So the big ones are not going to want to be bound by things going on in Link. But on the other hand, every now and again they'll be wanting to do things together (Interviewee 3).

It is important to recognise that the advantages of working in coalition may be more apparent in the context of NGO advocacy as opposed to other types of strategic NGO intervention. Two of our interviewees alluded to this, using litigation and campaigning as examples. For one interviewee collaboration on case work, including judicial review, is 'a nightmare because organisations want to do their own press work, they want to get their policy messages into their [...] proofs of evidence, you know, that I find really challenging' (unattributed).[34] In Greener UK's collaboration with The Climate Coalition on *The Time is Now* Campaign, one interviewee noted that:

> an area where perhaps it's more difficult, because it's things that are more done by organisations and more relate to their membership

and their brand and how they speak to their members. So it's maybe one of the areas where it's more challenging to get collaboration, whereas on some of the inside track stuff, the advocacy, it's easier (Interviewee 16).

Alignment of interests and compromise

Collaboration is much more likely if interest groups are able to adopt a jointly agreed position when lobbying power-holders. But finding a shared policy goal, as well as agreeing upon the strategic approach to be taken, is not always easy: 'an alignment of interests is really hard' (Interviewee 17). This can lead to tension and compromise. These points were made by a number of our participants. There is a danger of 'lowest common denominator viewpoints' (Interviewee 13) emerging from coalition. Where interests are aligned and concessions are made, this can in turn impact on the extent to which individual coalition members can pursue their intended goals to the full. According to one interviewee, 'sometimes it just means that coalition itself, because we're a product of consensus, can only go so far on some of these issues, publicly at least' (Interviewee 6).

The environment sector was described by one as 'generally ... a consensual sector' (Interviewee 13), with a shared overarching commitment to environmental protection and nature conservation. It has, however, been 'vexed over the years by, sort of, badge waving' (Interviewee 13). This is perhaps unsurprising. Individual organisations inevitably focus on their own particular issues and interests:

> [T]here's just difference of emphasis. So if you're the Wildlife Trust, you think the most important bit's the nature restoration target. If you're ClientEarth, you think the most important bit is the World Health Organisation clean air targets. If you're Friends of the Earth, you think it's, you know, climate, or whatever. So there's differences of emphasis (Interviewee 11).

Some of our interviewees recognised this in speaking to their own organisational position:

> But it does also mean that when we're sitting in a meeting and we're trying to agree a strategy, that there may be times when we as XXX have to be a bit awkward and say, 'Do you know what, we can't support that. We're really sorry, that's going beyond what we're

comfortable with saying as XXX. You know, can we find a compromise? Do we have to step back from this on this occasion?' (Interviewee 9).

Compromise and concession are therefore important parts of building an effective coalition: 'you have to make significant compromises all the time about things that you think are important to your organisation that others in the coalition may not think are so important' (Interviewee 14). Reaching consensus may also be more difficult in larger coalitions. In comparing, for example, Greener UK and Link, 'I think it's much easier for the big NGOs to operate as a coalition through Greener UK than Wildlife Countryside Link, purely because it's a smaller group that needs to reach agreement' (Interviewee 15). It may also be more difficult for coalitions of interest groups and business organisations to reach consensus, although in these more heterogeneous coalitions, the underlying purpose of and approach to collaboration may be different:

> I think there's less desire to find common ground, like if there is common ground, great – there's common ground, let's talk. If there's not common ground, well we're not entering that relationship to try and necessarily convince them all to find that common ground … The possibility to change – not change – or to work with NGOs to find that common ground is more pressing I suppose (Interviewee 7).

Another interviewee, in talking about Greener UK's work with business groups commented that:

> the way that we've approached working with those collaborations is to, I guess, number one, keep the channels of communication open so that everyone knows what they're doing. Number two, try and find as much common ground as possible, and number three, just be really open and transparent about, you know, any areas where we may not always agree (unattributed).

Pre-empting our discussion of Greener UK in the next chapter, our interview data is indicative of at least broad agreement around the big Brexit picture: 'I think the NGO community probably is largely at a consensus on the overall impact of Brexit. I think it considers it's bad for the environment, because of the way in which European environmental law has been designed and implemented' (Interviewee 17). For one interviewee, Brexit itself seems to have led to an 'exceptional willingness to bury, you know, individual organisational interests' (Interviewee 3) and was seen as so fundamental to the sector that groups put aside their individual interests and worked in collaboration:

> It's an emotional issue as well as an intellectual one for people. I think there is a sense that most NGO people, they're on the same side on this really ... So that whatever differences they have, it was just totally fundamental. And I think there were not major differences of view about it. And I think everyone knew that the environmental progress we'd made was at threat, you know. That was a bigger problem than their own issues. So, yes, I think it was a bit of a watershed in that way (Interviewee 3).

Only one of our interviewees suggested, albeit tentatively and whilst acknowledging consensus within Greener UK, that 'other NGOs lobbying in that space. I don't feel they have that strong consensus' (Interviewee 17). Nevertheless Brexit would appear to again be 'special', with members of the Greener UK coalition (at least) setting aside fundamental differences in light of the threat posed by the UK's withdrawal from the EU. The referendum result imposed on the sector an issue that was extraordinarily salient for them, and where most of the community was already 'on the same side on this really' (Interviewee 3).

Alignment over the big picture, and even much of the detail, of governance and principles after Brexit seems to have been relatively unproblematic. Speaking in July 2019 one interviewee commented that: 'I don't think that so far it's been particularly bad. Because particularly when we were working on the Withdrawal Bill, to some extent what we needed to do was get the environment inserted into that piece of legislation. So we all needed to work together' (Interviewee 2).

In addition to the governance elements, however, the Environment Bill was widely perceived as the opportunity of a lifetime for getting environmental values and objectives into primary legislation. We expected to see more challenges around collaboration on the substantive elements of the Bill:

> I think the Environment Bill will potentially lay some of those tensions a bit more open, because it's a big, important piece of legislation. It's very broad. And trying to get all of the coalition to agree on what the priority is on that legislation, at the expense of anything else, I think is going to be ... (Interviewee 2)

And there certainly were some tensions. But overall, our interviews suggest that even collaboration around the more substantive (water, waste, nature) elements of the Environment Bill remains largely consensual. We should be somewhat cautious about this conclusion, in part because our participants were much more circumspect about Link than they were about Greener UK. Furthermore, the very narrow framing and segmentation of the environmental issues may limit the number of individuals and organisations with a strong view on each separate part of the Bill. Related to that, and importantly, at the time of our interviews, the prioritisation of some elements of the Environment Bill over others, was at an early stage.[35]

One element of the Bill that came up most frequently in our interviews was targets. Targets ended up being successfully framed as a governance issue, as below; but targets also involved at times a discussion about which specific targets on which environmental issues the coalition should argue for legislative action on. 'It's quite difficult to keep the whole coalition on the same page on targets generally' (Interviewee 3):

> I think it's fair to say, not all organisations are entirely happy with, not only the topic areas but also the way that the targets need to be, well drafted, for want of a better word. There's still a lot of debate and I think [XXX] is pulling [their] hair out. [...] So each organisation, you know, somebody wants a bee specific one, someone wants a soya specific one, someone wants, you know. So I think that has been a huge, huge challenge (Interviewee 12).

Focusing on the legal architecture for targets, as opposed to the setting of specific targets in particular areas was significant: the 'wording we need to see on the face of the Bill that would give confidence that it would deliver across, you know, all of these areas' (Interviewee 2). There was, according to this same interviewee, 'a bit of work to do, and that's ongoing, about explaining and trying to give confidence that a target-setting framework, which is by its very nature not specific will deliver what, you know, colleagues working in specific policy areas want' (Interviewee 2).

Collaboration and consensus-building around trade has been difficult, for different reasons. As discussed earlier, its technical complexity is likely a resource and capacity challenge for environmental groups. Furthermore:

> some of the Greener UK coalition have got a clear interest or position, a history of working in this area, and see trade as

something impinging on their objectives. And others [...] not traditionally involved in trade, wouldn't necessarily see it as a priority (Interviewee 3).

On the one hand, 'there's still a sense I think amongst those organisations that do wish to work on trade – they want to do it together' (Interviewee 3) and common ground has been established. But it has been acknowledged that there are some aspects of trade policy in which consensus was either unachievable or even undesirable, and different organisations will take different positions, within a common framework.

Profile, competition and identity

Collaboration may imply not just the pooling of resources, but also the 'pooling' of outcomes (credit, policy impact, profile, relationships); working in coalition may threaten interest groups' drive to remain competitive, specialised and autonomous. Groups may 'avoid alliances with other groups in order to enhance their own reputations as advocates and to distinguish themselves from other organizations representing similar interests'.[36] A key factor in ensuring the survival (and organisational maintenance) of an NGO is that it has a strong and appealing organisational identity, in the eyes of both supporters and those it seeks to influence.[37] Group identity, which 'flows both from how an organization understands itself and how it is understood by others'[38] is especially important in a crowded environment in which NGOs are competing for income, resources and influence. Although the emphasis placed on identity will vary from one group to another, it is an important factor in the decision to work in collaboration or work alone. Organisational identity may relate to a group's policy position or special expertise on a particular issue,[39] or its favoured political strategy (for example litigation, lobbying or protest), or may be linked more broadly to whether or not the group defends radical positions or prefers more moderate positions that are suited to political compromise. Describing the environment sector as 'like an ecosystem' in which 'we all have slightly different perspectives ... slightly different views', Interviewee 9 went on to say that:

> you have those that are what you might describe as at the extreme end, who want to really push forward, who want to do big public campaigns, lots of sort of disruptive stuff. And then you have [others] at the other end of the spectrum, who are very much on

> board with the kind of principle, but actually you know [...] in a different place. (Interviewee 9).

Whilst they may share end goals, environmental NGOs must weigh the advantages of collaboration against the fact that they will also likely be competing (with their collaborators) for income and indeed, influence; without resources, an audience, members and supporters, groups are unable to pursue their strategic objectives. In the words of one of our interviewees:

> whilst environmental NGOs obviously all work together, there is also an underlying element of competition, I think. And because obviously they all work in the same sector, they're all trying to get the same members and they're all trying to become the lead organisations, if you like, in the environmental sector domestically. So there is always going to be a little bit of an element of competition, and that does sometimes manifest itself in organisations trying to take ownership of particular areas and lead in those areas (Interviewee 15).

Albeit in the context of litigation, one of our interviewees alluded to this 'strategic positioning' when there is the potential to work collectively on a particular high-profile case:

> ... there's lots of dialogue about who's going to argue what and how is it going to work and don't shaft us, and that kind of thing. [...] some of that becomes about organisational positioning; it's not elegant, it's not pretty. It is proper, you know, People's Popular Front of Judea kind of stuff. Because they're jostling for position and jostling for recognition. They're jostling for money, they're jostling for members. So it isn't beautiful sometimes (Interviewee 5).

Some interviewees explicitly acknowledged the clear 'profile sacrifice' (Interviewee 2) that has to be made when NGOs are working in coalition: 'coalition work didn't allow enough room for the oak leaf to shine or the panda to stand out' (Interviewee 13). To take another example:

> So I spend quite a lot of my time drafting stuff or kind of working in coalition, attending meetings on behalf of or with the coalition. That's, you know, it does come often at the expense of profile for XXX. So there is a tension. (Interviewee 2)

This may be especially challenging at high-profile moments when coalition members look for their contribution to be explicitly acknowledged and recognised. One of our participants made this point when talking about the 'internal pressures' s/he faced during the second reading of the Environment Bill in February 2020:

> it's questioned why there were only [X] references to XXX whereas there were twenty to Greener UK. And does everyone know that XXX is basically tied into Greener UK? And I'm sure that other organisations are having equally tricky conversations, you know, they want that name recognition (unattributed).

We see 'competition between coalitions' (Interviewee 15) in the relationship between Link and Greener UK. Getting two large coalitions to work together (and indeed reach a level of consensus which, as discussed above, it seems they did) is no small task:

> we've managed to inspire quite a high level of trust and collaboration amongst thirteen organisations, you add fifty-two more into that mix, you think, 'How on earth can you do that?' So it's been a case of needing to ensure that all of the organisations are brought on board, whilst not creating something totally unwieldy (unattributed).

A number of our interviewees spoke of tensions between the two coalitions, certainly during the earlier stages of advocacy around Brexit-environment, although some also noted improvement: 'I think they seemed to have found their roles now [...] that relationship seems to be improving 'cause they're working out how they can complement each other' (Interviewee 15). For another interviewee there was a sense that early in the process, although relations were 'perfectly friendly', 'Link kept feeling they were being excluded from things and they should have a bigger role' (Interviewee 3). We are conscious that our interviews may not have picked up on any broader resentment of Greener UK in the sector.

And the competitiveness between NGOs sometimes manifests in a very personal way. Not speaking specifically about Brexit, Interviewee 12 told us:

> We are all human and I do find myself getting a bit competitive when maybe other organisations seem to be doing things in their

own name, when we have agreed to work together and be in collaboration. [...] other organisations might want to make sure that people know that they are working on something and therefore they want to do their own reports, they want to do their own lobbying or their own meetings with different organisations [...] so yes, I do get quite annoyed.

We may assume that the greater the competition, the less likely it is that groups will form coalitions. However, the literature suggests the opposite: competition stimulates coalition forming, perhaps because groups in competition often share important policy objectives.[40] 'Organisational salience' is an important explanatory factor for coalescing.[41] The shared objectives and high salience of Brexit, discussed in the next chapter, bear considerable explanatory weight in respect of collaboration over Brexit: political alignment around the post-Brexit governance mechanisms seemingly outweighed any costs to organisations' own interests. Furthermore, the need for strong accountability mechanisms post-Brexit was important for environmental NGOs, in terms of maintaining their own political and legal opportunities in the future.

But the challenge is not just about the immediate question of profile. In the longer term, collaboration may inhibit the extent to which NGOs are able to build their own relationships with power-holders, which are so important in the world of lobbying. So, 'whilst it's useful to be talking with one voice, in another sense ... over the longer term, that's not useful because we're not generating our own relationships with government. Which of course, is the stuff that we live on' (Interviewee 14). And yet:

You can't set up a coalition and say 'we want you to represent us' and when we do that say 'ah but, you know, we want be there too'. So there are many benefits of a coalition, but there are also inevitably tensions along the way as well, and I think that's one of them. How you achieve meaningful representation and advocacy without cutting off rightful ties that organisations need to have on their own basis (Interviewee 6).

Both the literature on collaboration and our interview data points to membership organisations as facing particular competitive risks around collaboration and identity.[42] The type of membership model might be significant. Much of the work identifying membership pressures as a deterrent to collaboration is about collaborations whose members are themselves organisations rather than mass membership organisations like ours.[43] But the impact on membership was explicitly acknowledged by some of our interviewees, for example:

> by having to put a lot of effort into the coalition, more dynamic NGOs may have lost investment and members on their own profile. They probably have, you know, if I was really being clinical about it. You know, they would have been able to perform. [...] 'Cause they're all, you know, they're free-market organisations, NGOs. They do need to keep their profile up, keep their members up. And if they're always saying things in coalition, it's kind of boring and it's not good for membership (Interviewee 3).

We might expect membership groups to work in coalition less frequently than, say, groups with incomes from other sources,[44] although we should note wider competition for finance, for example philanthropic funding. However, members may query an NGO's commitment to a particular goal if it fails to work in coalition with other like-minded groups: 'they've also been able to demonstrate to their memberships and to the interested parts of the public, "Look, we collectively ..."' (Interviewee 11). A very large majority of Greener UK members are membership organisations, again perhaps signalling that collaboration around Brexit is 'special'. An important and related point, raised by a range of interviewees working within and outside membership organisations, is that membership organisations 'need to tread really quite carefully' around Brexit, due to its sensitivity for their membership. Collaboration may have given them 'a space to kind of debate those issues and they're not necessarily leading that debate. Sometimes it maybe might help them to push the boundaries of what their own kind of positioning might be' (Interviewee 6).

Conclusions

Collaboration is important and the environmental NGO sector is calling for more of it.[45] Our case study has provided a useful lens through which to observe the 'benefits of a coalition', but also the 'tensions along the way' (Interviewee 6). Greener UK is a key feature of the Brexit-environment collaborative landscape. We can however point to a range of other collaborations, both formal and informal, which have enriched the debate and are likely to have contributed to shaping the post-Brexit environmental landscape.

One of the interesting features of the Greener UK collaboration from the perspective of our work is its impact on legal expertise. It has made pockets of specialised expertise available to the community. But it has also deepened that expertise through deliberation, creating more than the sum of its parts. And it may have contributed to foregrounding legal expertise within member organisations. We surmise that collaboration may play a similar role with respect to other thinly spread areas of expertise, such as expertise in parliamentary procedure and tactics.

Whilst the focus of our work has been on principles and governance, we can see that collaboration is continuing with the broader Environment Bill. The scope of the Bill (not to mention the Covid-19 pandemic and shifts in the political landscape) has made collaboration more complex and has demanded greater resource from both Greener UK itself and its member organisations. Greener UK's important alliance with Link has facilitated a grand pooling of expertise but has raised new and additional challenges.

Notes

1. Browne 1990. See also Sorurbakhsh 2016.
2. Sorurbakhsh 2016.
3. See e.g. Hojnacki 1997, Sorurbakhsh 2016, Beyers and De Bruycker 2018.
4. Heaney and Leifeld 2018.
5. Beyers and De Bruycker 2018, 961.
6. Beyers and De Bruycker 2018, 960, citations omitted.
7. For examples of early collaboration at the EU level see Chichowski 2007, 237–9. See also Richards and Heard 2005 for a discussion of the widespread collaboration around marine campaigns by European environmental NGOs.
8. Over one-quarter of NGOs who responded to the European Funders Network 'pulse taking' survey of the sector indicated that they had participated in collaboration related to Brexit; Miller, Cracknell and Williams 2017.
9. Wildlife and Countryside Link is the English part of a coalition of LINK groups in Scotland, England, Wales and Northern Ireland. Greener UK also collaborates with the groups in the other countries.
10. Environmental Audit Committee 2019; Environment, Food and Rural Affairs Committee 2019.
11. HM Government 2018.
12. Aldersgate is a member of Greener UK.
13. At our closing event, 24 June 2020.
14. https://www.wcl.org.uk/our-members.asp accessed 1 July 2020.
15. Beyers and De Bruycker 2018, 961.
16. https://www.aldersgategroup.org.uk/ accessed 7 December 2020.
17. https://www.iema.net/broadway accessed 7 December 2020.
18. Both coalition groups represent multiple stakeholders from the private and public sector, and civil society organisations. They are engaged in advocacy work around the environment and climate change, and have been very much involved in scrutinising the UK government's response to environmental protection post-Brexit.
19. We think it is fair to say that they can also be glimpsed in Goodman and Thornton 2017.
20. https://greeneruk.org/about/board accessed 1 July 2020.

21　This may not always be the case. Mahoney 2007, 51, for example, finds that activity in a coalition bears no relationship to lobbying success.
22　Beyers and de Bruycker 2018, 960.
23　Baumgartner 2009.
24　Weiler and Reibmann 2019, 93.
25　Beyers and De Bruycker 2018, 960.
26　Heaney and Leifeld 2018.
27　Weiler and Reibmann 2019, 95.
28　See Miller, Cracknell and Williams 2017 for a discussion of the trends in NGO resource and income.
29　Weiler and Reibmann 2019, 95 find that collaboration, because it allows for the pooling of expertise, is especially helpful for insider strategies.
30　Weiler and Reibmann 2019, 96.
31　See chapter 2 for a discussion of the role of organisational identity in NGO thinking.
32　Coen 1997.
33　Sorurbakhsh 2016.
34　This was said in the context of discussing how important individuals were to making the collaboration on Brexit work, rather than the nature of the debate.
35　So not: 'What should the Bill say on conservation covenants?', but: 'Is it more important to influence the provisions on air quality or conservation covenants?'
36　Hojnacki 1997, 62.
37　Weiler and Reibmann 2019.
38　Heaney 2004, 615.
39　Niche theory observes interest groups developing 'issue niches', distinctive areas of interest and expertise that will set their group apart from others in the same or similar policy domain, thus shielding themselves from competition and ensuring their own survival. See Baumgartner and Leech 2001; Beyers and De Bruycker 2018; Heaney 2004.
40　Beyers and De Bruycker 2018.
41　Issue salience can also be considered from a media and public perspective. See Beyers and De Bruycker 2018, 965–7.
42　Also see chapter 5 (page 117) for a discussion of additional pressures faced by membership groups when framing the Brexit debate.
43　Sorurbakhsh 2016. These are often business groups.
44　Beyers and De Bruycker 2018.
45　See Miller, Cracknell and Williams 2017.

7
Greener UK: influence and collaboration

Introduction

As we discuss in chapter 6, collaboration brings with it both challenges and rewards. Whilst it has enabled the environmental NGO community to pool and develop resource and expertise (including legal expertise), it requires groups to reach consensus on end goals and may come at a cost, both financial and in terms of organisational profile. In this chapter, we focus in more detail on the Greener UK coalition, which has played a central role in Brexit-environment advocacy. Greener UK has been the key forum in which many of the large UK environmental NGOs have developed their thinking on Brexit, and has led the debate for NGOs in the corridors of power. Collaboration through Greener UK was a recurring theme of our interviews, with almost everyone volunteering positive assessments of its work. That is of course in part a result of our sample; almost anyone working on Brexit-environment, especially on governance and principles, will be aware of, and probably directly working with, Greener UK, and no doubt some of Greener UK's choices or objectives might be contested. But we do think we would have heard any complaints and disappointments from our own participants.[1] Collaboration has been a 'bright side' (Interviewee 13) of the Brexit-environment journey, and Greener UK has been 'exceptionally well-organised, very disciplined' (Interviewee 3).

We assess the Greener UK coalition's success along two lines. First, and this is the subject of the next section, it influenced the public debate and some outcomes on Brexit-environment. As discussed in chapter 1 (pages 10–14), and as is recognised by our interviewees, determining the influence of NGO advocacy on specific outcomes is extraordinarily difficult: 'it's always very hard to know how powerful [environmental

NGOs] are, and what influence you have and what you can do' (Interviewee 8). Attributions of causation are complex and often contested. We have already explored some significant political factors at play in the Brexit process, and many other actors, including academics and other public and private interest groups have contributed to the debate alongside environmental NGOs, as have individuals in parliament and government. Having said that, and taking these limitations as read, we explore the influence of Greener UK on the Brexit-environment debate and the development of the Environment Bill. We see Greener UK's influence from the early stages of the post-referendum debate, right through to the version of the Environment Bill introduced to Parliament in 2020. As discussed in chapter 5, we do not try to establish the precise impact or influence of legal argument. However, the heavy reliance on legal expertise by the environmental NGO community, coupled with what we have to say about the relative success of Greener UK, provides some indirect evidence for the influence of that expertise.

A second measure of success, which is probably related to Greener UK's influence and effectiveness, is that this is a collaboration that has 'worked' *as* a collaboration. It has held together, it has been active, people have contributed and found that contribution rewarding. It has been properly 'collaborative' in any sense of the word. Indirect benefits of the coalition, beyond immediate or even delayed outcomes on the objectives of Greener UK, may include improved relationships, and the development of expertise at an individual and collective level. Drawing heavily on our interviewees' perceptions and experience of working together through Greener UK, we explore some of the key features that may have contributed to this collaborative ethos. In particular, and developing our discussion in the previous chapter, we identify three crucial features of the Greener UK coalition: the nature of Brexit and its salience for the sector; people and trust; and resourcing. And finally, we consider the 'footprint' (Interviewee 3) of Greener UK and the possible future of collaboration between environmental groups.

Influence and impact

Adapting Michelle Betsill and Elisabeth Corell's definition, influence can be attributed when environmental groups 'intentionally transmit information' to those making decisions, and that information alters the process and the outcome.[2] We are a little more modest in our aspirations than Betsill and Corell. We have observed an enormously complex, diverse and dynamic set of influences on Brexit-environment, and we do not attribute sole responsibility for process or outcome to Greener UK (or even environmental NGOs generally), or engage in any philosophical or practical debates about causation.[3] So when we refer to influence, we mean that we can see a link between Greener UK and debates or outcomes, but accept that other influences may also be significant. And of course, it would be impossible to separate Greener UK's influence from the influence of other NGOs and coalitions, as well as individuals (including academics) advancing similar arguments.

We use Greener UK as a reference for a number of reasons. First, as we discuss in chapter 3 (page 63), our interviews have revealed the 'unprecedented' nature of 'access' (Interviewee 6) to government and parliament during our period of study. According to DEFRA transparency data, Greener UK met with ministers on nine occasions between January 2018 and December 2019, and there would have been many more meetings with officials than with ministers.[4] Maria can attest to very frequent meetings between Greener UK and officials in DEFRA and other government departments. Second, Greener UK is made up of, and gets its resources (of expertise as well as finance[5]) from a number of major environmental groups, representing a significant part of the community on the issues at the heart of our case study. Third, and more prosaically, for the purposes of our research, Greener UK provides a convenient marker of NGO demands.[6]

As we say in chapter 1 (page 13), we do not intend to suggest that Greener UK is responsible for all of the positive outcomes of the sector's work in this area. In addition to the challenges of attributing causation noted above, the active and energetic collaboration by a large number of NGOs is what made Greener UK what it is.

We did not set out in our interviews to assess influence. However, although our interview data provides an impressionistic and subjective account of influence, our participants did have interesting and insightful things to say on the subject. Along with our interview data, our analysis in this section of the progress of Greener UK demands provides a good sense of influence. 'Process tracing' is subject to a significant literature,[7] and is broadly an effort 'to assess causality by recording each element of the causal chain'.[8] Although we are making limited claims on causation, we borrow from this methodology to explore influence. We start from Greener UK's Manifesto, and explore the progress of their objectives on governance through key moments, into government policy, and into the Environment Bill as it stands in June 2020. As the sector's demands become more detailed and refined, rather than trying to follow through the whole of the Greener UK Manifesto, we focus on a single objective, the need for a new body to replace as far as possible the role of the European Commission.

We use Select Committee reports as milestones against which to assess the evolution of Greener UK's objectives, and responses to them. This is of course a major simplification, not least because of the mutual influence between the Select Committees and environmental groups, with Select Committees amplifying, and being amplified by, the NGO community on Brexit. Nor was there a single leap in Greener UK's demands between these milestones. Rather, the demands were subject to constant refinement and iteration, and Select Committee submissions are very far from Greener UK's only interventions on the subject. Despite these caveats, Select Committees provide a useful way of organising the material and are a good place to observe political activity around Brexit: they are a 'key site of influence for external pressure groups'.[9] We have not systematically analysed 'behind closed doors', face-to-face or written interactions with government and parliamentarians, simply placing public-facing work alongside what our interviewees told us. We shall explore in this chapter the Environmental Audit Committee Inquiry into the *EPG Consultation*,[10] the pre-legislative scrutiny of the draft Environment (Principles and Governance) Bill[11] and interventions on the Environment Bill published in January 2020.[12]

Notwithstanding the inevitable methodological limitations, we are confident, from our interview data, our personal observations and our analysis of the progress of its demands (to which we return below) that Greener UK was in a broad sense very influential in the Brexit-environment debate. Simply keeping environmental governance on the agenda, at a time when the excitement of the Brexit drama was almost overwhelming of media, public and political attention, was an extraordinary achievement. Many of our interviewees referred to this, with varying levels of surprise: 'So recognition of the governance gap and things […] it was much more successful than I expected it to be in terms of the discussions we started at the end of 2016' (Interviewee 16). In 2018 (before Greta Thunberg or Extinction Rebellion hit the headlines), anyone would have expected the parliamentary agenda to be exhausted by the high constitutional and political drama of Brexit, and yet 'you've got cross-party debate on the environment in the context of the EU Withdrawal Bill' and that significant debate itself 'was a big sort of win' (Interviewee 16).

Many elements of the Environment Bill (arguably even any prospect of primary legislation) can be linked to the work of Greener UK and its allies. This came through in our interviews: 'Greener UK has had a really profound influence on DEFRA's thinking, in terms of its approach to Brexit' (Interviewee 11); Greener UK has been at 'the sharp end of things, sharp end of delivery ... that's allowed the somewhat more jelly-like enviro sector to gain a hard edge at the front' (Interviewee 13).

Greener UK also became a trusted interlocutor with parliament. As well as public briefings and evidence to Select Committees, Greener UK had many private communications with parliamentarians and their staff. Our interview data points to Greener UK's influence in parliament, with one participant noting that: 'You can see that people are on a journey, we're all on a journey together. And so I think the support [in parliament] was there but it had to grow and it had to be broader than it was, and [Greener UK] helped make that happen' (Interviewee 6). With appropriate reservations about our sample, we heard only one overtly negative comment about Greener UK in our interviews, and that might be attributed to a difference of opinion on a particular decision, and may even speak to Greener UK's effectiveness in driving the debate.[13] That there seems to be some commitment to continuing with a formal collaborative arrangement in the sector post-Brexit is also perhaps indicative of the seeming success and influence of Greener UK.

The Manifesto objectives

The top headline of the Greener UK Manifesto, published in February 2017, is to 'Secure the benefits of existing environmental laws as the UK leaves the European Union, and pass an ambitious new Environment Act'.[14] The issues set out under that headline are, in full (references added), as follows:

1. Fully transpose and maintain existing EU environmental laws and principles through the Repeal Bill,[15] and ensure we have the necessary governance arrangements in place for robust implementation and enforcement in future.
2. Lead the world by setting measurable milestones for environmental restoration and high standards for pollution and resource efficiency, as part of a strong 25 year plan,[16] reinforced in law in an ambitious new Environment Act.

We pursue four basic Greener UK objectives from this statement: maintenance of environmental laws; maintenance of environmental principles; governance arrangements for implementation and enforcement; and targets ('milestones') in 'an ambitious new Environment Act'. This necessarily simplifies the sector's environmental asks, which were not pre-packaged, waiting to be inserted into a decision-making process. Rather, they were developed collaboratively, and partly precisely in response to the fora available to make the case, and the receptiveness of those fora: the political and hybrid political–legal opportunities discussed in chapter 3.

When the Greener UK Manifesto was published in February 2017, as discussed in chapter 3 (page 61), the Government of the day was implacably opposed to making any interventions to address changes to the structures and governance of environmental law that would result from Brexit. They had undertaken to 'retain' existing law after leaving the European Union, and argued that this, together with existing domestic mechanisms of political and legal accountability, would be adequate. The General Election in June 2017, and the appointment of Michael Gove as Secretary of State for DEFRA, changed that. In a November 2017 article in *The Daily Telegraph*, the Secretary of State promised a consultation on establishing 'a new, world-leading body to give the environment a voice and hold the powerful to account. It will be independent of government, able to speak its mind freely. And it will be placed on a statutory footing, ensuring it has clear authority.'[17] He also undertook to ensure that 'environmental enforcement and policy-making is underpinned by a clear set of principles'. And by contrast with his predecessors, Gove acknowledged that judicial review and parliamentary scrutiny are not sufficient to respond to concerns about the loss of EU Member State accountability mechanisms.[18] We know from personal experience and our interviews that Greener UK (including its members) was in close contact with DEFRA in the period between the General Election and this major and public shift of policy. Public documents, including a Greener UK briefing published in August 2017 for Parliamentarians and policy-makers on the 'governance gap' enlarged on the Manifesto.[19]

The Secretary of State's article addresses, in broad outline, two elements of the Greener UK Manifesto. It promises the retention of environmental principles after Brexit, and proposes a new body to scrutinise the implementation of environmental law. And whilst he is silent here on future environmental targets, a *25 Year Plan on the Environment* had been expected since 2014, and this article promised legislation (albeit only for the new body, not for the plan).

As we discuss in chapter 3 (page 66), the maintenance of environmental laws after Brexit was achieved in a minimalist way by the EU (Withdrawal) Act 2018. If by 'maintenance' of environmental law,

Greener UK had intended a longer-term maintenance of standards, that is non-regression after leaving the EU, Greener UK continues in 2020 to argue that a non-regression provision should be introduced into the Environment Bill.[20] Even the retention of EU law had begun to fall apart a little by the time that the UK left the EU, given the amendment of provisions on EU case law in the EU (Withdrawal Agreement) Act 2020, discussed in chapter 3 (page 73). Equally questionable are the problems with the 2018 Act's provision, also discussed in chapter 3, for secondary legislation to deal with 'any failure of retained EU law to operate effectively', or 'any other deficiency in retained EU law'.[21] For example, EU environmental laws routinely contain review and revision clauses, to ensure that the legislation remains up to date and effective. Andy Jordan and Brendan Moore highlighted in May 2020 that these had not been 'retained' effectively. The role of the Commission in reviewing legislation needed to be addressed, but rather than giving that role to another body, these provisions were removed entirely.[22] The review and revision clauses of the Environment Bill, such as they are, fall short of what is required.[23]

Moving into detail

The *25 Year Plan* was published in January 2018.[24] It is 151 pages long, covering a wide range of policy areas. Its overall ambition was broadly welcomed by the environmental community. Criticism focused on the absence of a statutory underpinning for the commitments and targets (also one of Greener UK's manifesto objectives), weak or even backsliding commitments, and a general vagueness. The Environmental Audit Committee launched an inquiry focused on the 'ambition and architecture' of the *25 Year Plan*, foreshadowing what became the provisions on environmental targets and Environmental Improvement Plans in Chapter 1 of the Environment Bill. We return to Greener UK's response to this inquiry below. The *25 Year Plan* further committed DEFRA to holding a consultation on 'plans to set up a world-leading environmental watchdog, an independent, statutory body, to hold Government to account for upholding environmental standards'.[25] This provided some demanding language against which environmental groups judged Government intentions.

The DEFRA consultation on Environmental Principles and Governance (the *EPG Consultation*) was finally published in May 2018,[26] including questions on creating a new body to monitor government performance on the environment, and options for bringing the environmental principles into the post-Brexit domestic legal system. We should not understate the influence (subject to all the provisos above) of the environmental NGO community in achieving this. The Consultation Paper was, however, deeply disappointing in its detail.

Staying with the big picture for a moment, the introduction of section 16 to the EU (Withdrawal Act) 2018 was a major achievement for Greener UK and its allies: 'I said, "Who's been briefing you?" He said, "Greener UK"' (Interviewee 10). As Interviewee 3 put it:

> not wanting to kind of blow all our own trumpets around the work that we did on the Withdrawal Act, I don't think we can understate what we managed to achieve there. Which was to get an amendment into a piece of legislation that Government really, really didn't want to amend and to get that amendment on policy into a procedural Bill and to get commitment for legislation to come out the back of it.

Ruth Chambers of Greener UK said at our closing event that this achievement 'should never ever be forgotten and never ever be diminished' because 'the law is stacked against being changed by civil society from start to finish'.[27]

Passed before the *EPG Consultation* had been completed, section 16, as discussed in chapter 3 (pages 67–68), required Government to produce draft legislation (what became the draft Environment (Principles and Governance) Bill) within six months.[28] The Secretary of State had been much more equivocal in front of the Environmental Audit Committee: 'he would "hope, but of course it is subject to the agreement of my Cabinet colleagues, that we would bring forward an Environment Act [...] by 2020"'.[29]

As discussed above, and to avoid making this section too lengthy, rather than trying to follow through the whole of the Greener UK Manifesto, we focus here on the proposed new body, which (see chapter 3) was to replace, as far as possible, the role of the European Commission in scrutinising and enforcing the implementation of environmental law by the state (regulating the regulators). The sector's objectives for the new body continued to be developed in much more detail, in outputs such as blogs and briefings, as well as responses to the Consultation Paper. We take Greener UK's submission to the Environmental Audit Committee,[30] which expands significantly on the bare starting point of the Manifesto, as the framework for our discussion.

Greener UK argued that 'it is essential that recourse to legally biting mechanisms is available'. The new body 'must be able to initiate legal proceedings, and to intervene in proceedings brought by others where appropriate'.[31] Binding notices must be available, and 'would be of most value if they arose from a consideration of the merits of government decision-making'. Greener UK criticises the absence of any details on how Government will ensure that the new body will be independent, and in oral evidence, said that this suggests that independence has been 'kicked into the long grass'. Greener UK argued that the new body must have 'legal powers over all public bodies, not just central government', as had been proposed by DEFRA. It also rejected the exclusion of climate change[32] from the remit of the body.

Many of these points are picked up in whole or in part by the Environmental Audit Committee's Report and Recommendations.[33] Spelling out mechanisms for independence from government, the new body should report to parliament, and be overseen by a parliamentary committee who would also set its budget and 'endorse' its Chair. Further:

> The Government should ensure that the draft Environmental Principles and Governance Bill includes effective and proactive enforcement powers, with the power to fine government departments and agencies that fail to comply. [...] The enforcement function should investigate compliance with environmental law, including complaints brought by the public, which the courts can then adjudicate.[34]

Government published the draft Environment (Principles and Governance) Bill on 19 December 2018, at which point, the 'new body' becomes the Office for Environmental Protection (OEP). Some of Greener UK's detail was accepted by Government, and included in the draft Bill: Government purports to have put in place mechanisms to ensure the independence of the OEP; the OEP's remit is extended to all public authorities; it is able to issue 'decision notices', and bring what amount to judicial review proceedings. The reliance on judicial review means that there is no merits review at the hard enforcement end of the OEP's activities. There is no express provision on intervening in others' litigation, although a catch-all provision in the schedule would allow the OEP 'to do anything ... it thinks appropriate for the purposes of, or in connection with, its functions'.

In its submissions to the joint Environmental Audit Committee/EFRA Select Committee pre-legislative inquiry into the draft Bill, Greener UK again held the proposals up against Government promises. It states that the provisions do not amount to 'equivalence with the current EU oversight, scrutiny and enforcement arrangements', and do not meet 'the government's ambition for a "world-leading body to give the environment a voice and hold the powerful to account" and "a pioneering new system of green governance".[35] On independence, Greener UK focuses on funding, appointments and status. As quoted by the Environmental Audit Committee, three of Greener UK's 'critical' measures on funding are: a strong and visible commitment to multi-annual budgets; the OEP to determine what funding is sufficient by preparing and publishing its own supply estimate; and the OEP having the right and the independence to say how much money it thinks it needs at the start of the process.[36]

On appointments, the draft Bill provides for the OEP Chair and Board members to be appointed by the Secretary of State. An undertaking to consider a pre-appointment Parliamentary hearing for the Chair was, however, not sufficiently reassuring for Greener UK, which argued that 'Parliament must play a greater role in the appointment of the OEP Chair. There is no reason why the Chair could not be appointed either directly by Parliament or the appointment approved by the relevant Select Committee.' Greener UK also argued that the Chair's appointment should be made directly by the Monarch, rather than by the Secretary of State, 'following a proposal to Parliament for a preferred candidate by the Secretary of State, supported by the Chair of the relevant Select Committee.' The other non-executive members should be appointed by the Chair, and not by the Secretary of State. And on status, the draft Bill provides for a non-departmental public body (NDPB);[37] for the sake of independence from Government, Greener UK argued that the OEP should be a Parliamentary body.

These arguments around funding, appointments and status are all to some degree supported by one or both of the Select Committees. On funding, the Environmental Audit Committee 'recommend that the Government makes a political commitment to providing the Office for Environmental Protection with a five year budget in line with spending reviews', subject to its own estimate.[38] The EFRA Committee also recommends a 'multi-annual budgetary framework'.[39] The EFRA Committee recommended that: 'The Chair and all non-executive members of the board should be appointed by the Secretary of State only with the consent of the Environment, Food and Rural Affairs Select Committee. The Chair should be subject to a pre-appointment hearing prior to the Committee consenting to her appointment.'[40] The Environmental Audit Committee concludes that a committee of Parliament 'should set [the OEP's] budget, scrutinise its performance and oversee its governance', with a new Parliamentary Committee having a veto over certain appointments. The EFRA Committee recommends that:

'The Government should revisit the legal status of the Office for Environmental Protection to provide greater independence than a standard Non-Departmental Public Body allows.'[41]

Turning to enforcement, Greener UK supported the draft provisions on information and decision notices, but expressed concern that the 'proposed enforcement provision' would not provide 'an adequate and effective means for enforcing environmental law'. More specifically, the OEP should have express powers to initiate its own investigations, rather than having to wait to receive a complaint. They propose 'dedicated and bespoke enforcement processes', including the possibility for binding decision notices against all public authorities, which can require particular steps 'such as the publication of action plans, the implementation of certain policies or compensation payments'. Enforcement action must be available if decision notices are not complied with: 'The most appropriate forum for this could be the specialist Environmental Tribunal rather than the High Court', 'operating an improved system of Judicial Review with tailored rules on standing, costs, intensity of review and remedies and in which specialist judges (possibly with technical advisers) could sit'. Remedies should include 'fines, relocation of powers or introducing "special measures"'. Greener UK seeks transparency of the OEP's decisions. It seeks 'greater clarity' on the meaning of 'a serious failure' to comply with environmental law, a phrase that sets the boundary on the OEP's remit; and a review of the definition of 'environmental law', so that it includes climate law and law 'relating to' rather than 'mainly concerned with' environmental matters. The OEP should also develop and publish its own enforcement policy.

Again, much of this finds its way into the reports. The EFRA Committee recommends that:

> the Bill should be redrafted to ensure the OEP has the power to proactively carry out investigations into a serious failure to comply with environmental law on its own initiative, rather than just in response to a complaint. [...] The word 'serious' in relation to a breach of environmental law should be clarified on the face of the Bill.[42]

The Environmental Audit Committee proposes that the definition of 'environmental law' 'should be changed from "is mainly concerned with" to "relating to"'.[43] Both Committees recommend more attention to 'international law'.[44]

The Environmental Audit Committee describes the draft Bill's enforcement procedures as 'too slow and inflexible', says that judicial review is 'not appropriate for environmental problems', and calls for a 'bespoke enforcement procedure' and 'an expansion of the role and remit of the General Regulatory Chamber in the First-tier Tribunal'. It suggests that the OEP should be able to issue notices 'at first advisory, then latterly binding', including 'a range of compliance recommendations'. A decision not to comply with the notice could be challenged by the OEP in 'substantive review of the authority's decision not to comply with the notice' by the tribunal (so looking very like a merits review).[45]

The response of Government to pre-legislative scrutiny was limited. The Environment Bill put before Parliament in January 2020 (which for current purposes is almost identical to the October 2019 version) continued to include in broad outline the relevant initial Manifesto objectives of Greener UK as discussed above; and picked up many of the more detailed objectives, although by no means all. Greener UK, jointly with Link, produced a number of briefings on the Bill.[46] The changes that are called for are indicative of arguments not yet accepted. On the OEP, Greener UK seeks a number of changes, including: the consent of the EFRA and Environmental Audit Committees to the appointment of the Chair, who would then appoint the other members; a legislative commitment to five-yearly budgets, the OEP's ability to make its own estimate, and direct funding from Parliament; a number of improved institutional protections of independence, including 'the maintenance of a log of substantive contact with government'; a specific power to carry out broad reviews into substantive issues; clarity that the tribunal can 'consider technical facts and issues, with experts who are able to thoroughly review the substantive matter at hand'; improved transparency around the OEP's processes; a definition of environmental law as law 'related to' rather than 'mainly concerned with' environmental matters.[47]

The Covid-19 pandemic has had a significant impact on the progress of the Environment Bill through the Public Bill Committee. As discussed in chapter 3 (pages 73–74), all Public Bill Committees were suspended in March 2020, in response to the lockdown. There is enormous pressure on parliamentary time and physical space for progressing Bills.[48] At the time of completing this manuscript, the Bill has not returned to Committee, and the Secretary of State has said that it is unlikely to return before September 2020.[49]

Success, failure and influence

It is a little premature to call victory or failure. Not only has the Covid-19 crisis derailed progress on the Environment Bill, but legislation is not the end of the journey. Even a fabulous Environment Act would not be self-executing and would require ongoing scrutiny and engagement by environmental groups. The environmental NGO community should take any opportunity presented by the provisions of a future Environment Act to contribute to shaping the rules of the environmental governance game.[50] Some of the things not successfully achieved during passage of the Bill may be advocated as part of the day-to-day practice of the OEP, and that may be helped if the debate during the Bill leads to ministerial assurances from the dispatch box.

And it is difficult at the best of times to agree what success would look like. An NGO's objectives may be unclear, in part because they evolve during a process, but also because they may take public positions that go beyond what they would privately be content with. Interviewee 3 says that in some meetings with government, 'you might be there to represent a position, even if it's a more extreme position than you think you're going to get'. And as should be clear from the above, NGO positions evolve during a process. An Environmental Funders Network survey of environmental groups brings out the ambiguity of success:

> Some of the work that features in the sector's collective list of successes also appears in the list of the top ten failures, reflecting the fact that while [civil society organisations] may have helped put issues on the agenda there is much that remains to be done. For example, some respondents saw campaigns against fracking as a failure because the government has not shut the door on shale gas development. To others, this work is a success – not only because fracking has not yet moved forward at anything like the scale its supporters would like – but also because a strong, vibrant grassroots movement has been built around this issue.[51]

There are similarly distinctive ways of thinking about success in the Brexit-environment debate. We are confident that Greener UK, and the sector, have been influential in the Brexit-environment debate, keeping that debate alive and shaping its progress over a lengthy and challenging period; the resilience and persistence of the individuals and institutions involved should not be under-estimated. The very existence of the first major Environment Bill for a generation is at least a partial victory, and its contents in many respects reflect the objectives of Greener UK. If the Covid-19 pandemic means that the Bill is killed or weakened does this still count as a success? On its own terms, it must, and shaping the debate over this period lays some groundwork for the future.[52] The expectation is that the Bill will survive and become an Environment Act; Greener UK may yet exercise further influence. For now, an Environment Act that is passed as the Bill stands could, as far as the OEP is concerned, be categorised a success for the influence of Greener UK and the sector. Imperfect, and incomplete, but a good thing, a body whose job it is to make sure that Government (in all its parts) ensures compliance with environmental law.

It is not really a criticism to say that Greener UK (or its allies, including academics) did not address all of the significant governance questions. In fact, it may indicate just how much Greener UK has driven the debate to observe that issues like the 'review and revision' clauses discussed above, which received little or no attention from Greener UK, also received little or no timely attention in public debate. Whilst it is impossible for us to robustly evidence this negative, we believe that this particular gap reflects the constraints on legal expertise in the sector. Not only was the issue not recognised (or at least not at the right level at the right time), but the capacity to carry out a comprehensive assessment of the statutory instruments as they went through Parliament, and then to raise the flag and fight the battle, was simply not there.

The targets/milestones objective from the initial Greener UK Manifesto are a mixed story. The Environment Bill is lengthy, and addresses many of the sector's key issues, and to that extent is a success. The architecture of the targets in the 'governance and principles' part of the Bill is also a significant achievement, albeit with some major and concerning gaps from Greener UK's perspective, as is apparent from its briefings. The provisions on principles are much more difficult to categorise as an achievement. The principles are present in legislation, and they certainly formed a part of what was a hugely important debate, which evidences influence of a sort. But they have lost their legal status, are subject to worrying exceptions, and are more or less entirely within the control of the Secretary of State. Battles won along the way are not therefore terribly significant in terms of the legislation's overall approach to principles.

The qualities of collaboration

'Success' may translate literally, as we discuss above, into achieving specific legal or public policy goals such as governance arrangements post-Brexit, either in the short term or by laying the ground for the longer term. But there have also, as suggested in the Introduction, potentially been more indirect benefits to collaborating through Greener UK. We discussed in the previous chapter the way that relationships between

NGOs, particularly ClientEarth, evolved and deepened through this process. Our sense is also that Greener UK has contributed to a deepening and foregrounding of legal expertise. Greener UK may also have played an important role in building capacity in the sector. Junior colleagues have had the opportunity to learn from more experienced individuals across the sector, and perhaps to be stretched with more robust support than might otherwise be available, or in strategic spaces that are less familiar to them. This learning could be significant for individuals and for the sector, especially given the relative inexperience we noted in chapter 4 (pages 93–94).

In this section, we explore the features of Greener UK that may have contributed to its success as a collaborative exercise, as something that held together and was resilient to the extraordinary challenges that the four years of our case study threw at it. We explore our participants' perceptions of collaborating in Greener UK, or their reflections on this collaboration from outside. It is important to remember, as we discuss in chapter 6, that collaboration is not easy and that it brings with it both opportunities and challenges. It will not always be successful, in any of the ways explored in this chapter. We identify three key factors that contributed to the success of Greener UK: the nature of Brexit and its salience for the sector; people and trust; and resourcing.

The nature and scope of Greener UK's work has not remained static and has, as we note in chapter 3, required the coalition to be agile in its response. The broadening of the Brexit-environment debate, the fast-paced shifts in the political landscape during our period of study and the pandemic lockdown have all played a part in shaping Greener UK and its work:

> It's been like tales of the unexpected and the unpredictable, hasn't it? So we've had to be quite adaptable, and adapt as we've gone along. Not only react to all of the things that nobody knew were coming, but also to try and be as proactive and strategic as we could amongst that (unattributed).

Generally, 'Brexit has turned into a major project in terms of legislation and policy beyond legislation – trade policy, politics, negotiations with the EU. It's become a very big topic' (Interviewee 3). The Environment Bill itself, our focus in this monograph, is huge and addresses a wealth of issues. Despite these new challenges, the sector's commitment to Greener UK and its work has continued. Here, we can see two things going on. First, 'a recognition that no one organisation can deal [with all elements of the Bill]' (Interviewee 3). This extended even to the Greener UK collaboration itself, and led to the important alliance with Wildlife and Countryside Link, as outlined in chapter 6. And second, the perceived success of Greener UK, 'the sense that Greener UK's track record has been quite good, they have actually managed to achieve some things' (Interviewee 3) also led to continued commitment to the coalition.

The nature of Brexit: salience for the sector

In the previous chapter, we discussed the importance and the challenge of consensus, and Greener UK's success in building consensus around both the governance and the substantive elements of the Environment Bill. We do not want to repeat the discussion in chapter 6, but it is important to highlight the contribution of the extraordinary salience (and associated broad consensus) around Brexit to the success of the collaboration. Several of our interviewees seemed at least a little surprised by the sector's commitment to collaboration around Brexit: 'the NGOs did organise better than I thought they would. You know, the coalition came together, and it was quite disciplined and quite effective' (Interviewee 3).

Our interview data suggests that Greener UK is different from previous collaborative efforts. Whilst one interviewee acknowledged that the sector has 'always collaborated' (Interviewee 6), s/he went on to state that historically 'it's done so at a much more technical policy level ... to do, you know, joint letters to ministers and that kind of thing' (Interviewee 6). For that same interviewee, collaboration on this 'political journey ... it's been on a different scale and the appetite for it has been different and, you know, that's because of Brexit I think' (Interviewee 6). The scale of the challenge posed by Brexit, its technical novelty (not 'bread and butter' issues, below) and the pace of the debate, have intensified the interest in collaboration. That the nature of Brexit has forced a different kind of 'political' collaboration was acknowledged by other interviewees:

> So it took this political crisis moment to force that kind of collaboration, rather than an environmental [crisis] [...] 'cause the organisations were already set up to do environment, that was their bread and butter, and they were doing that. But they weren't doing that collectively, in the way that they have worked on Brexit (Interviewee 8).

We can conclude, albeit tentatively, that the Brexit project has led to a different kind of collaboration: 'there's gotta be a big enough threat, or maybe a big enough opportunity, but at the time it felt like the threat, I think, was the thing that pushed everyone together' (Interviewee 8), what Ruth Chambers of Greener UK described as 'an ethos of organisational selflessness'.[53]

The changing nature of the debate, once there was a broader Environment Bill to discuss, added a layer of complexity for Greener UK and its member organisations. As discussed in chapter 6, the search for consensus around the broader sectoral elements of the Bill required intense coordination and effort.

People and trust

Ultimately, collaboration is about people. Almost all of our interviewees (unprompted) identified the same individual as being central to the success of collaboration through Greener UK; we return to the importance of resourcing some key roles below. Many also pointed to the importance of higher-level individual and organisational leadership in the instigation of the collaboration, albeit without coalescing in the same way on where that leadership lay. But generally, good relationships and good communications are crucial:

> [Greener UK] try to be a lot more consensual [...] if we have to say, 'No, we can't sign up to that.' We try not to do that unless we really have to. And you know, we've kind of got good enough relationships that actually people still understand why we're doing it. [...] So it's all about relationships, it's all about being clear and communicating as well as we can, compromising in both directions where we need to (Interviewee 9).

There is also 'something about the spirit and the culture in which it's done' (Interviewee 6) in Greener UK. There seems to have been a strong commitment by Greener UK members to work together, at an organisational and an individual level. Trust within a coalition (or any team) is generally considered important. Greener UK seems to fit with the idea that 'closely connected, recurrent relations embedded in intricate social structures'[54] enhance trust. Greener UK had a number of active groups, which met regularly and worked on specific tasks over a lengthy period. Maria has witnessed impressive chairing of formal meetings, meticulous inclusion, careful and considerate management of meetings with external actors such as government officials. Open discussion and debate have been the norm. Similarly, one of our interviewees acknowledged that 'there's a lot of, a huge amount of trust between the individuals around that table to be able to debate in a very respectful and thoughtful way' (Interviewee 8).

We also see the importance of people and personalities in the tension discussed in chapter 6 around early relationships between Link and Greener UK. These personalities worked positively in that members of both groups worked hard to forge a stronger relationship between the two coalitions, but also less positively: the early tensions were 'partly aggravated by personalities', although 'all this seems to have been ironed out now', again largely by dint of the involvement of particular personalities (Interviewee 3). Another participant expanded on that:

> largely it's a personality thing, so each individual comes in at the beginning with what they think should be in [the Bill]. But with anything, when you've been working on it for over a year, two years, and you see little movement in areas or you see acceptance of something, you become more comfortable with what's been in front of you for a length of time. So it might not necessarily be an institutional thing with the member organisations but a personality thing where people are sort of giving up ground to reach that consensus (Interviewee 15).

Despite all of the challenges, collaborating through Greener UK has been personally rewarding for our participants:

> yes personally I've rather enjoyed the level of collaboration. It makes it more worthwhile. So I think for the people involved in doing it, it is quite rewarding, and it makes their jobs richer. I think quite a lot of us will miss it if it goes, and probably be a little bit biased towards maintaining it because of its personal qualities. And I think we've been lucky in the personalities. Just that is fortuitous to some degree. Although you do get more collaborative people coming into these collaborative roles, it doesn't always work that way (unattributed).

But the 'people' question cannot be left to chance, even if this participant suggests that it was 'fortuitous to some degree' in this case. It requires commitment by member organisations, and strategic thinking about which people to devote to the collaboration (and we discuss possible limitations in that respect in chapters 4 and 5), and it requires commitment to individuals to hold the coalition together. This feeds directly into our discussion of resources, below.

In addition to diverting some of Greener UK's attention away from Brexit-environment to work on the impact of Covid-19 on the environment and on the sector, the pandemic has impacted the sector's way of working. For one interviewee, the move online is a positive development and will facilitate more collaboration: 'I'm hoping that actually people will see that it is literally just a click of a button and we can all work together and chat easily, which I hope will make it easier to work together' (Interviewee 15). For another, this was more problematic:

> Obviously we're gonna do more video conferencing and that allows us to speak to people more quickly, more easily. But video conferencing is not the same as being there in person. You can't build the same kind of personal relationships as you can in person, it's less chit-chat, certainly when it's a big meeting, when you have twenty-five people on the meeting to begin with, you can't have little side conversations (Interviewee 7).

In light of the crucial role that people play in making coalitions work, and the importance of communication and building trust in collaboration more broadly and within Greener UK in particular, this could be detrimental to the sector in the longer term.

Resources

In chapter 6, we discuss how collaboration enables the pooling of resources, including legal expertise. We conclude that the investment of resource (both financial and human) in Greener UK as a coalition has contributed to its success. As we know, lobbying in coalition is a resource-intensive strategy:

> All the coordination takes a lot of time and effort. And you can't just say, 'Oh we all want to collaborate.' It means that everybody has to invest time which has then a resource attachment. And if you're the organisation that's doing the convening and collaborating, you need to be resourced. And I know that Green Alliance would sometimes find that people would say 'collaboration' but then they weren't necessarily willing to put in the resource that would be required to really support that to flourish (Interviewee 16).

Notwithstanding the efficiency gains of collaboration, discussed in chapter 6, if shared goals are to be accomplished, then at least a subset of members must contribute resources to the work of the group: 'it takes a lot of resource, you know. [...] yeah, you've gotta pay for people's time and you've gotta put your own staff time into going to working groups and thinking through building consensus and all that stuff' (Interviewee 8); collaboration takes 'energy' and, 'if you have a focus on collaboration, you inevitably don't have a focus on what you otherwise would be doing' (Interviewee 6). The extent of an organisation's contribution to coalitions is generally thought to vary depending on the level of their commitment to the issues, the availability of staff and resource, and the prospects of success. There must also be a genuine intention to make it work. As noted by one interviewee:

> Collaboration, it really is the only way to win anything but it comes at a cost and it takes time and it takes resources and you've gotta invest in that collaboration if you're really serious about it. So you can't just pretend you're collaborating; you really have to collaborate and it's got to be meaningful, and you know, it takes time (Interviewee 6).

Another interviewee points to the growth of Greener UK as a particular challenge: 'And you know, that's a huge resource and capacity issue for all of us' (Interviewee 14). Greener UK took the strategic decision to work on the Bill in its entirety, 'which some might say is a fool's errand when you consider just how many clauses are in the Bill' (Interviewee 6), albeit in a collaboration with Link that allows it to focus on particular issues. The complexity and scope of collaboration has almost certainly also become more challenging for individual organisations and indeed individuals working intensely in the Greener UK coalition. Interviewee 9 emphasised the challenge in 'keeping track of everything', especially when internal resources are limited. This, and the 'new kind of politics' (Interviewee 16) that emerged after the 2019 election, has brought with it some quite significant challenges for the coalition.

From observation and our interviews, it is clear that individuals from across the coalition have worked extremely hard on Brexit, specifically within the structures of the coalition. Brexit has 'sucked up a lot of resource, a lot of people's time and effort' (Interviewee 14) and for some, 'the day job's carried on' (unattributed). A number of organisations contributed significant (human and expert) resources. Maria has observed some ebb and flow in both respects; the Brexit process has been going on for a very long time, punctuated only by a global pandemic. But this serious commitment from member organisations, and the individuals within those organisations, has been crucial to making the coalition work.

The resource demand of a coalition is not just in the in-kind contributions of personnel from the partner organisations. Importantly, by contrast with ad hoc collaboration, certain people are actually responsible for making the collaboration work, without other organisational demands. The resourcing of the Greener UK *unit* has clearly contributed to the success (in all senses) of Greener UK. At a very practical level, 'that going back and constantly involving people and checking that they're on message. And not everyone is onboard, so then you have to get all of that constant iteration […] it's driven by the unit' (Interviewee 6). This direct resourcing of Greener UK itself is closely connected to the people point above, and as suggested above, our participants clearly consider the community to have been fortunate in the individuals involved. The 'kind of actual coordination and collaboration role' is a 'job that does have to be valued in order for it to exist' (Interviewee 16). This is not an administrative role. There is a huge amount of effort and of skill in holding the coalition together, and inspiring people to work for the coalition, including paying attention to the external competence and reputation of the coalition.

We think that it has been extremely important for Greener UK's success that these roles were both valued and resourced. By contrast with Greener UK, one of our interviewees described Link as 'a sort of true coalition in that it's the members who are doing the work themselves' (Interviewee 15). This emphasises the sense that the spirit and culture of collaboration through Link was different, that there was more scope and space for individuals within Link to shape the coalition's focus. Our participants spoke very positively of Link, but we got a strong sense that this flexibility meant that things had not always happened when they needed to. The culture of Greener UK was more 'can do' (Interviewee 16) and 'disciplined' (Interviewee 3), which may well be attributable to Greener UK's specific resource (both financial and expertise) for the support of coalition working.

The future of collaboration and Greener UK

The collaboration around Brexit has clearly left behind a 'footprint' (Interviewee 3). Important organisational links have been strengthened and individual relationships have developed. Greener UK has demonstrated what can be achieved when groups work together. So despite all the challenges and tensions, our interviewees see a future for collaboration in the sector, beyond Brexit: 'the positive experiences around coalition show what we can achieve if we work together and if we put our minds to it' (Interviewee 2).

There was less certainty as to the vehicle through which collaboration would take place. Greener UK was of course formed in response to the Brexit crisis. As to its future role:

> As Brexit becomes a fact, and as the primary legislation moves through Parliament and presumably is adopted eventually, I think there'll be another question about whether Greener UK at that point ceases altogether. Which would be logical. Or whether there's some kind of ongoing collaborative structure. And I think that's a question on a lot of people's minds and there's not a completely clear answer as yet (Interviewee 3).

The future of collaboration will ultimately be decided by the collaborating organisations themselves, and the future of Greener UK is 'really up to the groups' (Interviewee 16). As we know, building a successful coalition requires funding. It requires commitment in terms of time and resource, and effective leadership. The profile sacrifice inherent in collaborative working is part of the assessment of the future of collaboration:

> They've seen, they've created, they've co-created something together, that's been really powerful and effective. But there is an opportunity cost for them, in that a lot of the time with government or, you know, the parliamentary airtime on whatever you might want to say has been created for the many, sometimes at the expense of the individual organisations. Is that something that they are happy with, continue to do, or is it in prescribed circumstances, and if so, what are they? And I guess that's a question more for [the organisations] than for the [individual] collaborators as it were (unattributed).

One interviewee emphasised the importance of larger NGO commitment to collaboration:

> But the real value of it has been all the big groups are members and I think if you were to lose even really one of, some of, the big

names [...] I dunno, it's hard to see it working in the same way (Interviewee 7).

Coalitions 'rarely end with a bang', they fade away, with a gradual withdrawal of energy and support.[55] That Brexit created a clear and significant focus (salience as above) was an important contributor to the perceived success of Greener UK. Perhaps, in the absence of such 'big events or big moments', collaboration will continue but will be smaller, 'certainly in terms of taking on less resource and capacity from members', without the necessity of 'a shared view on everything', but just 'a space where we can come together to share ideas, to share intelligence, in a trusted way' (Interviewee 7). Whilst such a space may have value, and may even be all that is available in the absence of a highly salient joint project, it is clear that it would not have the drive of Greener UK. On similar lines, we wonder whether the delay in the Environment Bill, certainly if it goes on for too long, will lead to some dissipation of energy and focus from the coalition.

And so that leads us to the question of whether there will be another issue with the salience and common ground of Brexit. Sadly, collaboration may be most attractive and most productive in a crisis:[56]

If the government comes out of Covid with a kind of deregulatory phase [...] If it can encompass an economy first, you know, reduce the role of the state, I think the NGOs will stay together. You know, the pressure to collaborate will be greater. If it's a sort of new world of endless opportunities and ambitious new carbon targets and so forth, maybe less pressure to work together and more opportunity to kind of get one's own idea to the front of the pack (Interviewee 3).

Conclusions

Whilst we are not seeking to establish unique causal connections, Greener UK's contribution seems to be clear to our participants, and we have been able to trace some influence through the public debate. We suspect that there may be further significant indirect benefits of collaboration over Brexit, in particular around learning and support, including on legal expertise. This needs to be recognised and valued by organisations and funders.

Our interviewees indicated a strong interest in continuing to collaborate after Brexit, albeit recognising that that would be both difficult and different; there was less consensus about what the vehicle for collaboration would be. It is clear from our case study that working in coalition requires commitment. The threat to the environment from the UK's departure from the EU provided a big enough incentive for coalition members to set aside any differences and commit fully to the Greener UK agenda. Collaboration is about people working together to achieve common goals, and key people have worked hard to build trust and a sense of purpose. The relationships that have been forged during collaboration around Brexit will be central to the success (or failure) of any coalition moving forward. And finally, collaboration must be properly resourced by the organisations involved and will be enhanced where the coordinating unit is itself appropriately funded and led.

Collaboration is not new to environmental NGOs, but our interviewees have perceived collaboration through Greener UK as being different, more intense, special, with plenty of lessons for the future. Memories are short, and individuals move on. Interviewee 6 emphasised that it is important 'to take some space and time to actually write [the lessons] down and check that we've got them right and socialise them amongst the movement' (Interviewee 6). The benefits we have witnessed are most likely to accrue if the sector (or more specifically their funders) consciously capitalise on the Brexit experience.

Notes

1. We have, for example, heard concerns about Greener UK's insider approach (chapter 2 and chapter 3), and about the focus on governance and principles rather than on contesting Brexit (chapter 4).
2. Betsill and Corell 2001.
3. Vanhala 2017.
4. Data available at: https://www.gov.uk/government/collections/ministers-hospitality-gifts-meetings-overseas-travel accessed 1 July 2020.
5. Greener UK also received external grant funding.
6. Ensuring a systematic analysis of the demands of individual NGOs would be problematic as websites evolve and old material has been removed.
7. See the very useful review in Vanhala 2017. See also e.g. Bennett and Checkel 2015; Beach and Pedersen 2013.
8. Betsill and Corell 2001, 72 citing Zürn 1998, 640.
9. Russell and Cowley 2016, 133.
10. Environmental Audit Committee 2018.
11. Environmental Audit Committee 2019; Environment, Food and Rural Affairs Committee 2019.
12. https://services.parliament.uk/Bills/2019-21/environment/committees/houseofcommons publicbillcommitteeontheenvironmentbill201921.html accessed 1 July 2020.
13. Informally, we did hear some criticism of Greener UK's objectives.

14 Greener UK 2017. This is not the earliest moment we could have chosen. We discussed the contributions made by various groups at the end of 2016 to the inquiries by the House of Lords EU Select Committee and the Environmental Audit Committee in chapters 3 and 4, and various NGOs published blogs and briefings in 2016. As above, the way that the websites are organised means that it would be difficult to review those systematically.
15 What became the EU (Withdrawal) Act 2018.
16 Which had been promised since 2014.
17 Gove 2017b.
18 We have 'a vibrant democracy and robust legal system which allow individuals and parliaments to hold the powerful to account when they do the wrong thing – whether it's turning a blind eye to pollution or damaging our beautiful countryside. But when it comes to protecting the environment, this is not sufficient on its own'.
19 Baldock 2017.
20 Greener UK and Wildlife and Countryside Link 2020.
21 Section 8(1).
22 Jordan and Moore 2020.
23 Clauses 6 and 9 require the Secretary of State to review targets and Environment Improvement Plans. There are a number of ways in which these clauses could be improved, but one key problem is that the process, outputs and impacts of these reviews are too much in the hands of the Secretary of State.
24 HM Government 2018.
25 HM Government 2018.
26 Department for Environment, Food and Rural Affairs 2018.
27 24 June 2020.
28 There was much amusement in the sector that the deadline was Boxing Day 2018. Note that section 16 was repealed by the EU (Withdrawal Agreement) Act 2020.
29 Environmental Audit Committee 2018, para 15.
30 Environmental Audit Committee 2018.
31 Note that section 16(1)(d) EU (Withdrawal) Act 2018 included a requirement that the new body be able to take 'legal proceedings'.
32 Government excluded climate change on the basis that climate change is addressed by the Climate Change Committee; however it has no enforcement functions.
33 Environmental Audit Committee 2018.
34 Environmental Audit Committee 2018, para 73.
35 Submission to pre-legislative scrutiny, Environmental Audit Committee 2019 and Environment, Food and Rural Affairs Committee 2019, citing Gove 2017b and HM Government 2018.
36 Environmental Audit Committee 2019, para 76.
37 According to Government, a NDPB is a 'body which has a role in the processes of national government, but is not a government department or part of one, and which accordingly operates to a greater or lesser extent at arm's length from ministers', https://www.gov.uk/guidance/public-bodies-reform#ndpbs-executive-agencies-and-non-ministerial-departments accessed 1 July 2020. The Environment Agency and Natural England are both NDPBs.
38 Environmental Audit Committee 2019, paras 83–8.
39 Environment, Food and Rural Affairs Committee 2019, para 14.
40 Environment, Food and Rural Affairs Committee 2019, para 51.
41 Environment, Food and Rural Affairs Committee 2019, para 68.
42 Environment, Food and Rural Affairs Committee 2019, para 79.
43 Environmental Audit Committee 2019, paras 103–4.
44 Environmental Audit Committee 2019, paras 103–4; Environment, Food and Rural Affairs Committee 2019, para 28.
45 Environmental Audit Committee 2019, para 46.
46 https://greeneruk.org/briefings/environment-bill accessed 1 July 2020.
47 Greener UK and Wildlife and Countryside Link 2020.
48 For a discussion of the House of Commons and coronavirus see https://constitution-unit.com/2020/05/13/coronavirus-and-the-commons-how-the-hybrid-parliament-has-enabled-mps-to-operate-remotely/ accessed 1 July 2020.
49 In evidence to the Environmental Audit Committee, 18 June 2020, https://parliamentlive.tv/Event/Index/0aac96da-671f-4d75-9889-eaae882ff687 accessed 1 July 2020.
50 Galanter 1974. See also chapter 8.

51 Miller, Cracknell and Williams 2017.
52 Although some of our interviewees would be concerned that the very insider-y nature of Greener UK mean it is not in a good position to fight these sorts of battles, to 'win the politics', Interviewee 11.
53 At our closing event, 24 June 2020.
54 Heaney and Leifeld 2018 (citation omitted).
55 Brooker and Meyer 2019.
56 See e.g. Brooker and Meyer 2019 and Staggenborg 1986 on the importance of threat for collaboration.

8
Conclusions

Introduction

We write in strange and uncertain times. We had hoped that by the time we finished writing we would know the fate of the Environment Bill. No one who has been following Brexit for four years would suggest that we postpone completion pending certainty – even if the end seems within grasp. Although there will be much to say on the Environment Act (or indeed the failure of the Bill), and we hope to be part of that conversation, this book has a different objective. What we have learned about law and legal expertise in environmental groups and about the path to Brexit stands, regardless of what happens to the Bill.

Three tightly related themes have emerged most strongly from our work. First, the political and legal opportunities around Brexit have been fascinating, complex and unique, and our own work confirms the emphasis in the literature on the role of external factors in shaping interest group activity and achievement. Paying unusually close attention to legal mobilisation outside judicial and quasi-judicial fora has allowed us to add to ideas of political and legal opportunity, identifying hybrid political–legal opportunities that create space for legal expertise in political fora. Second, we draw two ostensibly contradictory conclusions about the role of legal expertise in the community. Legal expertise is thinly spread in environmental NGOs, and the understanding of the role and complexity of legal expertise is sometimes complacent. This may be linked in complicated ways to the sector's internal context, especially 'resources, identity, ideas and values'.[1] And yet at the same time, we saw intense and sophisticated rallying of expertise around Brexit and the Environment Bill.

Third, a very powerful collaboration between environmental NGOs on Brexit has been successful in a number of different respects, although the sector has not got everything it has asked for. The existing literature on collaboration and coalitions between NGOs is limited, and the value of collaboration is largely assumed both in the scholarship and by practitioners such as the Environmental Funders Network.[2] Our work does bear out those assumptions, and we have also been able to explore a little more the different ways in which that value can manifest, and to identify some of the elements of a successful collaboration.

In this chapter we address each of these three themes in turn (although in reality they cannot be so easily separated). We then turn again to our case study. The heterogeneity and complexity of the area we are examining (the nature of the sector, the nature of the problem), and the unique circumstances thrown up by Brexit, means that the caution necessary for drawing conclusions from any case study is especially pertinent here. All of our conclusions are therefore subject to the proviso that they have emerged in the rather distinctive context that Brexit provided for NGO advocacy. That distinctive context has, however, made legal expertise especially visible; and whilst 'proof is hard to come by [...] learning is certainly possible'.[3]

Political and legal opportunity

We set our case study, the debate about the environmental impact of Brexit, and the resulting Environment Bill, in the context of the literature on political and legal opportunity. The political context in which Brexit played out has been extraordinary. At times, parliament has had a good deal of power, making it possible for environmental groups to leverage (hard-won) relations with individual and groups of parliamentarians. The hefty Conservative majority in the December 2019 election changed the parliamentary context in which environmental groups operate. In addition, government (or at least DEFRA) has engaged unusually actively with the environmental community around some shared objectives. In this, the dynamics of the General Election 2017, which galvanised the governing Conservative Party to improve its 'green' credentials, were crucial.

In addition to conventional political and legal opportunities, we have also identified what we call hybrid political–legal opportunities, where the nature of the political space augments the role of legal expertise in argument. So the framing of Brexit as a question of (legal) equivalence and the acceptance of the 'governance gap' by parliament and government, both emphasised legal expertise, as did the heavy legislative agenda associated with Brexit.

For much of the period of our case study, especially the two and a half years between the 2017 and 2019 General Elections, political dynamics opened space for environmental groups pursuing careful and quiet advocacy with the powerful. This book would be telling a very different story if a different set of political opportunities and hybrid political–legal opportunities had emerged during this period. But political opportunity is complex, shifting subtly and quickly, simultaneously hampering and enabling environmental groups. Environmental groups need to be extremely agile to make the most of any external environment.

Law and legal expertise in the environmental community

We set out in this project to understand better the uses of law and legal expertise in environmental NGO advocacy. Our analysis shows that law and legal expertise have been heavily utilised in the Brexit-environment debate, and in the development of the Environment Bill. Some of this has been extremely sophisticated. Although it is probably impossible to draw absolute conclusions on the impact of particular arguments, legal expertise can be a powerful tool of advocacy and we share the perception of many of our participants that the environmental community's legal expertise had some impact in the Brexit process.

The conclusions we reach on the limitations of environmental group appreciation of legal expertise in this section need to be read alongside the nuance of earlier chapters. Further, ClientEarth is an obvious outlier, to which we return below. Having said that, although the NGO community enjoys the benefits of skilful and effective legal experts, our sense is that this area of expertise is generally under-utilised and under-resourced. There is just not that much legal expertise in the sector, and what there is, is thinly spread, and relatively early career. We also identified a limited understanding of the complexity and diversity of legal expertise, and a complacency around specialisation. The expertise necessary for a 'generalist' environmental lawyer to engage in debate on, for example, trade or constitutional law is not a trivial form of expertise, and the challenge of attaining it may be underestimated. Our interviewees had given limited thought to the role of law outside the courtroom, and when pressed, turned primarily to the role of legal experts in drafting legislation. More specifically, legal expertise seems not to have a strong role in leadership and strategy in the sector. On the contrary, law is generally perceived as instrumental, supporting a pre-articulated campaign need. This is surprising and revealing: this is a sophisticated and well-resourced sector, dominated in practice by complex regulation, and our sample of interviewees (connected with Brexit) is probably more than averagely sensitive to law. We would have expected more reflection about legal expertise.

Legal expertise can make a number of contributions to advocacy. In addition to work on cases and legislation, our interviewees pointed to contributions in education, translation and fact checking. Analysing submissions to Select Committees, we see the use of legal expertise as a path to credibility and authority, the identification of 'legal hooks' to provide evidence for arguments, the assessment of the impact of government promises or commitments within broader legal architecture and frameworks, and the comparison of government promises or commitments against the best from elsewhere. More generally, understanding both the detailed implications of law, and the overarching frameworks and institutions that govern outcomes, can provide a different way of seeing the world, and a different way of changing the world. Law and legal experts play a significant role in shaping the rules of the social and economic game, in setting out the way things are done. Economic interests and governments involve themselves in the rules of the game. Many of our participants emphasised the perceived authority and power of legal argument, and saw legal expertise in environmental groups as an important equaliser.

Our conclusion that NGOs are underpowered in terms of personnel and expertise is not straightforward, for a number of reasons: because there is strong legal work going on, because the situation varies across organisations and because it is possible that the situation might be evolving in ways that were not visible in our interviews – but also because the reasons are complex and self-reinforcing. Our conclusions fit neatly in the literature that argues that the approaches taken by environmental NGOs will be shaped by external factors (by political opportunities as above), but also by internal factors such as resource and organisational culture. The link between resource, capacity and culture has been an important observation from our work. Resources are not just a practical limit on what expertise is available, but also spill into the very understanding of what constitutes expertise, and the contribution it can make. Theoretically, this supports in a very concrete sense the idea that legal expertise is partially constructed in the process of developing and communicating that expertise. Practically, limited legal resource means limited appreciation of legal expertise, means limited ongoing investment in legal resource. An organisation's understanding of itself, and of law, is likely to be reflected in investment (or not) in legal expertise; and in turn, expertise in law reverberates in the understanding of law, in a self-perpetuating cycle. Intervening to reduce the overstretching of legal capacity in the sector could have effects throughout these chains. The point would be not just to allow for more of the same, but to create space for more creative thinking about law and its contribution to the objectives of the environmental community.

As we suggested above, ClientEarth is an outlier for many of our conclusions about legal expertise in the environmental NGO community. To really get to the bottom of what ClientEarth does, and how that affects the sector, would require a completely different (and very worthwhile) research project. But whilst we did not set out to study ClientEarth specifically, its place in the environmental NGO community is obviously significant. It should go without saying that ClientEarth takes a sophisticated and strategic approach to law (although of course there is space for disagreement about its approach). Its integration into the community has been slow, and sometimes tense, but enhanced by Brexit. If one accepts that legal expertise is not just a technical service for campaigners, but has a more substantive role to play in understanding and shaping the world, then one might conclude that it is not healthy for a single organisation to dominate the pool of legal expertise in the sector.

Forming a successful collaboration

Greener UK has been an important actor in the Brexit-environment debate, and an important theme in our research. Although there have been tensions and unachieved objectives, and its approach might be contested, Greener UK has been broadly successful across two dimensions. First, for all of the challenges of attributing influence to particular actors, and recognising that others were making similar points at similar times, we have demonstrated that Greener UK was influential in areas that mattered, from the existence and shape of the Environment Bill to many of its detailed provisions. Greener UK amplified political opportunity by speaking with a united voice and became a trusted expert insider with government and parliament.

Second, the success of Greener UK as a collaborative enterprise has been striking. This was a strong and recurring theme from our interview data. We identify three particular features of the Greener UK collaboration that have contributed to its success. First, consensus around the broad issues associated with Brexit, and the enormous salience of Brexit for the sector, meant that individual organisational pressures were temporarily set aside. Second, people are at the heart of collaboration. Without the right people, in terms of expertise and ability to build trust, collaboration is not going to work well. But this should not be left to chance, it must be managed. The careful attention to working relationships and trust between individuals was crucial – and, crucially, somewhat resourced. So third, Greener UK had some resource. The partner organisations contributed expertise and people to the exercise, and these individuals worked hard. Direct funding of Greener UK itself has also, we think, been crucial, valuing and resourcing the extraordinarily skilled roles that make a coalition work. That means partly the internal relationship building and ability to get work done. But it also means that those leading the coalition identified the expertise and people needed for the coalition's external work, and the importance of that significant work being done by the coalition rather than by an organisational representative. This links to our more tentative observation that early successes cemented commitment to the collaboration; and a concern that the delay to the Environment Bill risks diminishing the momentum.

Importantly for our purposes, we found that collaboration made a major contribution to the space in the community for legal expertise, in three main ways. First, thinly spread expertise was pooled, and available to the community. Second, collaboration deepened expertise, which became more than the sum of its parts as legal experts discussed issues with each other. The importance of these communities of expertise are presumably equally important in other areas where expertise is fragmented or dispersed. And third, the high profile of law within the coalition's activities may have its own impact. Whether it will encourage the sector to develop its understanding of legal expertise and to reflect upon a non-instrumental role for legal expertise, remains to be seen.

Brexit is special, but lessons can be learned

This book is specifically about environmental groups who are active in English-level advocacy and have an interest in Brexit; and it is specifically about Brexit, and the Brexit-oriented Part 1 of the Environment Bill. We set out to improve understanding of how and why NGOs use law and legal expertise in advocacy, by assessing their efforts to influence Brexit's impact on the environment. If we altered any of these features of our research, our conclusions would also alter. Our research has focused specifically on law and legal expertise, and it is of course possible that the strengths and weaknesses that we observe are not just about the sector's approach to law and legal expertise, but about the sector more generally.

But more importantly than the scope of our research, Brexit has been special. A number of issues stand out. First, over the four years between the referendum and June 2020, the political opportunities, that is the external context affecting access to and receptiveness of decision-makers, have been unusual. Notwithstanding the brutality and drama of the politics, the technical difficulty of leaving the EU, alongside the large and significant legislative programme, seems, during most of these four years, to have prioritised insider advocacy, expertise and law. Second, collaboration was surprisingly disciplined in part because Brexit was special, with members of the Greener UK coalition (at least) setting aside fundamental differences in light of the threat posed by the UK's withdrawal from the EU. Third, the relatively high status of law in the Brexit debate, beyond but including the environment, may have been a factor in elevating legal argument in NGO advocacy. Legal advocacy on Brexit may have been more appealing to ambitious and energetic lawyers than usual. It involved working with a community of peers over a long period, on an issue of huge significance and considerable profile, with the glamorous interludes of appearing before Select Committees and attending important meetings. Fourth, it might also be that because stability was precisely one of the aspirations of advocacy in this case, the criticism of law, with which we have some sympathy, that it will often favour incremental, status quo solutions over radical change, actually made legal expertise especially apposite.

All of these special features of Brexit, and of our research, mean that there is a limit to what we can claim about legal expertise in the sector generally. However, the nature of our case study means that the barriers to using law, and limitations in the understanding of legal expertise here, are very likely to be replicated in cases where the significance of law is less obvious or less strongly argued. Further, the special circumstances of Brexit have allowed us to shine a brighter light than usual on law and legal expertise. Even if the strength of law may not be perfectly replicated in other cases, it should be considered for what it *can* do. Law is not limited to enforcement, is not merely a service, is not only relevant when there is a case or a Bill to be getting on with. Legal institutions and structures are not deterministic, but they contribute to shaping the world we live in, in very profound ways; being able to see and critique and offer alternatives to those institutions is a crucial role for environmental civil society.

Conclusions: the future

The detailed provisions of the Environment Bill are not finalised at the time of writing. There is currently no indication that Government intends to abandon or weaken the Environment Bill, although the environment may be vulnerable to efforts to stimulate the economy through deregulation, post-lockdown. In any event, careful and considered scrutiny of the Bill as it continues through Parliament is vital. But it is more difficult than ever, due to the Covid-19 delay to the Bill process and the difficult working conditions in Parliament and Government. Furthermore, the impact of the virus on environmental NGOs means that their continued robustness cannot be taken for granted. It was always unlikely that Parliament would be able to force amendments to the Bill, given Government's large majority. But shaping the debate and setting a direction of travel for the future will require enormous amounts of environmental group energy and expertise.

This once-in-a-lifetime legislation, although imperfect, contains important measures to protect the environment. But even an Environment Act is not the end of the story. Environmental groups have the opportunity to be the 'repeat players' of any future Environment Act, playing the long game rather than looking for immediate outcomes, and in that way shaping the rules, including the rules of the game.[4] This means influencing the OEP's enforcement activity by careful and strategic selection of complaints, but also by using the broader 'legal stock' of the Act: for example scrutinising and exposing the target setting and monitoring framework, or influencing the OEP's non-legally binding powers around the implementation of environmental law. The whole point of the 'governance gap' exercise was to provide a framework to assist civil society in holding the powerful to account. That will require yet more sustained, disciplined, careful, collaborative and at least partly legal work.

Notes

1   Hilson 2002, 239 and 240.
2   E.g. Miller, Cracknell and Williams 2017.
3   Flyvbjerg 2006, 224.
4   Galanter 1974.

Bibliography

Aagaard, Todd S. 'What Legal Scholarship Can Contribute to Environmental Law'. In *Perspectives on Environmental Scholarship: Essays on Purpose, Shape and Direction*, edited by Ole W Pedersen, 10–25. Cambridge: Cambridge University Press, 2018.
Abbot, Carolyn and Maria Lee. 'Economic Actors in EU Environmental Law', *Yearbook of European Law* 34 (2015): 26–59.
Affolder, Natasha. 'Domesticating the Exotic Species: International Biodiversity Law in Canada', *McGill Law Journal* 51 (2006): 217–51.
Affolder, Natasha. 'Contagious Environmental Law Making', *Journal of Environmental Law* 31 (2019): 187–212.
Bailey, Cathy, Catherine White and Rachel Pain. 'Evaluating Qualitative Research: Dealing with the Tension Between "Science" and "Creativity"', *Area* 31 (1999): 169–83.
Baldock, David. *The Governance Gap: Why Brexit could Weaken Environmental Protections* https://greeneruk.org/sites/default/files/download/2018-07/Greener_UK_Governance_Gap.pdf (accessed 12 October 2020).
Baumgartner, Frank R. *Agendas and Instability in American Politics*. Chicago: University of Chicago Press, 2009.
Baumgartner, Frank R. and Beth L. Leech. 'Interest Niches and Policy Bandwagons: Patterns of Interest Group Involvement in National Politics', *Journal of Politics* 63 (2001) 1191–213.
Baumgartner, Frank R. and Beth L. Leech. *Basic Interests: The Importance of Groups in Politics and in Political Science*. Princeton: Princeton University Press, 1998.
Beach, Derek and Rasmus Brun Pedersen. *Process-Tracing Methods: Foundations and Guidelines*. Ann Arbor: University of Michigan Press, 2013.
Bennett, Andrew and Jeffrey T. Checkel. 'Process Tracing: From Philosophical Roots to Best Practices'. In *Process Tracing: From Metaphor to Analytic Tool*, edited by Andrew Bennett and Jeffrey T. Checkel, 3–37. New York: Cambridge University Press, 2015.
Benton, Megan and Meg Russell. 'Assessing the Impact of Parliamentary Oversight Committees: The Select Committees in the British House of Commons', *Parliamentary Affairs* 77 (2013): 772–97.
Berny, Nathalie and Christopher Rootes. 'Environmental NGOs At a Crossroads?', *Environmental Politics* 27 (2018): 947–72.
Betsill, Michelle and Elisabeth Correll. 'NGO Influence in International Environmental Negotiations: A Framework for Analysis', *Global Environmental Politics* 1 (2001): 65–85.
Beyers, Jan. 'Voice and Access: Political Practices of European Interest Associations', *European Union Politics* 5 (2004): 211–40.
Beyers, Jan and Iskander De Bruycker. 'Lobbying Makes (Strange) Bedfellows: Explaining the Formation and Composition of Lobbying Coalitions in EU Legislative Politics', *Political Studies* 66 (2018): 959–84.
Binderkrantz, Anne Skorkjaer. 'Interest Group Strategies: Navigating Between Privileged Access and Strategies of Pressure', *Political Studies* 53 (2005): 694–715.
Binderkrantz, Anne Skorkjaer and Simon Kroyer. 'Customizing Strategy: Policy Goals and Interest Group Strategies', *Interest Groups and Advocacy* 1 (2012): 115–38.
Boon, Andrew. 'Cause Lawyers and the Alternative Ethical Paradigm: Ideology and Transgression', *Legal Ethics* 7 (2004): 250–68.
Boukalas, Christos. 'Politics as Legal Action/Lawyers as Political Actors: Towards a Reconceptualisation of Cause Lawyering', *Social & Legal Studies* 22 (2013): 395–420.

Boutcher, Steven A. and Holly J. McCammon. 'Social Movements and Litigation'. In *The Wiley Blackwell Companion to Social Movements*, 2nd edition, edited by David A. Snow, Sarah Anne Soule, Hanspeter Kriesi and Holly J. McCammon, 306–21. Oxford: Wiley-Blackwell, 2019.

Bouwen, Pieter and Margaret Mccown. 'Lobbying versus Litigation: Political and Legal Strategies of Interest Representation in the European Union', *Journal of European Public Policy* 14 (2007): 422–43.

Bradshaw, Carrie. 'England's Fresh Approach to Food Waste: Problem Frames in the Resources and Waste Strategy', *Legal Studies* 40 (2020): 321–43.

Bright Blue. 'Tories must be greener to win younger voters, says Bright Blue', https://brightblue.org.uk/tories-must-be-greener-to-win-younger-voters-says-bright-blue (accessed 12 October 2020).

Brooker, Megan E. and David S. Meyer, 'Coalitions and the Organization of Collective Action'. In *The Wiley Blackwell Companion to Social Movements*, 2nd edition, edited by David A. Snow, Sarah Anne Soule, Hanspeter Kriesi and Holly J. McCammon, 252–68. Oxford: Wiley-Blackwell, 2019.

Browne, William P. 'Organized Interests and Their Issue Niches: A Search for Pluralism in a Policy Domain', *Journal of Politics* 52 (1990): 477–509.

Cane, Peter. 'Taking Disagreement Seriously: Courts, Legislatures and the Reform of Tort Law' *Oxford Journal of Legal Studies* 25 (2005): 393–417.

Carter, Neil and Mike Childs. 'Friends of the Earth as a Policy Entrepreneur: "The Big Ask" Campaign for a UK Climate Change Act', *Environmental Politics* 27 (2018): 994–1013.

Carter, Neil and Mitya Pearson. 'A "Climate Election"? The Environment and the Greens in the 2019 UK General Election', *Environmental Politics* 29 (2020): 746–51.

Chambers, Ruth. 'What does Brexit mean for Defra?' *Inside Track* (Green Alliance, 2019) https://greenallianceblog.org.uk/2019/12/05/what-does-brexit-mean-for-defra/#more-12954 (accessed 12 October 2020).

Chambers, Ruth. 'Where is the Environment Bill?' *Inside Track* (Green Alliance, 2020) https://greenallianceblog.org.uk/2020/06/08/where-is-the-environment-bill (accessed 12 October 2020).

Chi, Michelene T. H. 'Two Approaches to the Study of Experts'. In *The Cambridge Handbook of Expertise and Expert Performance*, edited by K. A. Ericsson, N. Charness, P. J. Feltovich and R. R. Hoffman, 21–30. Cambridge: Cambridge University Press, 2006.

Chichowski, Rachel A. *The European Court and Civil Society: Litigation, Mobilization and Governance.* Cambridge: Cambridge University Press, 2007.

Clifford, David, Frida Geyne-Rajme, Graham Smith, Rebecca Edwards, Milena Buchs and Clare Saunders. 'Mapping the Environmental Third Sector in England: A Distinctive Field of Activity?', *Voluntary Sector Review* 4 (2013): 241–64.

Coen, David. 'The Evolution of the Large Firm as a Political Action in European Union', *Journal of European Public Policy* 4 (1997): 91–108.

Collins, Harry M. 'Bicycling on the Moon: Collective Tacit Knowledge and Somatic-Limit Tacit Knowledge', *Organization Studies* 28 (2007): 257–62.

Collins, Harry M. *Are We All Scientific Experts Now?* Cambridge: Polity Press, 2014.

Collins, Harry M. and Robert Evans. 'The Third Wave of Science Studies: Studies of Expertise and Experience', *Social Studies of Science* 32 (2002): 235–96.

Collins, Harry M. and Robert Evans. 'King Canute Meets the Beach Boys: Responses to the "Third Wave"', *Social Studies of Science* 33 (2003): 435–52.

Collins, Harry M. and Robert Evans. *Rethinking Expertise.* Chicago: University of Chicago Press, 2009.

Conservative Party. *The Conservative Party Manifesto: Strong Leadership; A Clear Economic Plan; A Brighter, More Secure Future.* Conservative Party, 2015.

Corell, Elisabeth and Michele M. Betsill. 'Analytical Framework: Assessing the Influence of NGO Diplomats'. In *NGO Diplomacy: The Influence of Nongovernmental Organizations in International Environmental Negotiations*, edited by Elisabeth Correll and Michele M. Betsill, 19–42. London: MIT Press, 2008.

Cracknell, Jon, Florence Miller and Harriet Williams. *Passionate Collaboration?: Taking the Pulse of the UK Environmental Sector.* Environmental Funders Network, 2013.

Craig, Paul. 'Brexit A Drama: The Endgame – Part 1', *European Law Review* 45 (2020): 163–82.

Cremona, Marise. 'The Withdrawal Agreement and the EU's International Agreements', *European Law Review* 45 (2020): 237–50.
Cummings, Scott L. 'The Social Movement Turn in Law', *Law & Social Inquiry* 43 (2018): 360–416.
Curtis, Chris. 'How Britain Voted at the 2017 General Election', *YouGov* (2017). https://yougov.co.uk/topics/politics/articles-reports/2017/06/13/how-britain-voted-2017-general-election (accessed 12 October 2020).
De Bruycker, Iskander and Jan Beyers. 'Lobbying Strategies and Success: Inside and Outside Lobbying in European Union Legislative Politics', *European Political Science Review* 11 (2019): 57–74.
De Búrca, Gráinne and Joanne Scott (eds). *Law and New Governance in the EU and the US*. Oxford: Hart Publishing, 2006.
Department for Environment, Food and Rural Affairs. *Consultation on Environmental Principles and Governance After EU Exit*. London: HM Government, 2018.
Doherty, Brian and Graeme A. Hayes. 'Tactics and Strategic Action'. In *The Wiley Blackwell Companion to Social Movements*, edited by David A. Snow, Sarah Anne Soule, Hanspeter Kriesi and Holly J. McCammon, 271–88. West Sussex: Wiley-Blackwell, 2018.
Duxbury, Neil. *The Elements of Legislation*. Cambridge: Cambridge University Press, 2012.
Edelman, Lauren B., Gwendolyn Leachman and Doug McAdam. 'On Law, Organizations and Social Movements', *Annual Review of Law and Social Sciences* 6 (2010): 653–85.
Ekins, Richard, 'The Legal Problem with Boris Johnson's New Brexit Withdrawal Agreement Bill', *The Spectator* 6 January 2020 (2020).
Enderlein, Henrik, Sonja Walti and Michael Zurn (eds). *Handbook on Multi-Level Governance*. Cheltenham: Edward Elgar, 2010.
Enright, Máiréad, Kathryn McNeilly and Fiona de Londras. 'Abortion Activism, Legal Change, and Taking Feminist Law Work Seriously', *Northern Ireland Legal Quarterly*, forthcoming 2021.
Environment, Food and Rural Affairs Committee. *Pre-legislative Scrutiny of the Draft Environment (Principles and Governance) Bill, 14th Report of 2017–19 HC 1893*. London: House of Commons, 2019.
Environmental Audit Committee. *Assessment of EU/UK Environmental Policy, 3rd report of 2015–16 HC537*. London: House of Commons, 2016.
Environmental Audit Committee. *The Future of the Natural Environment after the EU Referendum, 6th Report of Session 2016–17 HC 599*. London: House of Commons, 2017.
Environmental Audit Committee. *The Government's 25 Year Plan for the Environment, 8th Report of 2017–19 HC 803*. London: House of Commons, 2018.
Environmental Audit Committee. *Scrutiny of the Draft Environment (Principles and Governance) Bill, 18th Report of 2017–19 HC 1951*. London: House of Commons, 2019.
Environment Bill Committee https://services.parliament.uk/Bills/2019-21/environment/committees/houseofcommonspublicbillcommitteeontheenvironmentbill201921.html (accessed 12 October 2020).
Environmental Funders Network. 'Covid-19: Emergency Funds Available to Environmental Groups', https://www.greenfunders.org/2020/04/20/covid-19-emergency-funds-available-to-environmental-groups (accessed 12 October 2020).
Epp, Charles. *The Rights Revolution: Lawyers, Activists, and Supreme Courts in Comparative Perspective*. Chicago: University of Chicago Press, 1998.
Epp, Charles. 'Law as an Instrument of Social Reform'. In *The Oxford Handbook of Law and Politics*, edited by Keith E. Whittington, R. Daniel Kelemen and Gregory A. Caldeira, 595–613. Oxford: Oxford University Press, 2008.
Ericsson, K. Anders. 'An Introduction to Cambridge Handbook of Expertise and Expert Performance: Its Development, Organization, and Content'. In *The Cambridge Handbook of Expertise and Expert Performance*, edited by K. Anders Ericsson, Neil Charness, Paul J. Feltovich and Robert R. Hoffman, 3–20. Cambridge: Cambridge University Press, 2006.
Evetts, Julia, Harald A. Mieg and Ulrike Felt. 'Professionalization, Scientific Expertise, and Elitism: A Sociological Perspective'. In *The Cambridge Handbook of Expertise and Expert Performance*, edited by K. Anders Ericsson, Neil Charness, Paul J. Feltovich and Robert R. Hoffman, 105–24. Cambridge: Cambridge University Press, 2006.
Ewing, Keith. 'Covid-19: Government by Decree', *King's Law Journal* (2020): 1757–8442.
Expert Group on Science and Governance. *Taking European Knowledge Society Seriously*. Brussels: Directorate-General for Research Science, Economy and Society, 2007.

Eyal, Gil. 'For a Sociology of Expertise: The Social Origins of the Autism Epidemic', *American Journal of Sociology* 118 (2013): 863–907.
Fisher, Elizabeth. 'The Rise of Transnational Environmental Law and the Expertise of Environmental Lawyers', *Transnational Environmental Law* 1 (2012): 43–53.
Fisher, Elizabeth. 'Climate Change Litigation, Obsession and Expertise: Reflecting on the Scholarly Response to Massachusetts v EPA', *Law & Policy* 35 (2013): 236–60.
Fisher, Elizabeth. 'Back to Basics: Thinking about the Craft of Environmental Law Scholarship'. In *Perspectives on Environmental Scholarship: Essays on Purpose, Shape and Direction*, edited by Ole W. Pedersen, 26–40. Cambridge: Cambridge University Press, 2018.
Flyvbjerg, Ben. 'Five Misunderstandings About Case-Study Research', *Qualitative Inquiry* 12 (2006): 219–45.
Freeguard, Gavin, Marcus Shepheard, Benoit Guerin, Thomas Pope and Ketaki Zodgekar. *Whitehall Monitor 2020*. London: Institute for Government, 2020.
Fuchs, Olivier. 'REACH: A New Paradigm for the Management of Chemical Risks'. *Health and Environment Reports No 4* (IFRI, 2009).
Furlong, Scott R. 'Interest Group Influence of Rule Making', *Administration and Society* 29 (1997): 325–47.
Galanter, Marc. 'Why the "Haves" Come Out Ahead: Speculations on the Limits of Legal Change', *Law and Society Review* 9 (1974): 165–230.
Ghose, Katie. *Beyond the Courtroom: A Lawyer's guide to Campaigning*. London: Legal Action Group, 2005.
Gieryn, Thomas F. *Cultural Boundaries of Science: Credibility on the Line*. Chicago: University of Chicago Press, 1999.
Gordon, Jennifer. 'Concluding Essay: The Lawyer is not the Protagonist: Community Campaigns, Law, and Social Change', *California Law Review* 95 (2007): 2133–45.
Gove, Michael. 'The Unfrozen Moment – Delivering a Green Brexit.' https://www.gov.uk/government/speeches/the-unfrozen-moment-delivering-a-green-brexit (accessed 12 October 2020), 2017a.
Gove, Michael. 'Outside the EU We Will Become the World-Leading Curator of the Most Precious Asset of All: Our Planet', *The Daily Telegraph* 11 November 2017, 2017b.
Grant, Wyn. *Insider Groups, Outsider Groups and Interest Groups Strategies in Britain*. Warwick: University of Warwick, Department of Politics, 1978.
Grant, Wyn. *Pressure Groups, Politics and Democracy in Britain*. Hemel Hempstead: Philip Allen, 1989.
Grant, Wyn. *Pressure Groups and British Politics*. Basingstoke: Macmillan, 2000.
Grant, Wyn. 'Pressure Politics: The Changing World of Pressure Groups', *Parliamentary Affairs* 57 (2004): 408–19.
Gravey, Viviane, Andrew Jordan and Charlotte Burns. *Environmental Policy After Brexit: Mind the Governance Gap*. Brexit and Environment, 2016. https://www.brexitenvironment.co.uk/2016/08/10/environmental-policy-after-brexit-mind-the-governance-gap (accessed 12 October 2020).
Greener UK. *A Manifesto for a Greener UK*. London: Greener UK, 2017.
Greener UK. 'The Time is Now' Mass Lobby, https://greeneruk.org/time-now-1 (accessed 12 October 2020).
Greener UK and Wildlife and Countryside Link. Briefing for Commons Second Reading of the Environment Bill (2020). https://greeneruk.org/sites/default/files/download/2020-02/Greener_UK_and_Link_briefing_for_second_reading_of_the_Environment_Bill_February_2020.pdf (accessed 7 December 2020).
Greener UK and Wildlife and Countryside Link. *Briefing for Commons Second Reading of the Environment Bill*. London: Greener UK, 2017.
Gunningham, Neil. 'Environmental Law, Regulation and Governance: Shifting Architectures', *Journal of Environmental Law* 21 (2009): 179–212.
Harlow, Carol and Richard Rawlings. *Pressure Through Law*. London: Routledge, 1992.
Heaney, Michael T. 'Outside the Issue Niche: The Multidimensionality of Interest Group Identity', *American Politics Research* 32 (2004): 611–51.
Heaney, Michael T. and Philip Leifeld. 'Contributions by Interest Groups to Lobbying Coalitions', *Journal of Politics* 80 (2018): 494–509.
Hilson, Chris. 'New Social Movements: The Role of Legal Opportunity', *Journal of European Public Policy* 9 (2002): 238–55.

Hilson, Chris. 'Framing the Local and the Global in the Anti-Nuclear Movement: Law and the Politics of Place', *Journal of Law and Society* 36 (2009): 94109.

Hilson, Chris. 'The Courts and Social Movements: Two Literatures and Two Methodologies'. *Mobilising Ideas* (2013). https://mobilizingideas.wordpress.com/2013/02/18/the-courts-and-social-movements-two-literatures-and-two-methodologies (accessed 12 October 2020).

Hilson, Chris. 'Framing Fracking: Which Fames are Heard in English Planning and Environmental Policy and Practice?', *Journal of Environmental Law* 27 (2015): 177–202.

Hirschl, Ran. 'The Judicialization of Politics'. In *The Oxford Handbook of Law and Politics*, edited by Keith E. Whittington, R. Daniel Kelemen and Gregory A. Caldeira, 119–41. Oxford: Oxford University Press, 2008.

HM Government. *A Green Future: Our 25 Year Plan to Improve the Environment*. London: HM Government, 2018.

Hojnacki, Marie. 'Interest Groups' Decisions to Join Alliances or Work Alone'. *American Journal of Political Science* 41 (1997): 61–87.

House of Commons Library. *The 25 Year Environment Plan, CBP8196*. London: House of Commons, 2018.

House of Lords European Union Select Committee. *Brexit: Environment and Climate Change, 12th Report of Session 2016–17 HL Paper 109*. London: House of Lords, 2017.

House of Lords Select Committee on the Constitution. *Brexit Legislation: Constitutional Issues, 6th Report of Session 2019–2021 HL Paper 71*. London: House of Lords, 2020.

Irwin, Alan. 'STS Perspectives on Scientific Governance'. In *The Handbook of Science and Technology Studies*, edited by Edward J. Hackett et al., 583–608. Cambridge, MA: MIT Press, 2008.

Jasanoff, Sheila. 'NGOs and the Environment: From Knowledge to Action', *Third World Quarterly* 18 (1997): 579–94.

Jasanoff, Sheila. *The Fifth Branch: Science Advisers as Policymakers*. Cambridge, MA: Harvard University Press, 1998.

Jasanoff, Sheila. 'Breaking the Waves in Science Studies', *Social Studies of Science* 33 (2003): 389–401.

Jasanoff, Sheila (ed.) *States of Knowledge: The Co-Production of Science and Social Order*. London: Routledge, 2004.

Jasanoff, Sheila. *Designs on Nature: Science and Democracy in Europe and the United States*. Princeton, NJ: Princeton University Press, 2005.

Jasanoff, Sheila. 'The Practices of Objectivity in Regulatory Science'. In *Social Knowledge in the Making*, edited by Charles Camic, Neil Gross and Michèle Lamont, 307–37. Chicago, IL: University of Chicago Press, 2011.

Jasanoff, Sheila and Hilton R Simmet. 'No Funeral Bells: Public Reason in a "Post-Truth" Age', *Social Studies of Science* 47 (2017): 751–70.

Jordan, Andrew, Charlotte Burns and Viviane Gravey. 'Three Brexit Governance Gaps No one is Talking About'. *Inside Track*. (2017). https://greenallianceblog.org.uk/2017/12/06/three-brexit-governance-gaps-no-one-is-talking-about/ (accessed 3 December 2020)

Jordan, Andy and Brendan Moore. *Regression by Default? An Analysis of Review and Revision Clauses in Retained EU Environmental Law*. Brexit and Environment, 2020.

Jordan, Grant. 'Lobbying'. In *The Oxford Handbook of British Politics*, edited by Matthew Flinders, Andrew Gamble, Colin Hay and Michael Kenny, 365–82. Oxford: Oxford University Press, 2009.

Kelemen, R. Daniel. 'The EU Rights Revolution: Adversarial Legalism and European Integration'. In *The State of the European Union: Law, Politics and Society*, edited by Tanja A. Borzel and Rachel A. Cichowski, 221–34. Oxford: Oxford University Press, 2003.

Kennon, Andrew. 'Pre-Legislative Scrutiny of Draft Bills', *Public Law* 447 (2004): 477–94.

Kinghan, Jacqui and Lisa Vanhala. *Case Study of the Personal Independence Payment Legal Challenge*. London: The Baring Foundation and Lankelly Chase, 2019.

Kingston, Suzanne, Veerle Heyvaert and Aleksandra Cavoski. *European Environmental Law*. Cambridge: Cambridge University Press, 2017.

Kitschelt, Herbert. 'Political Opportunity Structures and Political Protest: Anti-Nuclear Movements in Four Democracies', *British Journal of Political Sciences* 16 (1986): 57–85.

Koopmans, Ruud. 'Political. Opportunity. Structure. Some Splitting to Balance the Lumping', *Sociological Forum* 14 (1999): 93–105.

Kriesi, Hanspeter, Anke Tresch and Margit Jochum. 'Going Public in the European Union: Action Repertoires of Western European Collective Political Actors', *Comparative Political Studies* 40 (2007) 48–73.

Lang, Andrew. 'New Legal Realism, Empiricism, and Scientism: The Relative Objectivity of Law and Social Science', *Leiden Journal of International Law* 28 (2015): 231–54.

Latour, Bruno. *Pandora's Hope: Essays on the Reality of Science Studies*. Cambridge, MA: Harvard University Press, 1999.

Latour, Bruno and Steve Woolgar. *Laboratory Life: The Construction of Scientific Facts*. New York: Sage, 1979.

Lee, Maria. *EU Environmental Law, Governance and Decision-Making*. Oxford: Hart Publishing, 2014.

Lee, Maria. 'GMOS in the Internal Market: New Legislation on National Flexibility', *Modern Law Review* 79 (2016): 317–40.

Lee, Maria. 'Brexit and Environmental Protection in the UK: Governance, Accountability and Law Making', *Journal of Energy and Natural Resources Law* 36 (2018a): 351–9.

Lee, Maria. *Public Service, Environmental Law Academics and Brexit* (2018b). https://papers.ssrn.com/sol3/papers.cfm?abstract_id=3267300

Lee, Maria. *The New Office for Environmental Protection: Scrutinising and Enforcing Environmental Law After Brexit* (2019a). https://papers.ssrn.com/sol3/papers.cfm?abstract_id=3312296. (accessed 12 October 2020).

Lee, Maria. *The Environment Bill: A Framework for Progressive Environmental Law?* Brexit & Environment (2019b). https://www.brexitenvironment.co.uk/2019/10/18/framework-progressive-environmental-law/ (accessed 12 October 2020).

Lee, Maria and Carolyn Abbot. 'The Usual Suspects? Public Participation Under the Aarhus Convention', *Modern Law Review* 66 (2003): 80–108.

Lee, Maria and Liz Fisher, 'Environmental Governance after the EU: The Need to Ensure Accountability', Brexit & Environment (2016). https://www.brexitenvironment.co.uk/2016/11/28/environmental-governance-after-the-eu-the-need-to-ensure-accountability/ (accessed 12 October 2020).

Lee, Maria and Eloise Scotford. *Environmental Principles After Brexit: The Draft Environment (Principles and Governance) Bill* (2019). SSRN: https://papers.ssrn.com/sol3/papers.cfm?abstract_id=3322341

Lehoucq, Emilio and Whitney K. Taylor. 'Conceptualizing Legal Mobilisation: How Should We Understand the Deployment of Legal Strategies?', *Law & Social Inquiry* 45 (2020): 166–95.

Levi-Faur, David (ed.). *The Oxford Handbook of Governance*. Oxford: Oxford University Press, 2012.

Lloyd, Lewis. *The Brexit Effect: How Government has Changed Since the EU Referendum*. London: Institute for Government, 2019.

Lynch, Michael. 'Circumscribing Expertise: Membership Categories in Courtroom Testimonies'. In *States of Knowledge: The Co-Production of Science and Social Order*, edited by Sheila Jasanoff, 161–80. Abingdon: Routledge, 2004.

Mahoney, Christine. 'Lobbying Success in the United States and the European Union', *Journal of Public Policy* 27 (2007): 35–56.

Maloney, William A., Grant Jordan and Andrew M. McLaughlin. 'Interest Groups and Public Policy: The Insider/Outsider Model Revisited', *Journal of Public Policy* 14 (1994): 17–38.

Marsh, David, David Toke, Clase Belfrage, Daniela Tepe and Sean McGough. 'Policy Networks and the Distinction Between Insider and Outsider Groups: The Case of the Countryside Alliance', *Public Administration* 87 (2009): 621–38.

May, Theresa. *The Government's Negotiating Objectives for Exiting the EU*. London: HM Government, 2017.

May, Theresa. *Major Speech on the Environment*. London: HM Government, 2018.

May, T. and T. Nugent. *Insider, Outsider and Thresholders: Corporatism and Pressure Group Strategies in Britain*. Kent: Political Studies Association Conference, University of Kent, 1982.

McAuslan, Patrick. *The Ideologies of Planning Law*. Oxford: Pergamon Press, 1980.

McCann, Michael. 'Law and Social Movements'. In *The Blackwell Companion to Law and Society*, edited by Austin Sarat, 506–22. Oxford: Blackwell, 2004.

McCann, Michael. 'Litigation and Legal Mobilization'. In *The Oxford Handbook of Law and Politics*, edited by Keith E. Whittington, R. Daniel Kelemen and Gregory A. Caldeira, 522–40. Oxford: Oxford University Press, 2008.

McConnell, Allan and Simon Tormey. 'Explanations for the Brexit Policy Fiasco: Near Impossible Challenge, Leadership Failure or Westminster Pathology', *Journal of European Public Policy* 27 (2020): 685–702.

McCrudden, Christopher. 'Legal Research and the Social Sciences', *Law Quarterly Review* 122 (2006): 632–50.

McHarg, Aileen. 'Climate Change Constitutionalism? Lessons from the United Kingdom', *Climate Law* 2 (2011): 469–84.

Meyer, David S. and Debra C. Minkoff. 'Conceptualizing Political Opportunity', *Social Forces* 82 (2004): 1457–92.

Mieg, Harald A. 'Social and Sociological Factors in the Development of Expertise'. In *The Cambridge Handbook of Expertise and Expert Performance*, edited by K. Anders Ericsson, Neil Charness, Paul J. Feltovich and Robert R. Hoffman, 743–60. Cambridge: Cambridge University Press, 2006.

Miller, Florence, Jon Cracknell and Harriet Williams. *What the Green Groups Said: Insights from the UK Environment Sector*. Environmental Funders Network, 2017.

Moorhead, Richard. 'Precarious Professionalism: Some Empirical and Behavioural Perspectives on Lawyers', *Current Legal Problems* 67 (2014): 447–81.

Moorhead, Richard, Steven Vaughan and Cristina Godinho. *In-House Lawyers' Ethics: Institutional Logics, Legal Risk and the Tournament of Influence*. Oxford: Hart Publishing, 2019.

National Audit Office. *Implementing the UK's Exit from the European Union: The Department for Environment, Food & Rural Affairs (HC 647, Session 2017–19)*. London: National Audit Office, 2017.

National Trust, *Annual Report 2018/19*. National Trust, 2019.

Oreskes, Naomi. 'Science and Public Policy: What's Proof Got to do With it?', *Environmental Science and Policy* 7 (2004): 369–83.

Page, Edward C. 'The Insider/Outsider Distinction: An Empirical Investigation', *British Journal of Politics and International Relations* 1 (1999): 205–14.

Paterson, Matthew. *Global Warming and Global Politics*. London: Routledge, 1996.

Philippopoulos-Mihalopoulos, Andreas and Victoria Brooks. *Research Methods in Environmental Law: A Handbook*. Cheltenham: Edward Elgar, 2017.

Polanyi, Michael. *The Tacit Dimension*. Chicago: University of Chicago Press, 1966.

Politico. 'The Greenwashing of Theresa May', https://www.politico.eu/article/the-greenwashing-of-theresa-may (accessed 12 October 2020).

Prosser, Christopher. 'The Strange Death of Multi-Party Britain: The UK General Election of 2017', *West European Politics* 41 (2018): 1226–36.

Reid, Colin. 'A New Sort of Duty? The Significance of "Outcome" Duties in the Climate Change and Child Poverty Acts', *Public Law* (2012): 749–67.

Reid, Colin. 'The Withdrawal Agreement Bill: New Legal Uncertainty?' (Brexit and Environment, 2020a) https://www.brexitenvironment.co.uk/2020/01/06/withdrawal-agreement-bill-legal-uncertainty/ (accessed 22 December 2020).

Reid, Colin. 'Environmental Principles, Governance and Alignment in Scotland: The New Continuity Bill (Brexit and Environment 2020b) https://www.brexitenvironment.co.uk/2020/06/24/environmental-principles-governance-alignment-scotland-new-continuity-bill/ (accessed 12 October 2020).

Revillard, Anne. 'Social Movements and the Politics of Bureaucratic Rights Enforcement: Insights from the Allocation of Disability Rights in France', *Law & Social Inquiry* 42 (2017): 450–78.

Richards, Jo and Jessica Heard. 'European Environmental NGOs: Issues, Resources and Strategies in Marine Campaigns', *Environmental Politics* 14 (2005): 23–41.

Rootes, Christopher. 'Environmental NGOs and the Environmental Movement.' In *NGOs in Contemporary Britain: Non-State Actors in Society and Politics Since 1945*, edited by Nick Crowson, Matthew Hilton and James McKay, 201–21. London: Palgrave MacMillan, 2009.

Rubin, Edward L. 'Thinking Like a Lawyer, Acting like a Lobbyist: Some Notes on the Process of Revising UCC Articles 3 and 4', *Loyola of L.A. Law Review* 26 (1993): 743–88.

Russell, Meg and Philip Cowley. 'The Policy Power of the Westminster Parliament: The "Parliamentary State" and the Empirical Evidence', *Governance* 29 (2016): 121–37.

Rydin, Yvonne. 'Re-examining the role of knowledge within planning theory', *Planning Theory* 6 (2007): 52–68.

Sargeant, Jess. 'The Sewel Convention Has Been Broken by Brexit – Reform is Now Urgent' (Institute for Government 2020), https://www.instituteforgovernment.org.uk/blog/sewel-convention-has-been-broken-brexit-reform-now-urgent (accessed 12 October 2020).

Saunders, Clare. *Environmental Networks and Social Movement Theory*. Bloomsbury: London, 2013.
Saunders, Robert. 'A Tale of Two Referendums: 1975 and 2016', *The Political Quarterly* 87 (2016): 318–22.
Scheingold, Stuart A. *The Politics of Rights: Lawyers, Public Policy and Political Change*, 2nd edition. Michigan: University of Michigan Press, 2004.
Scholzman, Kay Lehman and John T. Tierney. *Organised Interest and American Democracy*. New York: Harper and Row Publishers, 1986.
Scotford, Eloise. *Environmental Principles and the Evolution of Environmental Law*. Oxford: Hart Publishing, 2017.
Scotford, Eloise. 'Legislation and the Stress of Environmental Problems', *Current Legal Problems*, forthcoming 2021.
Scotford, Eloise and Stephen Minas. 'Probing the Hidden Depths of Climate Law: Analysing National Climate Change Legislation', *Review of European Comparative and International Environmental Law* 28 (2019): 67–81.
Scottish Government, *Protecting Scotland's Future: The Government's Programme for Scotland 2019–2020*. Edinburgh: Scottish Government, 2019.
Sennett, Richard. *The Craftsman*. London: Allen Lane, 2008.
Shaffer, Gregory. 'Comparative Institutional Analysis and a New Legal Realism', *Wisconsin Law Review* (2013): 607–28.
Shapiro, Sidney A. 'The Failure to Understand Expertise in Administrative Law: The Problem and its Consequences', *Wake Forest Law Review* 50 (2015): 1097–153.
Silverstein, Helena. *Unleashing Rights: Law, Meaning and the Animal Rights Movement*. Michigan: University of Michigan Press, 1996.
Sinclair, Alexandra and Joe Tomlinson, 'Brexit Delegated Legislation: Problematic Results' (UK Constitutional Law Association, 2020). https://ukconstitutionallaw.org/2020/01/09/alexandra-sinclair-and-joe-tomlinson-brexit-delegated-legislation-problematic-results/ (accessed 7 December 2020).
Sorurbakhsh, Laila. 'Interest Group Coalitions and Lobbying Environments: Toward a New Theoretical Perspective', *Interest Groups Advocacy* 5 (2016): 200–23.
Southworth, Ann. 'Lawyers and the Conservative Counterrevolution', *Law & Social Inquiry* 43 (2018): 1698–728.
Spiers, Shaun. 'Is the Government Going from Green to Grey?' *Inside Track* (Green Alliance, 2019) https://greenallianceblog.org.uk/2019/08/22/is-the-government-going-from-green-to-grey (accessed 12 October 2020).
Staggenborg, Suzanne. 'Coalition Work in the Pro-Choice Movement: Organizational and Environmental Opportunities and Obstacles', *Social Problems* 33 (1986): 374–90.
Stone, Christopher D. 'Should Trees Have Standing? Towards Legal Rights for Natural Objects', *California Law Review* 45 (1972): 450–501.
Taylor, Whitney K. 'On the Social Construction of Legal Grievances: Evidence From Colombia and South Africa', *Comparative Political Studies* 53 (2020): 1326–56.
Thompson, Helen. 'Inevitability and Contingency: The Political Economy of Brexit', *The British Journal of Politics and International Relations* 19 (2017): 434–49.
Thornton, James and Martin Goodman. *Client Earth*. London: Scribe, 2017.
Tierney, Stephen. 'The Territorial Constitution and the Brexit Process', *Current Legal Problems* 72 (2019): 59–83.
Tomlins, Christopher. 'Framing the Field of Law's Disciplinary Encounters: A Historical Narrative', *Law & Society Review* 34 (2000): 911–72.
Truman, David B. *The Governmental Process*. New York: Alfred A. Knopf, 1951.
UKELA. 'What We Do: About Us'. https://www.ukela.org/UKELA/About_Us/What-we-do/UKELA/About-Us/What-we-do.aspx?hkey=4e0ff2dc-d41d-4b29-997f-1014c3fb1a7a (accessed 7 December 2020).
Valverde, Mariana. 'Authorizing the Production of Urban Moral Order: Appellate Courts and Their Knowledge Games', *Law & Society Review* 39 (2005): 419–55.
Van Der Heijden, Hein Anton. 'Political Opportunity Structure and the Institutionalisation of the Environment', *Environmental Politics* 6 (1997): 25–50.
Vanhala, Lisa. 'Anti-Discrimination Policy Actors and Their Use of Litigation Strategies: The Influence of Identity Politics', *Journal of European Public Policy* 16 (2009): 738–54.
Vanhala, Lisa. *Making Rights a Reality? Disability Rights Activists and Legal Mobilization*. New York: Cambridge University Press, 2011.

Vanhala, Lisa. *The Baring Foundation: Working Paper No. 2 on Better Use of the Law by the Voluntary Sector*. London: The Baring Foundation, 2016.
Vanhala, Lisa. 'Legal Mobilization under Neo-Corporatist Governance: Environmental NGOs Before the Conseil d'Etat 1975–2020', *Journal of Law and Courts* 4 (2016): 103–30.
Vanhala, Lisa. 'Process Tracing in the Study of Environmental Politics', *Global Environmental Politics* 17 (2017): 88–105.
Vanhala, Lisa. 'Is Legal Mobilization for the Birds? Legal Opportunity Structures and Environmental Nongovernmental Organizations in the United Kingdom, France, Finland, and Italy', *Comparative Political Studies* 51 (2018a): 380–412.
Vanhala, Lisa. 'Shaping the Structure of Legal Opportunities: Environmental NGOs Bringing International Environmental Protection Rights Back Home', *Law and Policy* 40 (2018b): 110–28.
Vanhala, Lisa. 'Coproducing the Endangered Polar Bear: Science, Climate Change, and Legal Mobilization', *Law and Policy* 42 (2020): 105–24.
Vanhala, Lisa and Jacqui Kinghan. *Literature Review on the Use and Impact of Litigation, PLP Research Paper*. London: Lankelly Chase and Public Law Project, 2018.
Vaughan, Steven. 'Elite and Elite-lite Interviewing: Managing Our Industrial Legacy'. In *Researching Sustainability: A Guide to Social Science Methods, Practice and Engagement*, edited by Alex Franklin and Paul Blyton, 105–19. Abingdon: Earthscan, 2013.
Vaughan, Steven and Emma Oakley. 'Gorilla Exceptions and the Ethically Apathetic Corporate Lawyer', *Legal Ethics* 19 (2016): 50–75.
Waldron, Jeremy. *The Dignity of Legislation*. Cambridge: Cambridge University Press, 1999.
Walker, Jack L. *Mobilizing Interest Groups in America*. Michigan: Ann Arbor, 1991.
Weatherill, Stephen. 'The Protocol on Ireland/Northern Ireland: Protecting the EU's Internal Market at the Expense of the UK's', *European Law Review* 45 (2020): 222–36.
Webley, Lisa. 'Qualitative Approaches to Empirical Legal Research'. In *The Oxford Handbook of Empirical Legal Research*, edited by Peter Cane and Herbert M Kritzer, 927–50. Oxford: Oxford University Press, 2010.
Weiler, Florian and Jonas Reibmann. 'Interest Group Coalitions: How the Intensity of Cooperation Affects the Choice of Lobbying Strategies', *Interest Groups and Advocacy* 8 (2019): 91–119.
Weiler, Joseph. 'The Transformation of Europe', *Yale Law Journal* 100 (1991): 2403–83.
Weimer, Maria and Anniek de Ruijter. *Regulating Risks in the EU: The Co-Production of Expert and Executive Power*. Oxford: Hart Publishing, 2017.
Welsh Government Written Response by the Welsh Government to the Climate Change, Environment and Rural Affairs Committee's Report 'Environmental governance arrangements and environmental principles post-Brexit' (2020).
West, Tom. *Briefing on Non-regression in the Environment Bill*. London: Greener UK, 2018.
Willis, Rebecca. *Too Hot to Handle? The Democratic Challenge of Climate Change*. Bristol: Bristol University Press, 2020.
Woll, Cornelia. 'The Brash and the Soft-Spoken: Lobbying Styles in a Transatlantic Comparison', *Interest Groups & Advocacy* 1 (2012): 193–214.
Wynne, Brian. 'Risk and Environment as Legitimatory Discourses of Technology: Reflexivity Inside Out?', *Current Sociology* 50 (2002): 459–77.
Wynne, Brian. 'Seasick on the Third Wave? Subverting the Hegemony of Propositionalism', *Social Studies of Science* 33 (2003): 401–17.
Wynne, Brian. 'Public Engagement as a Means of Restoring Public Trust in Science – Hitting the Notes, but Missing the Music?', *Community Genetics* 9 (2006): 211–20.
Yamin, Farhana, 'This is the Only Way to Tackle the Climate Emergency', *Time* 14 June 2019.
Yong, Ben, Greg Davies and Cristina Leston-Bandiera. 'Tacticians, Stewards, and Professionals: The Policy of Publishing Select Committee Legal Advice'. *Journal of Law and Society* 46 (2019): 367–95.
Zürn, Michael. 'The Rise of International Environmental Politics: A Review of Current Research', *World Politics* 50 (1998): 617–49.

Index

25 Year Environment Plan ('25 Year Plan') 19, 51, 65, 109, 113, 128, 152, 153, 154

Aagaard, Todd 105, 108
academics, involvement in Brexit 59–60, 61
access to justice 53
accountability 6, 52–4, 60, 61, 62, 84, 144, 153
   in Climate Change Act 2008 114
   legal/political 53–4, 153
advocacy. *See also* lobbying
   definition of 10–11
   measuring impact of 11–12
Agriculture Bill. *See* Table of Legislation
Aldersgate Group 110, 128

Betsill, Michelle and Elisabeth Corell 12–13, 149
Beyers, Jan 34
   and Iskender De Bruycker 131
Binderkrantz, Anne Skorkjaer 34
Birds Directive. *See* Table of Legislation
Boukalas, Christos 109
boundary work 88, 106
Bouwen, Pieter and Margaret McCown 37
Box, Kierra 120
Brexit
   and costs and opportunities for environmental NGOs 51–6
   and expertise 74
   journey to 49–78
   and law, high status of 58, 85
   and leave/remain politics 70
   referendum. *See* EU membership referendum
   and the regulatory state 84
   salience for the environmental NGO sector of 138–39, 163–64
   sensitivity of for membership organisations 145
Broadway Initiative 128

Cameron, David 59
campaigning. *See* insider/outsider. *See also* The Time is Now Mass Lobby
career opportunities. *See* environmental NGOs
Chambers, Ruth 128, 155, 164
ClientEarth 4, 17, 20, 40, 42, 46, 102, 103, 105–06, 112, 117, 133, 134, 137, 162, 176, 178

collaboration 129–30
   impact on and relationship with the sector 17, 42–3, 105–06, 129–30, 178
   and select committees 114–15
Climate Change Act 2008. *See* Table of Legislation. *See also* accountability. *See also* Friends of the Earth. *See also* planning, reporting, reviewing.
Climate Coalition, The 30–1, 136–37
coalitions. *See also* collaboration. *See also* Greener UK
   coalitions of 126, 128
   definition of 126
   of environmental groups 127–30
   heterogeneous coalitions 128–29, 131, 138
   key features of 127–30
   legitimacy of 33
Coffey, Therese 60
collaboration 125–47. *See also* coalition. *See also* Greener UK
   access and influence 63–4, 130–31
   alignment of interests 137–41
   Brexit, salience of 138–39, 163–64
   as a challenge 136–45, 167
   collective resource 92, 130–36
   competition 137, 141–45
   definition of 126
   and efficiency and effectiveness 131–33
   and Environment Bill 139–40
   future of 168–70
   indirect benefits of 162
   investment in 166
   and legal expertise 22, 23, 133–36
   and membership organisations 145
   as an opportunity 130–36
   people, importance of 164–66
   and profile sacrifice 142–43
   qualities of a successful 23, 161–70
   and trust 164–66
Collins, Harry and Robert Evans 86, 92
Climate Change Committee 54, 114
Common Agricultural Policy (CAP) 5, 111
communication, role of law in. *See* Law
Conservative Party 20, 50, 57, 59, 62, 69, 70, 175
Consultation on Environmental Principles and Governance After EU Exit. *See* DEFRA
Coronavirus. *See* Covid–19

Covid-19, impact on
  Brexit 5
  collaboration 146, 166
  DEFRA 74
  Environment Bill 2, 12, 14, 20, 49, 73, 159, 160, 181
  environmental NGO sector 3, 74, 166, 170
  methodology 14
  political opportunity 50, 56, 73–4
culture. *See* identity

De Bruycker, Iskender 131
DEFRA
  Consultation on Environmental Principles and Governance After EU Exit 28, 65–6, 90, 117, 154–55
  experience / inexperience 63
  recruitment 63
  relations with environmental NGOs 37, 50, 63–4, 65, 132, 150, 152, 153, 175
Democratic Unionist Party 62
devolution. *See* territorial constitution
direct effect of EU law 53
draft Environment (Principles and Governance) Bill. *See* Table of Legislation
draft EU Withdrawal Agreement. *See* Table of Legislation

Earthfirst! 44
enforcement 52–5. *See also* implementation.
  draft Environment (Principles and Governance) Bill 156
  draft Withdrawal Agreement 69
  EU (Withdrawal Act) 2018 67
  EU law 6, 52–4, 60, 61, 62, 113
  and Greener UK Manifesto 153
  Office for Environmental Protection (OEP) 53, 156–57, 158–60, 181
Environment Bill. *See* Table of Legislation. *See* enforcement. *See* Office for Environmental Protection. *See* Targets and standards. *See* Environmental principles.
Environment Bill Public Bill Committee 19, 73, 109, 110, 159
Environmental Audit Committee 18, 19, 59, 60, 61, 69, 109, 111, 151, 154–59
Environmental groups. *See* NGOs
Environmental Improvement Plans (EIPs) 65, 69, 154
environmental NGOs
  characteristics of in UK 3–5
  competition between 23, 125, 131, 134, 136, 141–45
  definition of 3–4
  diversity of 4, 23, 175
Environmental Principles and Governance Consultation. *See* DEFRA
environmental principles 4, 6, 7, 61, 83–4, 153
  in the draft Environment (Principles and Governance) Bill 69
  in the draft Withdrawal Agreement 69
  in the Environment Bill 52, 55–6, 83, 155, 161

  in EU law 55, 83, 119
  and the EU (Withdrawal) Act 2018 52, 67–8
  in the Greener UK Manifesto 152
  success and failure of NGO campaign on 119, 155, 161
environmental targets. *See* targets and standards
Environmental Funders Network 4, 42, 160, 175
Epp, Charles 39
equivalence framing of Brexit 20, 50–51, 57–9, 60, 62, 63, 65, 69, 84, 85, 99, 105, 108, 112, 113, 118, 133, 156, 176
  demise of 70, 73
  by DEFRA 62–3, 65
EU environmental law 5–6, 51. *See also* environmental principles. *See also* enforcement.
  effectiveness 84
EU law. *See* direct effect of EU law. *See* supremacy of EU law
EU membership referendum 5, 7, 14, 20, 56, 59, 74, 105, 126, 149
  calling of referendum 59, 77
  EU Referendum Act 2015 77
  result of referendum 7–8, 49, 127, 139
EU (Withdrawal) Act 2018. *See* Table of Legislation
EU Withdrawal Agreement. *See* Table of Legislation
EU (Withdrawal Agreement) Act 2020. *See* Table of Legislation
EU (Withdrawal Agreement) Bills. *See* Table of Legislation
European Communities Act 1972. *See* Table of Legislation
Evans, Robert. *See* Collins, Harry and Robert Evans
experience. *See* legal expertise
expertise. *See also* legal expertise
  definition of 80–5
  fragility of 80–5
  identification of 85–9
  social construction of 80–1
  social context 86
Extinction Rebellion 11, 12, 151

financial resources. *See* resources
Fisher, Liz 80, 85, 86
Fisheries Bill. *See* Table of Legislation
framing 32, 38, 43, 84, 94, 107, 140. *See also* equivalence framing. *See also* governance framing
  definition of 51
Friends of the Earth 11, 44, 120, 137
  and Climate Change Act 2008 11, 103, 104
  campaigner led 103, 104
funding of NGOs 1, 3, 23, 41. *See also* Office for Environmental Protection, funding
  impact on strategy 44–5, 106, 117
  and collaboration 145, 169, 171, 179

general election 5
    of 2017 12, 20, 50, 62, 74, 118, 153, 175, 176
    of 2019 12, 20, 50, 57, 70, 74, 176
Gil, Eyal 85
Goodman, Martin 103
Gove, Michael 20, 50, 62–3, 64, 69, 71, 118, 153
governance framing of Brexit 50–1, 57–9, 60, 61, 62, 65–70. *See also* DEFRA; Consultation on Environmental Principles and Governance After EU Exit. *See also* draft Environment (Principles and Governance) Bill. *See also* Environment Bill
    by environmental NGOs and Greener UK 22, 61, 70–1, 105, 117, 126, 127, 133, 139, 140, 144, 151
    by DEFRA 62–3, 65
    and the future 160, 181
    and governance gap 6, 20, 24, 54, 57, 61, 72, 85, 104–05, 118, 176
    and Greener UK Manifesto 153–54
governance issues 51–56
Grant, Wyn 29, 31, 33
Gravey, Viviane 61
Great Repeal Bill 61
Green Alliance 4, 5, 30, 127, 166
'Green Brexit' 20, 50, 57, 62–4, 65, 70, 85
Greener UK 4, 22–3, 113, 125–73, 178–79
    access to government and parliament by 63–4, 131–32, 146–73
    board of 5, 61, 91, 105, 123
    Brexit Scenarios Group 4, 14, 91
    and ClientEarth 130
    and EU (Withdrawal) Act 2018 69, 155
    financing of 23, 166–68
    future of 168–70
    impact on Environment Bill. *See* influence and impact
    insider status 30–1, 45–6, 71–2, 136
    legal expertise 91, 105, 133–36, 146, 149
    legitimacy of 33
    Manifesto of 61, 152–54. *See also* enforcement. *See also* environmental principles. *See also* governance framing
    role in methodology 14–17, 150
    success and disappointment 13, 23, 148–73
    and Wildlife and Countryside Link 66–7, 127–28, 133, 138, 143, 146, 159

Habitats Directive. *See* Table of Legislation
Harlow, Carol and Richard Rawlings 35
Hilson, Chris 39, 44, 56
House of Lords European Union Select Committee
    Brexit: Environment and Climate Change 19, 59, 60, 61, 109
hybrid political–legal opportunity 20, 50, 62, 72, 74–5, 99, 100, 114, 118, 153, 174, 175–76
    definition of 2, 10, 58, 74–5

identity. *See also* legal profession
    and collaboration 141–45

culture and fit 102
    and link with leadership 102–03
    organisation and culture, and impact on strategy 9, 20, 43–4, 47, 104
impact. *See* influence and impact
implementation. *See also* enforcement. *See also* Office for Environmental Protection. *See also* Greener UK, manifesto of
    and enforcement and accountability 52–4
    Brexit implementation period 73, 75
    and governance post-Brexit 60, 61, 101, 153
    and role of environmental principles 55–6
influence and impact 11–12, 13–14
    definition of 150
    of Greener UK 148–73
    of legal expertise 100, 118–120, 149
insider /outsider
    and consultation 28–9
    characteristics of 29
    criticisms of 30–3
    and Greener UK 30–1, 46, 71
    and status 28–9, 31–3
    and strategy 33–6
interest groups. *See* environmental NGOs

Jasanoff, Sheila 32, 82, 86
Johnson, Boris 69, 70
Jordan, Andy and Brendan Moore 154

knowledge. *See* legal expertise

Labour Party 62
law. *See also* legal expertise.
    and case work in NGOs 101
    conservative 10, 103, 122
    and corporate work in NGOs 101
    definition of 79–80
Leadsom, Andrea 59
Lee, Maria
    and EU legal architecture / governance 59
    and Greener UK 14, 16, 91, 164–65, 167
legal expertise. *See also* influence and impact. *See also* legal mobilisation.
    and advocacy 21, 99–124
        assessment of government proposals 100, 111, 113
        comparison 100, 111, 113–14
        credibility and authority 22, 32–3, 82, 92, 100, 111, 112, 119–20, 177
        legal hooks and evidence 100, 109, 111, 112
    costs of 40–1
    and capacity in environmental sector 20, 39–40, 46, 66–7, 95, 121, 161, 176–78
    and career progression 41, 180
    collaboration. *See* collaboration.
    and communications 92–3, 100, 116–17
    complexity of. *See* specialisation and complexity.
    and educational role 103
    and evidence and legal hooks 76, 100, 108–9, 111, 112–13
    experience / inexperience in 41, 93–4
    identifying 85–9

INDEX 193

instrumental/supportive role of 103–4
composed of knowledge, skills and
experience 89–95
in leadership and strategy 22, 102–6
resource, capacity and culture, loop 21, 43, 92, 104, 135
specialisation and complexity 21, 60, 89–90, 104
understanding and valuing of 21, 80, 88–9, 90, 94–5, 100, 104, 106–7, 108, 121, 176–78
legal hooks. *See* legal expertise and advocacy.
legal mobilisation
and advocacy 106–16
definition of 8–9, 27, 34, 100–1
and focus on courts 9, 27, 34, 99, 100–1, 106–7
and legal expertise 39
and literature on 8–9, 100–1
in practice 99–124
legal opportunity theory 174, 175–76
definition of 10, 38, 58
EU (Withdrawal Agreement) Act 2020 67, 73
factors 38, 58
legal stock 38, 58, 73, 76, 114, 181
political–legal opportunity. *See* hybrid political–legal opportunity
legal profession 87–9
legal support structures 39
legal tactics 102, 118–9
legislation
academic neglect of 9
amending and drafting 107–8
importance of 9
Lehoucq, Emilio and Whitney Taylor 35, 122
Link. *See* Wildlife and Countryside Link
Litigation. *See also* legal mobilisation
and collaboration 142
and social change 35
lobbying. *See also* advocacy. *See also* influence and impact
definition of 10
and legal expertise or legal mobilisation 34
lockdown. *See* Covid-19

Mahoney, Christine 11
Maloney, William 31–2, 36
Marsh, David 33
May, Theresa 62, 78
appointment 59
Lancaster House speech 59
resignation 69
membership organisations. *See* Brexit
methodology
anonymity of data 17
case study 8
impact of Covid-19 on 14
Greener UK as part of 13, 150
interviews 14–8
limitations of 8, 13
Select Committee proceedings, analysis of 18–19, 110–11, 151
Michaels, Phil 103
monitoring. *See* planning, reporting, reviewing

Moorhead, Richard 99
Mount, Amy 105

NGOs. *See* environmental NGOs
non-regression 55, 68–9, 70, 76, 154
Northern Ireland
Backstop 68–9
and EU (Withdrawal Agreement) Act 2020 8
remain vote in 7

objectivity, elusiveness of 81–3
Office for Environmental Protection (OEP). *See also* influence and impact
distraction 53
evolution of 69, 156–9
funding of 117, 157, 159
and Greener UK, success and failure 59, 161
independence of 53, 156–57
monitoring by 158
resourcing of 53, 156–58
powers of 53, 76, 119, 156–59
organisational culture. *See* identity
outsider. *See* insider/outsider

Page, Edward 32, 37–8
pandemic. *See* Covid-19
parliament
relationship with government 49–50, 57, 62, 72–3
Select Committees. *See* Select Committees
Paterson, Matthew 12
philanthropy 44–5, 117
planning, reporting, reviewing
Climate Change Act 2008 54, 114, 122
Environment Bill 54
EU environmental law 53–4
political opportunity 41, 49, 174, 175–76
definition of 37, 47
and Brexit 19–20, 38, 49–78
in parliament 62
theories of 9–10
political–legal opportunity. *See* hybrid political–legal opportunity
principles. *See* environmental principles
pro-bono 40, 91
process tracing 12, 149–50
professionalism 88
Public Bill Committee. *See* Environment Bill Public Committee

referendum. *See* EU membership referendum
regression. *See* non-regression
Repeal Bill. *See* Great Repeal Bill
repeat players 181
reporting. *See* planning, reporting, reviewing
resource-based theories of influence 9, 32–3, 38–43
resources, impact of 39, 91–2, 131–36. *See also* legal expertise (esp cost)
retained law 6, 51
reviewing. *See* planning, reporting, reviewing
RSPB
Select Committee contributions of 114–15, 117
Rydin, Yvonne 80

Scholzman, Kay Lehman and John Tierney 36
Science and Technology Studies (STS) 79, 82, 86
Scotland
   and EU (Withdrawal Agreement) Act 2020 8
   remain vote 7–8
   UK Withdrawal from the EU (Legal Continuity) Bill 75
Select Committees 18. *See also* methodology
Sismondo, Sergio 86
skills. *See* legal expertise
standard-setting. *See* targets and standards
statutory instruments
   scrutiny of by NGOs 66, 161
strategies
   choice of by NGOs 36
supremacy of EU law 53
Sutherland, Rosie 101

targets and standards
   and collaboration 139–40
   in the Environment Bill 54
   in EU law 54
   and Greener UK 161
territorial constitution. *See also* England.
      See also Scotland. *See also* Wales.
The Time is Now Mass Lobby 136, 30–1

trade 7, 21, 73, 92, 112, 134, 176
   gaps in legal knowledge of 90, 140–41
Trade Bill 4, 51
Truman, David 32
Truss, Elizabeth 59

UKELA 114–15

Vanhala, Lisa 11, 38, 43–4, 83
Vanhala, Lisa and Jacqui Kinghan 102
Villiers, Theresa 70

Wales
   and EU (Withdrawal Agreement) Act 2020 8
Wildlife and Countryside Link 127–28, 168
   and Greener UK 66–7, 128, 133–34, 143, 146
   Legal Strategy Group 134
   and scientific and policy expertise 91
   and tensions of collaboration 136, 138
Willis, Rebecca 30
Withdrawal Agreement 5, 6, 8, 70
WWF
   Select Committee contributions of 113, 114–15

zombie legislation 60